Dangerous Women

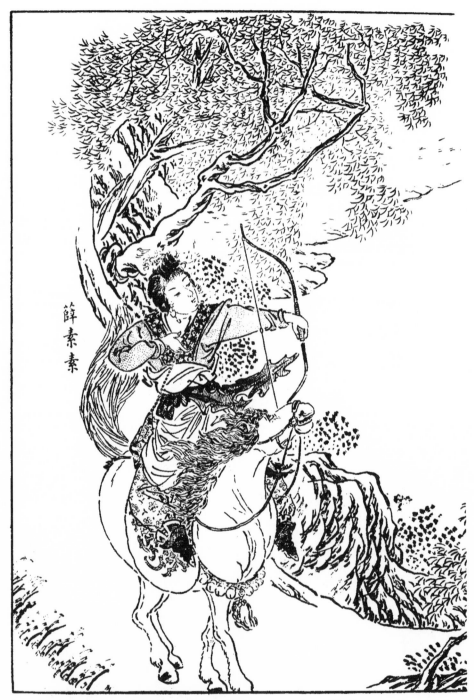

薛素素

The geisha Xue Susu on horseback performing the arrow shoot (*Wu Youru huabao,* vol. 1, "One Hundred Beauties Past and Present").

Dangerous Women

Warriors, Grannies, and Geishas of the Ming

Victoria Cass

ROWMAN & LITTLEFIELD PUBLISHERS, INC.
Lanham • Boulder • New York • Oxford

ROWMAN & LITTLEFIELD PUBLISHERS, INC.

Published in the United States of America
by Rowman & Littlefield Publishers, Inc.
4720 Boston Way, Lanham, Maryland 20706

12 Hid's Copse Road
Cumnor Hill, Oxford OX2 9JJ, England

British Library Cataloguing in Publication Information Available

Library of Congress Cataloging-in-Publication Data

Cass, Victoria Baldwin.
   Dangerous women : warriors, grannies, and geishas of the Ming
/ Victoria Cass.
     p. cm.
   Includes bibliographical references.
   ISBN 0-8476-9394-5 (cloth : alk. paper).—ISBN 0-8476-9395-3
(pbk. : alk. paper)
    1. Women—China—History. 2. Women—China—Language. 3. Women—
China—Social conditions. 4. China—History—Ming dynasty,
1368–1644. I. Title.
HQ1137.C5C37   1999
305.4'0951—dc21   99-19011
                                                     CIP

Printed in the United States of America

∞™ The paper used in this publication meets the minimum requirements of American
National Standard for Information Sciences—Permanence of Paper for Printed Library
Materials, ANSI Z39.48–1992.

To my mother and father,
Dr. Victoria M. Cass and Dr. Leo J. Cass

Contents

Figures and Color Plates

Color Plates

Preface

This is a study in the private language of women. In traditional China, such a language was given voice by female outsiders: by geishas, grannies, warriors, recluses, and demons. From their outside space, we hear an old woman ridicule a patriarch, a virago berate a husband, or a performer refuse to entertain. These women, of necessity, look at China from the other side of the mirror; their speech is the unsanctioned reflection or the overheard phrase. They reflect chaos and instinct, tell of life in a minor key; we hear them as shadow characters speaking out of turn, as they create the inside-out of the public text. Public language in China recommends and rewards, enumerates patriarchal benefits, and projects a world ordered by will, good intentions, and enforced decency.

Public language, however, though serviceable (as Howard Nemerov said), can provide a false lead: "Public language . . . imposes upon us a public dream, a fantasy written in a language that is neither right nor wrong . . . but makes no avail of our freedom of thought by telling us what we must have thoughts about, and by progressively and insensibly filling us with a low, dull language for thinking them."[1] Public speech is of high purpose, but finally echoes—on the large scale—Tolstoy's apparently guileless observation about domestic life: "All happy families resemble one another."

As philologists love to tell us, the logos of the insignificant also commands listeners. Public speech is helpful, positive, informative; but private speech reveals. Of course, some would say private voices have little importance; jibes and complaints seem a petty canon, one that can safely, in the interests of Great Thoughts, be ignored. Others discount this priority; they assert that the feminine counterpoint is, in fact, the one that makes sense. Henry Adams thought that the language of the silenced feminine had more authority than all the symbols of greatness that modernity was constructing. In "The Dynamo and the Virgin," Adams tells us that the Virgin—or Venus, or Diana, or fertility goddesses—was "the greatest of all mysterious energies. [They] had acted as the greatest force the western world ever felt." She was to Adams the fact of force itself, "as a compass-needle or a triangle was force."[2] But in the world of the dynamo—as in the world of any empire—when order and planning are the stamp of the enterprise, unchanneled power disrupts, and this is not good for the collective. So she is diverted; her influence is reduced and her speech muted.

Retrieving her language—"tracing the channels of her energies," as Adams put it—has been one task of this book. I have sought to reassemble her image from private journals and local histories, from popular fiction and Imperial accounts; and, indeed, despite her very unofficial and even heterodox life, she has survived in print with a powerful persistence. Having asserted that she was shoved aside, I must acknowledge that history in fact abounds with her: granny-healers, granny comics, granny troublemakers, and granny dowagers; magician-adepts, warrior-adepts, recluse-adepts, and reclusive poets. Like time-lapse photo studies, each myth has multiple identities, as if recreating itself in flattering self-mimicry, making shadow images and variations of itself.

My goal has not been, however, to list her multiple incarnations, but rather to show them off, to frame them sharply for the reader, to place them in their worlds so that they will speak coherently to the modern; for although these incarnations are not shy of direct speech, they do need context. For these dangerous women, the context is twofold: the universals of myth and religion, and the verities of the cultural landscape. But how to express this double context? The challenge has been to avoid failing them by succumbing to what A. L. Rowse, that wonderful academic writer, called "the academic disease," to avoid depicting them "in empty abstractions" with writing that is "weighed down by double adjectives and adverbialities," that is "colorless and humorless," "without savour or taste."[3] Although, like Adams, I am convinced of the high importance of these women, to plump up my explanations with high discourse might only serve to mask the women's own natural elegance and impede their vivid ways. So after locating them in the patterns of myth and culture as well as in the finer texture of specific events, I have sought to move out of the way and let them speak for themselves, with the hopes that, as they look down at us from myth and play out in history and culture, we might be attuned to the fine expressiveness of their lives; and that, as we turn aside briefly from that "low, dull" grammar of the public text, we will hear rather those asides and complaints and challenges and reservations—all those charming heroics of the dangerous.

* * *

I must here insert a note on the use of the word "geisha." Selecting the right translation for a term as complex as the Chinese word *ji* is extremely difficult. Although I am aware of the dangers of confusing a Chinese institution with a Japanese institution, I have, nonetheless opted for the Japanese term. The Japanese term "geisha" applied in the sixteenth and seventeenth centuries to performers, largely dancers, who entertained *as dancers* in aristocratic settings. In the nineteenth century, "geisha" also came to mean a courtesan. In both the Japanese and the Chinese cultures, this class of women received a rigorous artistic training. *Geisha* means literally "person of the arts" or "artist"; etymologically, the Chinese word *ji* connotes a performer, a person of training or talent. The western term "courtesan" is an excellent translation for *ji*, although I believe it does not convey as clearly as does "geisha" the sense that these women were trained primarily for the public presentation of artistic skills or works.

Acknowledgments

For her advice and guidance, and above all for her faith in this book, I would like to thank Susan McEachern. From among the many others to whom I also owe thanks, I would like here to single out my teacher and mentor, Edward Schafer. Many have been generous with their time and attention: Lin Li-chun has provided comments that have shaped my ideas on the folklore of the feminine in popular culture; Hugh Shapiro, friend and colleague, has helped me articulate ideas on the rhetoric of the exotic; and my husband, Stephen Dunham, has been a constant source of calm support. Mr. Tu Xinshi has created the map "The Great Ming" as well as the calligraphy for the chapter headings, and the artist Hung Liu has contributed two of her brilliant studies of early twentieth-century geishas to serve as front and back covers. Two people, however—Lynn Freed and Howard Goldblatt— have given me more than I can adequately acknowledge. Besides the support of many rereadings, they have given to me their ready reactions to the texts and language of others. With these friends I have explored a shared fascination with what language does. I would also like to recognize the contribution of my mother; she saw this book at an earlier stage, and I wish she were here to see it now.

Note on the Sources and on Translation

The majority of the translations in the book are my own. When I have used the translations of others, I have indicated so in the footnotes. The sources on this book's feminine outsiders are scattered throughout vernacular sources, in classical language sources such as short tales and hagiography, and in personal diaries or individual histories known as *biji*. Even orthodox histories contain much material on women; in particular the local topographies, known as *di fang zhi,* have biographies of local worthies. Although the material on such women is very scattered, it is important to note that the stories of these women did survive largely because the intellectuals were curious and observant. These men left accounts of friends, entertainment, clubs, business dealings, travel in their own and others' cities, Court life, married life, rural pastimes in reclusive settings, and visits to famous adepts.

Some of these scholars I used more than others. One of them was the very successful and much employed Xie Zhaozhe. He authored over thirty books of ethnographic and anecdotal history, largely based on his tenure in a succession of posts: Minister of Canals, Governor of Hunan, Imperial Attendant to the Region of Qu Fu, and others. In his studies of the worlds he governed, he took note of the varieties of women. In his far southern posts he saw that female shamans thrived; around the Yangtze cities he noted the prevalence of geishas; and in the North he observed how powerful were the Palace wet-nurses. He is a flawed observer, however, and his perspective on women is predictably anxious. He disliked viragos, mistrusted shamanesses, and loathed the woman warrior; but his historian's instincts served him well, for in his meticulous observations women of the sixteenth century survive.

Shen Bang was another observer I frequently turned to. He described life in Beijing, and, like Xie, he observed omnivorously. Shen Bang recorded the presence of mystics, nuns, doctors, midwives, tailors, and bearers. Economy and employment diverted him the most; so from his account of the Wan Shu district that encircled the Imperial Palace we learn how and where women were employed. Beijing was the heart of the Empire, and here women required all the pomp, circumstance, and base practicalities found in any great city. Shen Defu was another famous observer, although his account was known for its informality, for his is a very personal view of the Ming. He called his book *The Unofficial Gleanings of the Wanli Era,* and it is filled with Palace gossip and idiosyncratic observations about women of the Ming. There were female mystics who attracted the attention of the Empress and Emperor, were brought to Court, and set up with temples and patronage. There was the female physician who not only treated the Empress but remained at Court as royal confidante, only to be thrown out by an outraged Emperor.

Mao Xiang, Yu Huai, and Qian Qianyi were late Ming intellectuals who wrote about the lives of women of the theater and arts; they were interested in portraits of geishas and of geishas who became wives. Along with the poetry of such women and of the biographies and prefaces to their books, I have reconstructed portraits of such women and their worlds. Ultimately, the trail of evidence of such women is highly traceable; there might be a short anecdote about a warrior in a gossipy account of Court life, mention of a temple dedicated to her in a description of Beijing, and, in an account of local customs far from the capital, a version of her life among the descriptions of local religious leaders. There are traces of these women everywhere. If Pepys gossiped of the Court of London and Boswell adored society and wit, these Chinese chroniclers recounted the infinite specifics of a gregarious life in the Ming. Sober critics of the next era labeled the concerns of these authors frivolous, but it is because of this variety of documentation that the dangerous woman has a history.

If anecdote and journal entries gave glimpses of these women, fiction gave the most colorful accounts. Vernacular short fiction was especially concerned with the feminine. Women warriors, knowing grannies, domestic escapees, demons, and predators were the chief cast of characters for much Ming storytelling. Instead of the terse, classical notes about women, these stories provide richer portraits filled in with dialogue and background. One famous writer of the late Ming, Feng Menglong, wrote often about women. Feng has been called a "literary vacuum cleaner," a Daniel Defoe of the late Ming. Among his many books, he wrote or edited a three-volume collection of stories told in the vernacular language, an eccentric anthology of stories about love, a collection of folk songs, one joke book, a conventional local history of an area he governed, and, from the first days of the Qing era, an account of the final cataclysm of the collapse of the Ming. It is just because of his variety of interests that we have so many portraits of women.

Feng Menglong was not the only self-appointed biographer of the feminine. Other writers found the woman warrior, the demonic bride, or the granny interesting. The readership of Ming short fiction was apparently eager for stories of women, and authors of fiction did not disappoint them. One collection, *The Rocks Nod Their Heads*, depicted women in unusual solutions to the orthodoxies of the age. In the collection of fiction by the writer Ling Mengchu, there is a range of women from granny to goddess. The women in all these collections are of every archetype and occupation: demons, geishas, transcendents, artisans, powerful matriarchs, femmes fatales, and the ever-present granny matchmakers.

If short fiction depicts stories of women, one long novel of the Ming peers down into the domestic with astonishing detail. The novel *Jin Ping Mei* tells about the lives of many women and a few men in a vulgar but prosperous merchant family. This long novel of domestic intrigue and political disaster provides a storehouse of data on aspects of the feminine in the Ming. This book details precisely how the women of this class lived, from the floor plan to the furniture—the bed-hangings, the trunks, the silver, and the rugs. The author leaves nothing to the imagination; he has written not only of the drama of Ming life, but also of the boredom of it, with the details laid out like bolts and bolts of cloth, unfolding for five volumes. In the midst of all this trivia is a household of women: one first wife and four concubines acquired in series. The personae of the novel are almost all female, and the locus of the story—Ximen Qing's estate—is, in essence, a gyneceum. One of the most infamous women in the Chinese imagination leads the cast. Pan Jinlian, Golden Lotus, is the lethal bride who destroys a series of lovers and husbands; she is synonymous with the archetype of the dangerous woman. But there are also nuns and healers, matriarchs and cooks, all set against the background of domestic holidays and intrigues. The novel is an astonishing document of women's lives in the sixteenth century at the end of an era.

Timeline of Dynasties

Shang: c. 16th–11th centuries B.C.

Zhou: c. 11th century–256 B.C.

Qin: 221–207 B.C.

Han: 206 B.C.–A.D. 220

Three Kingdoms: 220–280

Jin: 265–420

Northern and Southern Dynasties: 420–589

Sui: 581–618

Tang: 618–907

Five Dynasties: 907–960

Northern Song: 960–1127

Southern Song: 1127–1279

Yuan: 1206–1368

Ming: 1368–1644

Qing: 1644–1911

Figure 1.1   Map of China, "The Great Ming," by Tu Xinshi (author's collection).

1

Background: The Great Ming, 1368–1644

> The city of Peking has twelve gates: all rarities in China are brought thither, so that the city abounds in everything either for pleasure, or humane sustenance. Several thousand Royal vessels are continually employed to fetch all manner of wares and Curiosities for the Emperour and his Council at Peking.
>
> Johan Nieuhof in 1644[1]

The Ming dynasty—or "the Great Ming" as it was called—was a glorious age for China. From 1368, when it was first established, until 1644, when it was destroyed, the Ming was a vital and dominant international force, a confident participant in the world economy (see Figure 1.2). Trade was the new language linking the globe, and China was a powerful new partner. Ming products—spices and teas, silks and ceramics, as well as the exotic carved woods from the southern regions—were shipped from Hangzhou to Macao, then to Hormuz and Isfahan, or to Basra and Istanbul, or even on to Cadiz, Lisbon, Amsterdam, and London. And as the fame of Ming wares stretched far abroad, the goods became a magnet for specie; Europeans lamented that almost half the silver removed from the Americas ended up in the vaults of the Forbidden City.[2] Within its own borders, the Ming was no less accomplished, no less exalted. Officials and historians praised its achievements. The Great Ming had restored China to its own "Han" people; it had thrust the nomads from the civilized world and sent the Mongols back to their yurts. Even the word "Ming" reflected a proud self-assertion, its claim for Han glory; it connotes in Classical Chinese the "radiance of great virtue."

Yet despite its brilliance, stability, and wealth, the Ming was anxious about its women. "Don't let the six grannies into your house," a local official warned, "they bring trouble and discontent"; and one patriarch anxiously counseled the men of his family, "Men are weak, and listen to what their women say, bringing strife and discord to our estates." Even generals could be worried: "Beware of meeting women in battle," one cautioned, "they always use magic arts." One father even complained bitterly about his own daughter. When she refused to remarry after the death of her spouse, he said, "Her heart is like iron and stone." Men of

1

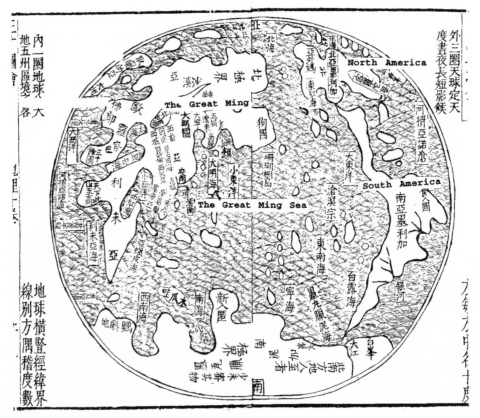

Figure 1.2   Map of the globe from the late Ming encyclopedia *The Illustrated Encyclopedia* (*San cai tuhui* [Illustrations for All in Heaven, on Earth and among Man]), completed in 1609. The map is based on the world map brought by Matteo Ricci from the Vatican to China (*San cai tuhui, juan* 1).

the Ming period were worried. They were not, however, amiss in their anxieties, for an unregulated woman was a disaster for the collective. Whether she was the fertile daughter-in-law, the granny at the bedside, the warrior outcast, or the seductress, she threatened disorder.

Opposing such women, however, was no small matter, for all these women were informed by powerful forces and deeply established traditions: the granny relied on the importance of fertility and of the lineage, the warrior on ancient religions, the predator and the geisha on the power of desire, and the recluse on the inherent fanaticism of the solitary woman. In other words, these marginal figures in the shadows of the Ming did not arrive as unexplained exceptions to the culture; rather, they echoed larger and powerful realities of the Ming. These dangerous women inherited the same mythologies that legitimized the male adept, the effete literatus, and the daring merchant. To introduce these excluded women, I will thus look first at the heart of the Ming, shifting the focus to center stage, to look at the men and women who prospered, who governed, and who obeyed. I will review the larger stage where the granny, the daughter-in-law, the predator, and the troublesome cast of dangerous women played their parts.

For our overview of this era, it is necessary to read the Ming like a map—but not a map of the physical landscape, rather a map of the cultural landscape. We will take in three features of the Ming map, three important prominences. The first feature is the life of piety, a life consecrated to the cult of the family and to the altars of the state. The second is a life of the secular and sophisticated city dweller. The Ming was justly famous for its vast and prosperous southern cities that grew fat on local, national, and international trade; Ming citizenry created an urbane and gregarious life in their markets and estates. Finally, the third feature to explore will be the cult of solitude: the detached, inward world of the artist and recluse.

Piety

Central to the Ming was the life of piety: a life of reverence for parents and ancestors, of respect for learning and for the past. Piety was the guiding ethic of the sober official and matriarch; piety meant a life of public service and private decency, structured around the many demanding details of both public and private ritual. (The usual term for this feature of Ming life is "Confucianism," a dryly masculine and overly philosophical term for a phenomenon that so deeply informed feminine identity.) The Chinese word for piety is *xiao*. The English term "pious" sounds deceptively benign, suggesting obedience or even submissiveness. In the Ming, however, piety connoted a constellation of values and practices, many of them fanatical.

In traditional China piety meant religious awe, for piety was not a philosophy, it was a cult. It meant that the child—male or female, of whatever age—was deeply reverent of the past, of the preceding generations, of both the living and the dead. The center of this cult of piety, this cult for the past, was the family. The family was where the worship of the past took place and where the gods of piety were feted. And, conversely, the home was not simply a place of domesticity, it was itself a sacred space. The gods of this cult were the family dead: parents and grandparents, once alive, now sanctified in death, made into deities of the hearth. The chief priests and priestesses were the elders who were still alive, and the acolytes of the cult were the children. In this sanctified space, domestic life was a form of sacred theater, a stage on which everyone assumed the role of the pious child, for the living performed constantly for the dead. In turn, the dead were a critical audience of the living. Ancestors noticed the studiousness of children, the dutiful responses of sons and daughters, the moral worth of an official's actions, the superiority of domestic arrangements. Household laxness was not a question of sloth; it was a question of sacrilege, a rift with the gods.

Childrearing was especially important, for the child was the inheritor of the cult, the essential link in the cosmic chain of order. Through counsel and discipline, mothers and fathers passed on the duties of the sacred past, lest an ignorant or arrogant child sever the ancestral conduit. The child—even as an adult—was always a child to the parent, always instructed, always corrected. One official composed instructions to his adult, married children on a plan of study for the examinations.

> Your father is forty-eight years old this year, and in no time he will be fifty. . . . Even if I should live to old age, I cannot possibly stay forever to teach you, and to work for you like horse and buffalo. You will be sorry if you don't resolve to establish yourselves by your own efforts.
>
> You will get up every day, never later than the hour of sunrise. Except for lectures, discussion, and the three meals, you will not go to see your teacher or friends and disturb [one another]. While I don't think the marital love of young people should be discontinued, it can be regulated by a departure in the morning and a return between nine and ten p.m. Periodically you shall sleep in the library, nor should you pay too many visits and waste time. . . .

Now a chart for daily assignments will be on hand. You will fill out the chart each day with the amount of work accomplished, number of essays composed, paragraphs of the classics comprehended, pages of *shiyi* and *guwen* read and studied. A reason must be given for any incomplete assignments, which is to be made up the next day.[2]

Rituals, however, were the core of the pious life. These were the distillation of *xiao* as well as occasions to display *xiao*, and they marked everything: how you ate, dressed, walked, and spoke; for though many of these rites had been laid down in texts two thousand years earlier, they determined conduct at every turn. Mourning rites were the most elaborate; for men they occurred at the death of a father. In these years of abstinence, the mourner consecrated his life, sons were expected to withdraw from office, and physical trauma was to be obvious.

For women piety meant much of domestic life was religious; women's roles as mother, daughter-in-law, daughter, and wife were all informed by the divine. "Confucian" domestic ritual constantly occasioned sober, and even grim, sacrifice. One woman licked the festering wounds of her sick husband; others cut pieces of their own flesh to feed a dying child or sick mother-in-law (see Figure 1.3). Countless biographies attest to these fanatical ideals. As in western medieval hagiographies, the reader is never spared the physical realities of devotion. The cult required that sacrifice be concrete, that there be actual denial and genuine physical maiming. Rituals were not empty, and piety was not an abstraction. Women conducted the most rigorous rites at the death of a betrothed or a spouse; mourning varied from ritual isolation and abstinence to suicide. In the pious life, marriage betrothals and marriage vows were sacred bonds; the bond, however, was not with the husband, but with the ancestors; hence remarriage was sacrilegious. The story of one woman of the Ming demonstrates the intensity of feminine piety. The young girl, Run Liefu, poisons herself, despite her own family's opposition. Her story is from the *Ming Dynastic History.*

> Run Liefu was widowed when she was twenty-three. She had no sons to raise, and so she wished to commit suicide by hanging. Her family was frightened she would take her own life, so they made sure she was never alone. Liefu, however, had heard that the jasmine plant had poisonous properties, and she set about locating some. No one in the family knew about her plan, and so in the day she collected a number of stalks. After one month, when the family was carrying out the mourning rites, the widow grieved violently as she performed her rites. Then at the fifth watch, when everyone's guard was relaxed, she boiled up her tea of poison and drank it. By daylight, she had died.[3]

These pious women were not merely local phenomena, however, nor was their cult confined to domestic life. Rather the cult of family piety also stamped public life; piety had political consequences as well as domestic. The state itself was constructed as a type of sacred family. The term for the Emperor—The Son of Heaven—was not empty rhetoric; the ancient term meant that the Imperial son was precisely that, a son: the offspring and subject of his parents and ancestors. Likewise, being the child was a role of religious and political significance. In the late Ming, when the Wanli Emperor entertained his principal mother, the Empress Dowager, and his natural mother, the Empress Ci Sheng, he had to kneel in the courtyard awaiting their arrival, "rising only when the empresses dowager had dismounted from their chairs."[4] When the same Emperor constructed a palace for his principal mother, her letter of thanks was read to him as he lay prostrate on the ground. The adult child's conduct, however, did more than order connections among generations; it potentially influenced the otherworldly. The child's behavior had magical importance and could invoke natural and celestial events. If the royal family was immoral, or court ceremony flawed, the heavens mimicked the imbalance, and the grotesque or disastrous followed. This was a sort of moral astrology in which the stars and every other celestial body imitated the rituals—failed or successful—of sons and daughters. Filial women played no small role in such cosmic influences. The piety of a wife could "touch heaven"; she could bring about miraculous cures or end natural disasters. A filial woman could become a kind of Imperial talisman, serving the way Daoists or Buddhists served—as a symbol of dynastic legitimacy.[5]

The pious woman was in essence a religious teacher, sister to the adepts and nuns of other teachings. Conversely, many religious teachers of Daoism or Buddhism and even local rebel leaders were filial women, famous for some episode of domestic sanctity. The term used for a filial woman reflected her impassioned sanctity, for although she was often referred to in English as "chaste," a term that means simply "sexually innocent," the Chinese terms are far more radical. The pious woman—the female suicide and strict mourner—was termed *lie*, which means "martyr" and connotes the meaning of "fierce"; or she was termed *zhen*, which means "sacred." These terms do not suggest chastity—chattel that has remained untainted by man— and in fact have nothing to do with men or mating. They have to do with a woman's relationship with the divine; they connote the cultic, the fanatic, and the religious, for the pious woman was, in effect, an adept in the religion of the family, a profoundly impassioned acolyte dedicated to her faith. For the pious woman domestic life was a religious experience and filial suicide an act of transfiguration. The community, in turn, viewed the female suicide as a deity. She was neither a sheltered bride nor a girlish innocent, nor was she ever considered a victim; for in suiciding she became a god, and a powerful one at that. The deity of a filial suicide could protect a community from predatory animals, from banditry, and from drought.[6] The martyr was thus transformed into a guardian spirit of the town; villagers prayed to her at the altar commemorating her pious act. Suicides were not done as angry refusals of community; they were carried out often as events of public worship. The entire village gathered at the woman's feet as she hanged herself, mourning her death and yet celebrating her martyrdom.

Not surprisingly, the Imperial government was concerned with the pious woman. Through its omnipresent Bureau of Rites, it subsidized piety in women. The Bureau collected and verified local reports of "filial women," gathering them from villages and towns throughout the Great Ming. When a report was verified, rewards followed. For the pious act of public suicide by hanging, families of the martyred widow received a stone arch erected before their houses, and for peasant families of the pious suicide the sons were exempt from corvée labor, the periods of service levied annually on the peasantry. From 1368 to 1644, the state compensated the families of over forty thousand female suicides.[7] The pious woman was a cult figure in the Ming, and the state was an ardent supporter.

All this state-sponsored piety could seem to some, however, to beget subservience. It is tempting to be cynical about this class of pious women and pious men, to regard their passion for morality as an uncritical dedication to orthodoxy, but this is a drastic oversimplification, for piety was not synonymous with obsequiousness, but with fervor and even martyrdom. The pious adult participated in a dangerous cult, dangerous because piety offers transcendence. Martyrdom, passionate commitment to doomed causes, death before dishonor—these were the hallmarks of the pious life. Sons and daughters existed in a moral universe; corruption, disloyalty, betrayal—these were unbearable disfigurements of the sacred. For them accommodation, capitulation, and cynicism were deeply repugnant.

At the collapse of the Ming in 1644, the intensity and passion of the pious life became clear. When the Emperor suicided and the state was overrun by the new Manchu rulers, thousands of officials committed suicide rather than serve the new Qing ruler, because service to the state was informed by religion. The issue in changing political masters was not simply one of treason nor even of ethics, but piety. The scholar-official Gu Yanwu contemplated becoming an *er chen*, a "twice-serving minister," when the Ming collapsed and the government became Manchu in 1644. He received advice on this matter of conscience from the one most able to speak on the propriety of this political act, the one closest to the sacred altars: his mother. She wrote to him: "Though I am only a woman, I personally received the country's benevolence. To perish together with the dynasty is to be righteous. You must never become an official of another dynasty. You must never turn your back on the generations of this dynasty's benevolence. You must never forget the instructions bequeathed you by the former ancestors. Then I can rest in peace under the ground."[8]

Nor was the matriarch of the family of Gu Yanwu alone in her pious demands. When the Ming armies abandoned cities, entire families committed mass suicides. Rather than "turn their backs on the dynasty's benevolence," the elders led their families to death. One family patriarch summoned his household to within the house, closed the doors, and set it ablaze. And one great matriarch led her family to the nearby river and commanded them to join her in a mass suicide in the rushing waters.[9] The filial adult was a volcanic idealist, her piety a potential catalyst for violent sacrifice.

Urbanity

The Ming, however, was not a culture frozen in time, a fixed and permanent civilization, a society governed only by the high principles of piety. The Ming was also sophisticated and urbane, secular and changing, infatuated with the new, crowded, self-indulgent, and cynical. This urbane culture was, not surprisingly, derived from Ming cities, which grew to have populations in the millions, becoming centers of business and manufacture. Ming city dwellers saw the full establishment of a mercantile economy, the growth of a middle class, as well as vast amounts of local, national, and international trade. In turn, these great population centers sheltered a thriving, highly complex city life. The Ming would have seemed in some ways quite familiar to a modern visitor: cities teeming with businesses and ringed with factories and workers' homes; downtown areas wide open with popular entertainment; a middle class with a definite sense of its own worth; and, the grim byproduct of urban success, an urban underclass — vulnerable even in times of prosperity, desperate in times of duress. Nor were the Ming citizens uninterested in their urban life; city life in the Ming was a self-aware subculture, a world that articulated its own values. Men and women bragged about their urban lives, wrote descriptions of their urban landscapes. Even city exploring was a favorite pastime. "Once you have finished the examinations in Nanjing," one scholar urged his nephew, "you certainly will be able to find an excuse to go out for a little sightseeing. . . . I know you don't want to be laughed at for missing the beautiful scenery."[10]

If city life was pleasurable, it was also influential; women were especially changed by city life. Cities saw the growth in women's associations, in opportunities for employment and subsequent independence for women. In cities, both women and men became entrepreneurs. Women were hired as healers and teachers or worked as merchants or midwives. As for men, cities were also places of anonymity and experimentation; there were more liberal ideas toward women and education, and literacy among women increased. In cities, women published books on an array of subjects: on medicine, on performances of plays, and on biography; and some saw their own collections of poetry achieve wide readership. Women of these great centers had access as well to feminine networks and associations; they read each other's published essays and formed clubs for writing poetry. Urban centers were a force that shaped the lives of both women and men.

The first city of the Empire was Beijing, a city that the Ming citizen both loved and hated. What they hated most was its weather. Vicious winter winds carried layers of dust from the steppes into clothes, hair, teeth, and eyes; nostrils became blackened by the grime. Men wore black veils for protection from the flying grit. Few of the streets were paved, and in the rains animal waste mixed with the loess soil to make travel by foot revolting.[11] Urban size also meant urban problems, for there were thousands of poor. Visitors were quick to note the misery of beggars — displaced farmers and unemployed laborers — who survived amid the temples and markets. Xie Zhaozhe, a relentless observer of his world, described the lives of the destitute as they sought shelter from the harsh northern winters of Beijing:

> Each borough of the city had warehouses in which local officials collected straw and animal fur. On the severely cold nights [the beggars] give the warehouse porter one copper coin [to sleep there], otherwise they freeze to death. Those who are bitterly cold and starving even dig pits in dry manure and live in them, or they swallow a lump of arsenic [to dull their senses to the cold]. But by spring months the poisons in the manure and arsenic break out and they invariably die. No less than several thousands die from poison or exposure each year, but there are as many beggars as ever.[12]

Grime and poverty notwithstanding, Beijing was still a mecca for the Ming citizen in search of power. Here the officials and clerks of the five branches of the government did everything from write official histories of preceding Emperors to review the progress of their colleagues. It was also where the final stage of the bureaucratic exams took place, where every three years the barren cubicles were filled with hopeful candidates. And Beijing was not only the seat of civil authority but the seat of military authority as well. Because of its proximity to the northern borders and the obvious necessity of maintaining an army poised to defend them, Beijing evolved as the center of power. As an emblem of its Imperial significance, and for obvious reasons of defense, the Emperor commissioned the still-standing and justly famous thirty-six-foot walls of the Forbidden City.

Beijing was more, however, than a bureaucratic and military center; it was a great religious center. Beijing was the stage for many cults and rituals; it was the locus for Daoist as well as Buddhist religious centers, for the elaborate cult of the Emperor, and for important monasteries; it was the central stage for the dazzling rituals held there to enlighten and entertain foreign visitors as well as aristocrats and subjects. Of course, all this pomp required circumstance; there was food, drink, music, costumes, acolytes and assistants, special vessels, and refurbished decor. At one famous religious banquet of the Jiajing period, in the year 1547, the court entertained twenty-four thousand Daoist monks;[13] as a religious center it was a very opulent city, a city in which "luxurious living became the hallmark of the age."[14]

A thriving and devout population was especially significant for women. Religious zeal in a wealthy community meant support for the feminine religious teacher. Beijing had important temples dedicated to female mystics; the court brought sacred women from the far reaches of the empire to be honored in the capital. Some of these divines were attended to by the Emperor himself; monasteries were established to sustain their sacred teachings after their deaths, and a large population of nuns and adept-disciples might be maintained for generations.

Elaborate devotions could help many other subjects as well, for opulence could sustain thousands of citizens. From tailoring to salt marketing, the trades and crafts of Beijing thrived. One official described one of Beijing's busiest commercial sections, which was visited daily by officials to make purchases for the Palace storehouses. The boulevard itself was filled with shops and restaurants, and the buildings had enormous signs, some as long as thirty feet, all decorated to catch the eye of the jaded officials in charge of court ceremonies. According to the official, the signs "were chased with gilt and color, or bordered with spotted bamboo; some are incised with golden oxen, white rams, black mules and every other form to signify [the trademark or brand]; some wine shops have horizontal placards that span the width of several columns, while others have hanging wooden pitchers or tin goblets festooned with garlands of colored feathers."[15]

Naturally, the wealth of the Imperial Treasury could benefit women as well as men. As Beijing grew fat on trade and foreign contacts, the city supported a population that required services. From midwives to palanquin bearers, from wet-nurses to florists, women found employment in the capital. If the city was a source of work, so was the Palace; the Forbidden City in particular was a gold mine. Many women entered into the great Imperial complex of the Forbidden City as healers and achieved great wealth.[16] The female physician was especially important; her skills rivaled those of her male counterparts, but the female was more desirable as a healer for the huge population of Palace concubines. Some women entered also as wet-nurses and wound up with aristocratic titles. Indeed, the influence of such women was a cause of great concern; male officials whose access was limited to official audiences were appalled at the intimacy a wet-nurse could have.

If Beijing in the North offered power and wealth, the cities of the South offered a degree of experimentation. The cities that sat along the eastern segment of the Yangtze River, in the region called the Jiangnan—the Yangtze Delta cities—were famous for variety and glamour. From the days of the Song Dynasty, cities such as Hangzhou and Suzhou were great population centers, famous for both the practicalities as well as the luxuries of life. Southern cities were centers for manufacture, shipping, banks, shipbuilding, and trading empires, but they were also known for art, theater, architecture, and publishing as well as for extravagant displays and romantic lives. Southern cities, by no means wealthy copies of Beijing, had their own distinct characters. Indeed, one writer of the late Ming wrote a history of one of the provinces of the South for which he claimed the status of a *guo*—a kingdom, a state with a distinguished history, a powerful aristocracy, natural borders providing military defense, and, above all, autonomy.[17]

The reasons for the special character of the South were many, but geography and business predominated. Geographically, the South was in an enviable position; the distance from the capital permitted independence from the more sober-minded center of power. Some have speculated that the exposure to foreigners, especially to foreign science, contributed to southern autonomy. Indeed, Hangzhou was famous for the new ideas from the European and Arab worlds that circulated freely. Matteo Ricci was himself a favorite among southern intellectuals, as were the maps and manuscripts he brought from the Vatican library.[18] Certainly, the contacts among merchants created a spirit of independence. Merchants knew the trade routes and welcomed the products of Portugal, Japan, Vietnam, and the Arab world; and Ming merchants left the Empire, traveling to Korea, Japan, the Pescadores, the Philippines, Annam, Cambodia, Malacca, and Siam.[19] This was a sophisticated world, not insular and landlocked like the North.

And then there was money, for southern independence was clearly sustained by the southern economy. Suzhou is perhaps the most dramatic example of southern wealth, southern autonomy, and southern innovation. Like its European counterpart of Venice, Suzhou was a city of canals, with a honeycomb of docks built in what was in effect a giant swamp. But access to water is access to trade. Flat boats carried Suzhou's most famous export—silk—directly from warehouses to Beijing via the chain of rivers and canals known as the Grand Canal. And silks were in great demand, not only for clothes but also for temple festivals and for gifts dispensed among the Imperial relatives, to visitors from abroad, and to court and military favorites. Likewise many of the southern cities of the Yangtze Delta fed, clothed, and furnished the North. In the year 1433, four hundred thousand pieces of porcelain were shipped along the canals to Beijing. Each year twenty-five to thirty thousand cotton quilted uniforms were delivered from the South. Silk, rice, bamboo mats and poles, wood for furniture and building materials, ceramic jars, and herbs—all these arrived from the South. Beijing was the Imperial center, yet it was, as one scholar observed, a "frontier outpost, retained in artificial splendor at the edge of the Steppe."[20]

Prosperity in crafts, trades, and private life also meant prosperity for women. Female healers and female matchmakers traveled through neighborhoods, earning substantial incomes from the wealthy of their cities. Women worked also as moneylenders and merchants; we hear of one woman who dressed as a man and traveled beyond the province with her male partner.[21] But these avenues paled in comparison to entertainment as a source of income. In this subculture of leisure entertainment became a real industry. The Ming cities became centers of theater, storytelling, and music—places where the wealthy spent days enjoying performances and thousands paying for them. The leisured and wealthy of all cities, North and South, made the popular stage a lucrative business. Established theaters staged performances lasting for several days, seating over a thousand patrons, and collecting from 100 to 1,000 cash per day. Shelley and Chun-shu Chang have noted that, North and South, there were great "entertainment cities." "The Tai'an Entertainment Center in Tai'an Prefecture of Shantung was a good example. Located at the foot of the scenic and famed Mt. Tai, it had: more than twenty playhouses; numerous quarters for storytellers, singers, and other entertainers; twenty special restaurants; special banquet buildings; specially designed hotels with beautiful resident . . . [geishas]; more than thirty stables for horses and donkeys, which provided transportation for the patrons."[22] In these centers there were few restrictions on females as performers. They worked as vaudeville-type performers (see Figures 1.3 and 1.4) and in the theaters (see Figure 1.5).

One of the places of entertainment was the geisha district, which was, however, not just a place for whoring; it was the theater district and the district for all forms—elegant and vulgar—of entertainment. Geishas worked there as theatrical performers, actresses, restaurant owners, and professional artists. In a world that had immense resources devoted to entertainment, geishas were highly valued. The geisha district in Nanjing was famous for its prosperity; "the market areas in the district were clean and of the highest class; merchants sold excellent products; there were perfumes, embroidered shoes, fine wines and teas, . . . pan pipes, doubleflutes, zithers or lutes."[23] The district also sustained an elaborate subsidiary network of crafts and service occupations, with a population of workers, cooks, and attendants, all of whom absorbed

Figure 1.3   A filial woman of the Ming cuts her flesh to prepare a magical soup to cure her aunt. Protective deities watch on from above. According to the anecdote, the soup cures the aunt and the niece earns divine blessings; she lives to the age of one hundred and produces five generations of sons and male descendants. At the end of her life, the Golden Boy and Jade Girl escort her to heaven. Many of the illustrations of the hagiographies of filial women include divinities watching over the filial woman's curative rituals (*Wu Youru huabao*, vol. 3, "Supplement to Customs").

a hefty share of Nanjing wealth. The writer Lu Ji noted that Suzhou and Hangzhou provided much new employment for boatmen, sedan chair carriers, male singers, and female dancers.[24] Women of the "education district" could also earn their livelihoods as instructors; one geisha, after retiring from performance, earned a living by teaching other women how to become musicians or performers.[25]

Figure 1.4   A female performer (*chang nu*) from the Ming on a high-wire act (*San cai tuhui*, vol. 1, "Ren shi").

With all this prosperity and all their leisure, southern cities changed. Since the Song they were known as urbane centers of urban entertainment, but in the Ming they became still more devoted to leisure, to conspicuous consumption, to "self assertion," as one scholar termed it.[26] Compared to the North, southern cities were places of pleasure, of diversion. "The traditional values . . . were replaced by materialist zeal—for opulent housing, expensive clothing, lavish eating and extravagant entertainment."[27] Contemporaries were aware of this transformation, calling it the *ju bian*, "the great change."[28] Now the great trade centers of the Yangtze Delta were thought to be great centers of fun; they were thought to be more sophisticated than the northern cities, with more troupes of professional entertainers, more poetry clubs, better tea, and better weather. The holidays were longer and noisier, and women were more beautiful; geishas were more noble, and men more artistic. If Beijing was the center of the cult of the permanent, the ancestral, and the divine, Hangzhou, Suzhou, Nanjing, and the many cities of the South symbolized the stunning. The educated, despite their sober responsibilities in the bureaucracy, became devotees of urban pastimes. From social clubs to street

Figure 1.5   A female performer from the Qing (*Dianshi zhai huabao*).

fairs to popular theaters and folk arts, and even to geishas and fabulous private parties, they became experts at entertainment.

The very spectacle of city life was a passion in and of itself. Descriptions of the city were a popular genre, especially of Hangzhou; this southern city inspired volumes describing its bridges, temples, parks, and neighborhoods. Even now, four hundred years later, you can reconstruct the city from the devout narrations of its famous sites. Urban life boasted a rich spectacle: there were storytellers, puppet shows, musical troupes, animal shows, fortune tellers, children's games, stalls for artisans and foods, multiple dialects, itinerant preachers, local doctors, and famous sites: bridges, lakes, groves and temples, parks and estates, shops, thoroughfares, and playing fields. Festivals were most clearly the times of public convocation and public display. The North may have claimed access to the gods through the Son of Heaven, but the citizens of the South claimed similar divine blessings through their own urban festivals. At the springtime festival of Qing Ming, city parks filled with strollers and picnic parties, and on the birthday of the Jade Emperor the faithful paraded through the streets to the Daoist temples. Yuan Hongdao thought the mid-autumn festival at Tiger Hill was spectacular: "From the families of high officials down to the people from the slums they all . . . walk down the roads. From Thousand Man Rock all the way up to the gateway to the mountain, the people are packed together like the teeth of a comb or scales on a fish."[29] At the Dragon Boat festival in midsummer, there were races and competitions. The Lantern Festival was perhaps the giddiest. The first full moon of the lunar year was like Christmas in old New York: brilliant, highly social, with goods displayed and goods traded. One scholar has suggested that the Ming Lantern Festival was the logical expression of the expanding Ming city—communal and bustling and raucous.[30] Here Xie Zhaozhe, who so dryly observed the misery of the poor of Beijing, describes the Lantern Festival of the cities of the far southern province of Fujian:

> Of all the people in the Sub-celestial Realm who light the lanterns of the High Prime, the people of the Southern area of Min [Fujian] are the most enthusiastic. As early as the eleventh of the month, they start to burn lanterns; and by the thirteenth of the first month the lanterns in front of all the houses shine out and glow as bright as day. The wealthy and high-born even decorate their back apartments and bedrooms with lanterns. Sometimes they leave the doors open so that people may come inside to enjoy the sight of their lanterns.[31]

Women were not excluded from these celebrations. During the Lantern Festival, "the men and women who come to amuse themselves in carriages and horseback rumble through the streets like thunder."[32] Women traveled the city on foot as well as in carriages; dressed in new gowns in brilliant colors, both gentry and middle-class women walked through the streets in the "walk of a hundred illnesses"; through the night they walked off past ills to greet the new year. Women participated as well in the street fairs that were part of the holiday— some as buyers, some as merchants. The celebrations of these urban holidays permitted women as well as men a degree of open exchange.

Of all these features of the city, however, none was more a mark of urbanity than the surge in the publication of books.[33] Innovations in woodblock printing in the Song, the dramatic increase in publishing houses, bigger markets, more money for leisure pursuits, greater curiosity for unusual subjects, as well a broader, more varied readership in the Song and Ming all caused an increased demand for books. In cities, there was a thriving and experimental publishing industry that put out works for an inquisitive audience eager for the new. From how-to books on gardening, to illustrated painting manuals, to medical books and popular romances, more books reached more eager readers. There even appeared, in the late Ming, an illustrated encyclopedia providing images of games, weapons, machinery, buildings and even a map of the world globe with the Great Ming and the newly discovered Americas face-to-face across the "Great Ming Sea" (see Figure 1.2).

This industry influenced women's lives, as it provided a public voice to previously silent women and made them authors. Collections of female poets were in great demand; the new romantic ideology favored feminine perspectives. "Poetry is a creature of serenity. Her body likes leisure, not toils. . . . Her sphere is to be secluded, not rowdy. No one can surpass females in these aspects," said one admiring critic.[34] Anthologies of female poets were in special demand, and two female publishers produced anthologies of women's writings. Stories about women were also circulated; there were accounts of the lives of women poets, painters, physicians, and warriors. In the prosperous Southern city of Wuxi, a female physician added her own voice. Dr. Tan Yunxian practiced medicine for many years, and at the end of her life she decided to publish the accounts of her many case histories, detailing the therapies she had developed in gynecology and obstetrics. Before the Ming there were certainly other female physicians; indeed, Dr. Tan had studied as a young girl with her own grandmother. But in the late Ming—now a world with books on every subject, even scientific and pragmatic, by every sort of writer—Dr. Tan could take the oral traditions of her grandmother and make them public. Tan said in her preface, "I have carefully written down what grandmother taught me as well as what I developed in my practice on my own; I have entitled the book, *The Comments of a Female Physician*. . . . I have arranged that my son Lian should transcribe it first, and then publish it in

Figure 1.6   Backstage with female performers; they are preparing a military play, as is evident from the woman sitting at the table putting on a military headdress (*Wu Youru huabao*, vol. 2, "Remarkable Women from All Over").

a block print form in order to disseminate it. I trust that my views will be of some use to physicians, and hope that my readers will not find the need to poke fun at it."[35] In the thriving and populated cities of the Ming, Dr. Tan had a readership.

For urban men and women, however, the innocent pleasures of the city were not enough; cliques of intellectuals did not just enjoy the convivial, they also used it. In these population centers, the Ming subject could meet not only friends but also political allies; together they could organize clubs, collect manuscripts of forbidden literature, sponsor dramatic performances, and, even in their domestic arrangements, defy conventional morality. Hence, if life in the Ming was urban, it was also urbane, liberal, and reformist. The city set the stage, in fact, for innovations: education, art, science, social organization, politics, philosophy, and especially women's roles all took new and startling forms in the Ming, for, as in all cultures, the city became the crucible for the culture. In Ming cities, wives became partners to their artistic husbands, and geishas became icons in the literati garden.

Notions of change took root especially in the salon society of southern cities. In the late Ming, elite life was dominated by an extensive web of clubs and societies; they were the hallmarks of intellectual life. Indeed, one scholar complained that he had hardly arrived in town when he was immediately enlisted in a society for discussion.[36] In these associations the educated passed around texts, ideas, rumors, plans for reform, and ideas from foreign lands. Even Matteo Ricci's map of the world entered China through the parlors of these intellectuals.[37] The novel *Jin Ping Mei*, the scandalous story about women and sexual intrigue, was "well known all over Suzhou," as one literatus remarked, before it ever received publication.[38]

In the salon society of the South, the elite interests had an edge to them, however, as many club memberships were deadly serious. In these associations, intellectuals converted fads into reforms and reforms into political opposition. Southern cities bred a subculture of troublemakers. In the southern town of Wuxi, the scholar Gu Xiancheng returned from his post in Beijing and reopened an old Song academy called the College of the Eastern Grove. He gathered fellow scholar-officials to discuss governmental reform, and they ultimately petitioned the Emperor to eliminate eunuch involvement in the Imperial administration. Their independence did not go unnoticed by the North, of course. As the College of the Eastern Grove became increasingly powerful, the eunuch faction grew increasingly intransigent. In the 1620s a reign of terror was carried out by the Inner Court against the members of the College.[39]

Southern cities thus became famous, as cities often do, for independence and liberalism—or, depending on whose account we read, for laxness, immorality, and subversion. The salon society became self-aware and restive, forming finally an avant-garde.[40] In the ideologies of urbane southerners, there was now an explicit contempt for the old and a new love of the experiment; Southerners championed the values of the marketplace—pragmatism, vulgarity, and the spirit of innovation.

Men and women now thought the old ideas were out of date; they became advocates for an ideology of the passionate and the personal. In the late Ming, this new ideology revolved around one word: *qing*. *Qing* meant passion, love, feelings, and romance. The educated and urbane southerner used the word as a banner, a herald that announced a morality based on powerful and impulsive feelings. Passion—*qing*—justified the man or woman; "passion is the string that ties up the many coins of life,"[41] said Feng Menglong in a fortuitously mercantile image. Instinct and impulse were at the heart of the new code; humaneness and loyalty were considered outdated. The "teachings of passion" created a cult of the natural. Raw emotion was true sentiment; ritual was only a filter impeding true feeling. Direct expression of love or hate was "natural and primal."[42] The subconscious took on new importance as well: dreams were revelatory, and eroticism was an essential expression of self, for there was something of the ecstatic and the Dionysian in this ideology. In the new philosophy, standards of conduct were radically redefined. If you were not moved by the powerful feelings of love, anger, admiration, sacrifice, or joy, you were weak in spirit and the deed was shallow. Ming writers even asserted that the ethic of *qing* constituted a school of thought that rivaled the ancient schools.[43] Feng Menglong called the morality a *qing jiao*, "teachings of passion," obviously echoing the teachings (*jiao*) of Confucius and the *jiao* of the Daoists. A few contemporary scholars have labeled this great shift in values a romantic movement.[44] To a twentieth-century observer, the cult of the passionate may seem a surprising feature of masculine culture, especially a culture associated with the "Mandarin" class. A lushly passionate life was not, however, anomalous to the southern literati; in the late Ming, a cultivated and passionate private life became a grand virtue.

The literati and their partners did not content themselves with theory, however; they applied *qing* to their lives. Indeed, the elaborations of this cult were vast. The literati used *qing* to make forays into the realms of state orthodoxies, attacking older forms of language and literature. Prefiguring the great reformers of the early twentieth century, the southern campaigners in the culture wars advocated new styles and new genres, as familiar forms were thought to be without *qing*.[45] They tampered with both the classical canon and the classical language, deeming them both old-fashioned. Vernacular language was the new experimental medium for poetry and prose, and folk poetry was now a better canon than the works of Confucius. "Folksongs . . . sung by women and children in the back alley, . . . compositions by ignorant but unaffected people," these were the new poems, said Yuan Hongdao.[46] The plebeian poets in their vernacular speech could "express themselves freely without inhibition; they are able to communicate . . . the feelings and desires of a human being."[47]

Women of the southern cities did not ignore this atmosphere of change; the "teachings of passion"—the new romanticism—opened a door for them. Gentry women and first wives from all levels had new roles. By the dictates of traditional morality, a wife's role was to be fertile, chaste, and reverential—there was nothing artistic and certainly nothing romantic in her role. In fact, a "virtuous woman" was often illiterate; reading for pleasure, composing poetry, and even painting were considered indecorous. Now, however, a certain romantic egalitarianism crept into the discourse of orthodox domesticity, as marriage between first wives and husbands became romanticized. Feng Menglong advised that "to be a wife means to form an equal match with someone [*Qi, qiye*]."[48] Gentry women were as moved by the new theories as gentry men. Some were captivated by the new heroines in the popular plays of Tang Xianzu; they found the eroticism and passion of the heroines to have special relevance for them.[49]

If wives became more romantic, geishas grew more legitimate. In the southern cities, geishas became less the tangential women of the theater and more the essential partners to the avant-garde artists. A few geishas even married into elite families as concubines, leaving the life of the demimonde for a life of marital legitimacy on the estates of the powerful,[50] joining the literatus in his study. Nor was the geisha just an icon; she was a necessity. Within the domestic space, the artistic-recluse needed the right mate, the right informant on the art of private living. If a passionate life was the new focus, the geisha was the new expert. Some, of course, entered as kept pets, with wealth lavished on them; but some entered as artists and painters, equal in artistic accomplishments to the men they married.[51] Eventually, they colonized elite life, becoming themselves poets, painters, scholars, and essayists, competitive with men in their skills and fame. Geishas, once silent in the quarters of the demimonde, now achieved renown as artists and authors in their own right.

Solitude

But if piety and urbanity do not present enough contrast, if the intense idealism of the pious life and the dynamic bustle of the urban life do not seem sufficiently at odds, there is a third state that defines the Ming. This is the state of reclusiveness. The reclusive life may sound to some to be a trivial life; the recluse seems merely an isolated hermit, odd, eccentric, but hardly destined to have great influence. Reclusiveness of the Ming, however, was a grand passion, a focus for subversive movements and a dangerously creative wellspring. Recluses were more than escapists; recluses were iconoclasts who had a corrosive disdain for the common. Nor were these recluses necessarily male—women claimed the status as well. Religious adepts or warriors were the typical female recluses; they inhabited mountain hideouts or temples built for them by devout worshipers. The state could sponsor these women with lavish appointments; Imperial patronage was an important resource for these women and their cults. Or some recluses could live a more mundane life—a scholar, a painter, a poet, a devout practitioner of the Dao or of Buddhism. She could even be a geisha, or simply a solitary traveler who lived in the mountains.

   In the Ming the recluse was a familiar figure. Everyone knew a recluse—or at least a would-be recluse—when they saw one. Recluses were the personifications of the mountains themselves: lonely, untamed, unkempt—storehouses of the secrets of nature. Caves, huts, and mountain temples were their lairs. From ancient times, the mysterious recluses had mysterious powers. They were often referred to as immortals; they could confer on the fortunate supplicant everything from military secrets and the warrior's arts to medications for healing and for transcendence, and even, as all Emperors were very aware, political legitimacy. Nor were these strange adepts confined to one religious camp. They were of every philosophical and religious caste; they could be Daoist, Buddhist, or even Confucian, for their essential affinity was not with humanity but with the wildness of the mountains. These figures were the inside-out of civilization: eccentric, bizarre, iconoclastic; they were the antiliterati whom the literati, along with almost everyone else, believed in (see Color Plate 1).

   Despite their solitary natures, they did not always remain alone. Intellectuals collected these strange adepts and their stories like artwork. One official entertained an infamous old man, scruffy and muttering, called charmingly "Elder Drunkard." The scholar invited the drunk to dinner and found him remarkably easy to entertain, for "Elder Drunkard" subsisted entirely on a diet of beetles and insects. "Elder Drunkard" did have standards, however—he refused to consume ants, because, he confided, "they depress me."[52] Of course, recluses were deeply antisocial—hence their strange behavior. They were odd, something their names reflected. Crazy Zhou, Mountain Recluse Ma, Bare-Belly Li, The Barefoot Immortal, Master

Big Belly, Crazy Immortal Zhang, and Ironcap Zhang all had hagiographies describing them.[53] Filthy Zhang was a particularly famous recluse-adept of the Ming, and he was indeed filthy: with the pills he formed from the dirt rolled from his skin he could cure disease. He had an immense popular following. Even the Emperor sought him, as Ming Emperors often sought the aid of these esoteric masters. For fourteen years an Imperial detective—the scholar Hu Ying—was dispatched from Beijing to find him.

Ultimately, these magicians were dangerous. They were a law, and indeed a religion, outside of the orthodoxies of state. Millenarian rebels would claim a hidden adept as their founder or informing guide. One female warrior-adept of the Ming, Tang Saier, was pursued throughout the Empire. During the Yongle period she collected a band of followers and captured cities in Shandong province. She called herself Buddha-Mother and had magical skills she used to defeat the Imperial troops. This adept was never apprehended; for despite the fact that every nun or female adept near the capital was rounded up for questioning, she escaped.

The behavior of the recluse was not confined, however, to the mountain adept or rebel. It became a practice available to almost everyone. From the early medieval period up through the Ming, some few educated men and women claimed reclusive status; indeed, for men, the cult of solitude was useful; and in the Ming, scholars were expected to be recluses, at least *pro tem.* The cult of the recluse became a fad that infected much of masculine and some of feminine culture. The aberrations of the recluse became conventions of the elite class. The eccentricity of the recluse was thought to add polish to one's style; the recluse-urbanite could clearly show there were higher ideals than the mundane and the common. Consequently the vocabulary of eccentricity became common coin in Ming cities, as much in circulation as the vocabulary of filial virtues. He is a "hidden adept" or a "man who blends to the times," one neighbor might observe of another. In some cases, a man could be truly "eccentric and mad" or of the "extraordinary class." Female poets or geishas might also qualify: they were said to be "adepts of the mountains" or "adepts residing in isolation" or cultivating "stillness" or practicing "free and easy wandering." You had to expect a bit of the mad even in your own neighbors, as retreat and solitary eccentricities became de rigueur. A wide range of eccentricities from chess playing to drunkenness would serve as hallmark. There was the painter who washed the rocks of his garden every day, the merchant who filled his garden with mechanical figures, the literatus who devoted his life to the study of archery. The artist Chen Hongshou embodied many of these southern predilections. Having failed out of a government career, he became the visual chronicler of southern places and southern values: drinking parties and club meetings, escapism and self-deprecation, the life of "unorthodox, bohemian . . . behavior."[54] His self-portrait as drunk suggests much about the detachment and eccentricity of the elites (see Color Plate 2). Ming reclusiveness required flexibility, however. Many of these "recluses" lived in cities and had businesses to manage; they had to make do with whatever city life afforded. So, despite the call of the craggy landscape, Ming hermits took to some very convivial places; they may have extolled the virtues of monkish solitude, yet they never left their own backyards. In the Ming, the popularity of the cult forced compromise on this emblem of alienation; the cult of solitude accommodated the urbanite. Urbanity and solitude formed a marriage of convenience.

The scholar Wen Zhenheng, in his how-to book on the scholar's life, *On Things at Hand*, showed just how such a marriage worked. In his book—a sort of "Compleat Recluse" of the Ming—he outlined for the Ming reader the standards for membership in the recluse's club, listing for the would-be escapist just where he might go. There are several possibilities: "To live out in the far country is best; next best is to live in the rural areas; and next comes the suburbs." But distance from the city is not always possible, so Scholar Wen hedges, "But if we are unable to dwell among cliffs and valleys and to follow the path of the hermits of old, and we have to settle in city houses, we must ensure that the doors, courtyards, buildings, and rooms are clean and smart, that the pavilions suggest the outlook of a man without worldly cares, and that the studies exude the aura of a refined recluse."[55] So "city houses" will suit the solitary, as long as they have the right "aura," are "clean and smart," and "suggest" the attitude of the untrammeled. Realism tempered Ming idealism. Now a useful pun was added to the vocabulary of eremitism. The standard expression for a recluse had always been a "hidden adept" (*yin shi*); but in the Ming a convenient pun was made on the ancient term. Instead of the expression *yin* (to hide away) *shi* (adept, master), a pun was made with the word *shi*; and the word "city" (*shi*) was substituted for "adept" (*shi*). Now, by the most convenient of linguistic rearrangements, the two opposites of being an adept and being an urbanite were linked. Instead of *yin shi*, "hiding as an adept," you could *shi yin*, "in the city, hide away."[56]

The ideal of the hermitage came to infect everyone, from lictor to Emperor. At the Imperial level, the Imperial architects ensured the recluse's escape; as the Yongle Emperor constructed the enormous Palace Compound with its massive walls, vast courtyards, and grand receiving halls, rows of government offices, magnificent residences, a hunting park, and no less than three lakes, he deemed it necessary to add also one simple thatched hut surrounded by a rustic fence.[57] Nor were merchants excluded; merchant-"recluses" lavished huge sums on the pristine environment and produced luxurious hermitages. Their gardens were often great productions, with rare boulders and dwarf plantings, finely carved walkways and handsome pavilions; some could cover acres of property and consume entire family fortunes.[58] The hermitage of the extremely rich could be built with exotic hardwoods and contain elaborate lacquerwork for screens and beds; there might be silks of every weight and detail for hangings and beautiful antiques and paintings. Some merchant clans had two homes, an estate in the city and a villa in the country, with the country garden expensively appointed to suggest the ascetic hermit.[59] One merchant-"recluse" paid one thousand ounces of silver—the price on a good-sized estate—for an antique incense burner used to create the perfect aura of the recluse.[60] Even the ordinary citizen participated in the cult. In observing the customs of the lowest level of local clerks, one official wondered what a humble runner for a local official could possibly do with a scholar's study in his house, all outfitted with wood paneling, and a courtyard with goldfish and pots of flowers.[61]

Of course, it got to be too much. "Why must they parade their oddities for public display?" complained one scholar. And another wrote a chapter on the "Stupidities and Excesses of the Hermits."[62] Indeed, many thought all the effete practices so much studied nonsense. Li Yu, the infamous parodist and playwright, composed a poem he called "Bu deng gao fu," "Rhapsody on Not Climbing Anywhere."[63] Not the least of the problems was the expense. Scholar Wen, who provided advice on city seclusions, was patronizing about the vulgarity of the wealthy who built great houses. "Those who only use large quantities of timber and paint are building themselves prisons and fetters,"[64] he counseled. But the urban sanctuaries of the Ming did not come cheap. Wang Shimin was a scholar and official who served in office and raised a family, but like many Ming men he played at the hermit's life. His only problem, however, was financial. Over the course of his life he managed to deplete his family inheritance: "I began in wealth and ended in poverty." His money—not spent on family or entertainments, nor on investments or bribes—was spent on his quiet hermitage and perfect garden surround. "I was," he admitted in his confessional essay, "fatally addicted to gardens."[65] The fad, however, prevailed.

The goals of all this "seclusion" was life "above the mundane"; it was an attempt to join the "untrammeled class," to achieve a perfected life of refined gesture and a superior setting. The garden was especially important to this "urban recluse," for the garden reflected most clearly his or her "untrammeled" nature. The garden was intended to be the replica of the sacred mountain and the site for the part-time sage's occasional apotheosis; "there should be fine trees and interesting plants, a display of antiquities and books, so that those who live there should forget about age," one scholar observed.[66] There "should be" a good deal more than that, however. Having the proper garden for exuding "the aura of a refined recluse" was no small matter. In fact, you had to bring the mountain to the city, albeit in miniature. Dramatic views, the illusion of distance, the look of untamed growth, and the antiquity of rocks were some of the desired features of a garden. This meant miniature mountain ranges, small forests, watercourses, lakes, caverns, and grottoes. Then you needed paths to take you through the manufactured wilderness, with bridges, covered walkways, and viewing spots laid out; and finally pavilions, small studios, and thatched huts for enjoying the flowers, the foliage, and the constructed views of imported mountains that were meticulously placed to suit the recluse at every change in the season (see Figure 1.7).

Figure 1.7   The Yu garden of Shanghai. Note the strange rocks forming a miniature mountain. (*Wu Youru huabao* vol. 3, "Famous Sites").

If the garden suggested the recluse, still more did the hermitage, with all its many props. The hermitage, or *zhai,* was where the garden aesthete studied and read, painted and composed poetry, greeted intimates and drank, where they led the "recluse's" life. Like the garden, the hermitage was not simply a location, however; it was the expression of the recluse's very nature. The *zhai* could be a thatched hut or it could be a studio retreat with many rooms all surrounded with a porch and railings from which to gaze out at the garden. The hermitage had to have the right "aura," exactly the correct tone; it was the recluse's signature. One Ming writer, Li Ruhua, described one:

> The library/study should be situated where the brook twists and bends between the hills. The total structure should not exceed two or three buildings, with an upper story to observe the clouds and mists. On the four sides there should be a hundred slender bamboo plants . . . [and a] gnarled old prunus with low twisting branches to come in through the window. . . . The east building houses the Daoist [canon] and Buddhist sutras, and the west building houses the Confucian classics. In the center, a bed and desk with a scattering of fine calligraphy and paintings. In the morning and evenings, white rice and fish stew, fine wine and tea, . . . [with] a strong man at the gate to reject social callers.[67]

If the hermitage and garden bore the recluse's stamp, still more did the objects of the hermitage. Like the rocks of the garden, the books and inkstones, brushes and antiques of the *zhai* were all props suggesting the drama of the recluse. They had to banish the ordinary to lift daily life out of the mundane; they could not be common. If god was in the details, then the objects of daily life needed to reflect it. In *The Mirror of Flowers,* one Ming scholar discussed the method of dwarfing trees, emphasizing the influence these miniature specimens exert: "The prominent man and the poet cultivate flowers in containers of reduced size, with the goal of thus escaping from the commonplace."[68]

This passion for the small became, in turn, a kind of aestheticism. If earlier generations debated endlessly about Confucian interpretations of ancient texts, late Ming literati—and literati imitators—reflected intensely on the special qualities of "things close at hand," becoming explicitly devoted to "superfluous things."[69] In this scaled-down, private realm, no object was too trivial; from incense to brushes, the literati were fascinated by all the objects of daily life, even devoting their scholarly lives to them. Countless books on small subjects proliferated; there were books on flower arranging, orchid growing, on rocks for the gardens or for the display pots; books on inkstones, chess, paintings, and dining tables; works on antiques and on bronze collecting; as well as tomes on aromatics and incense, on tea, food, fabrics, crafts, utensils, and domestic cats.[70]

The role of the garden and hermitage, however, was more than aesthetic, for the part-time "recluse" had higher ambitions than the pursuit of pleasure; these garden inhabitants were a good deal more than simple hedonists. Rather the goal of the escape was to eliminate the common and introduce the transcendent; there were overtones of a sacred search in the life of "seclusion" and a level of magical thinking in this garden life. Gardens existed on two planes—the mundane and the transcendent. The garden was a small recreation of the grand plan of Nature; it was a magical container that invoked the landscape of the cosmos; it both imitated and, in some sense, was the universe. One scholar termed the role of the garden-microcosm "parareligious,"[71] tracing its origins back thousands of years, and called the practice "universisme."[72] Ming writers themselves called these gardens sacred. The author and intellectual Li Yu describes the visit he made to a friend's garden: "It is now many days since I visited your famous garden, but even if my body has left it, my soul is still there. Revered Master, you have placed on the table of your studio Fang-hu and Peng-lai [islands of the immortals] on a small scale. That day, was it not like a stroll with the immortals, like a flight with the whole family to become immortal."[73] One Song text elaborated on just how the gardener encloses the cosmos in miniature. The author took special pains to explain the usefulness of rocks; these humble objects contain divine essences that may be usefully captured for domestic application. "The objects that are the purest quintessence of Heaven and Earth are found among rocks; penetrating the earth, they take on strange forms. . . . The big ones are worthy of being set out in a garden; the little ones are placed on stands or tables in a house."[74]

If gardening was the art of the microcosm, then it in turn made the gardener-recluse magical. Gardening was a form of sympathetic magic; the gardener created a magical container. Like Daoist adepts who contained the world in a gourd, the literati-gardeners had the power of the cosmos at their fingertips. They were adepts; and in turn the cult of the recluse gave the garden dwellers—male and female—a sanctity that legitimized all this attention to leisure, to the personal, and to the private. Despite the narrow realm of their private enthusiasms, it was a mystified realm of deep significance. Of course, there was something watered down about this magic—this was not the magic of the Imperial cult, nor of the great monasteries; but in transforming the private and personal into the "extramundane," the authority of the esoteric was made accessible. The urban "recluses" and their partners and friends did not have to train for years, learn an elaborate canon, nor move to remote areas for long periods of study. An ersatz religious legitimacy came to their gates.

For women, the cult of solitude brought two important changes. Solitude affected gentry women, who themselves became recluses or at least assumed, like Yuan Hongdao, the recluse's life. For these women, the ideal of solitude meant a place to work and meditate in a place that was outside the regulation of the family; some of these women even removed themselves from the community. The isolation of these women was not, however, the isolation of the lonely, for these women were not detritus. The female recluse was an outsider, but her status as outsider was informed by religion and magic, by the immense authority of the cult of solitude, by the value placed on the solitary and her eccentricities, and by the implied sanctity of her character. In the Ming, a women was not a pariah for her outcast status. Like the men who mimicked the recluse, she enjoyed the protection of the myth.

For geishas, the cult meant a new source of legitimacy. The cult of reclusiveness was, ironically, a rather gregarious cult; partners were required. If the merchant and literatus celebrated the cult in the cities, they certainly celebrated it with women. This provided an important forum for the geisha. She became the expert on the art of private pleasures; she knew about incense, folk songs, poetry, painting, fine teas, and good wines. There was also an inherent romanticism of the cult; reclusiveness joined with the ideals of *qing* to become a cult of affective and intimate life. Private life was no longer claimed only by the filial woman; the discourse of piety and the lineage did not dominate the ideals of domestic relations. Passionate attention to the lives of the artistic mates became a new ideal. Now geishas joined the recluses as poets and scholars; the geisha was no longer mistress of the stage, but mistress of the minutely appointed study. She joined the reclusive scholar as a poet-collaborator.

These women who have echoed the several features of Ming life seem to be of the same fabric as the men of the Ming. There is the pious wife to match the filial son, the esoteric mystic alone like her male counterpart, the romantic geisha mated with the talented scholar-artist, and the female healers, thriving in the urban prosperity in both the North and the South. Both women and men seem to have inherited the same conditions and inhabited the same meeting ground of myth and history. Yet these women are not die-cut copies of masculine archetypes; though they have inherited the traditions of piety and solitude and been sheltered in the cites of the Ming, they are different. Their chief difference is danger; these women are regarded as risky, seen to be perversely out of control. They have been regulated, banned, overlooked, and written out of the record; even the wet-nurse who dominated the Court has remained in the very margins of the historical record. It is no accident, however, that their lives have remained in the shadows. The men of the Ming had an empire to order, but they also had gender conflict that was often open warfare. For when piety, solitude, eroticism, and enterprising urbanity found expression in women, these women became deeply troublesome.

2
Geishas

One branch of soft golden hue, soon after the frost,
Half-open by the hedge in the pale evening sun.
Why fuss again to face the Southern Hills, with wine-cup in hand?
I'm sufficiently provided with dry food for the life of a recluse.

The geisha Xue Susu[1]

The degradation inherent in the life of the geisha was no secret to anyone in the Ming: "To be unchaste is my fate," wept one geisha, "but what is there I can do about it?"[2] For most geishas, life in the "education district" consisted of sexual servitude. Male "guests" selected a geisha and paid for sexual intercourse with her,[3] or paid for her presence at drunken, orgiastic parties.[4] Nor could the life in "the district" provide economic independence for most geishas. One Ming intellectual described many women who, though wealthy as younger women, died in poverty and difficulty.[5] They often entered the life through slavery; many women "descended into the education district" as war prizes. At the beginning of the Ming, for example, the wives of Mongol captives were forced into the geisha world; geishas with the names Dun or To were women of Mongol heritage, descended from their enslaved mothers and grandmothers.[6] Desperation typically marked a woman's entry into the geisha district; when the Mongol merchant Master Tie died at the end of the Ming, his daughters were left with few options: "When my father was killed, both my sister and I were forced into geisha life."[7] Even the very brilliant geisha entered the life against her will. One of the most famous artist-geishas of the late Ming was Wang Wei; Wang published a volume of travel accounts, earned her livelihood as a painter, and was acclaimed as a great poet. Yet her personal account was as bitter as all the others: "My father died when I was seven years old and I sank down into the Northern Quadrant (geisha area)."[8] Most women were forced to work in the district; it is no wonder that "dropping from the registration list" was the explicit goal of virtually every geisha.

Despite the humiliating and desperate origins of the geishas, however, some few of these women achieved a status as artists and urban cult figures. Starting as personalities of the pop-

25

Figure 2.1 *Flowers,* **by Xue Susu. (1564–1637), dated 1615, detail. Handscroll, ink on paper. 101.4 in. × 249 in. China, B66 D22 (The Asian Art Museum of San Francisco, The Avery Brundage Collection).**

ular stage within the education district, they became important characters in the urban dramas of late Ming intellectuals. Celebrated first as women dedicated to the arts, they became exemplars of talent in an art-obsessed age. These women joined the literati as "mates in excellence"; they were famous for their expertise in theater, music, painting, and poetry, and became the essential figures for the gathering of artistic males. Nor was their expertise limited to art; it extended also to the artful and passionate life. They functioned as counselors on matters of refinement, as the resident experts on the elaborate esoterica of a romanticized, affective life. Some of these women became public celebrities, urban folk heroes; crowds followed them, popular literature celebrated them, and an adoring public called them "River Consorts" or "Divine Women." Such adoration may seem trivial to contemporary observers, hollow praise from the fatuous men who exploited the women. Public acclaim, however, can translate into wealth and social status; cultural capital can mean real capital. Finally, some of this subset of geishas stepped out of the education district into the charmed circle occupied previously by the male intellectual. They became painters and poets, known for their own work; they edited books of scholarship and published volumes of poetry and letters. Some of these women took to the reclusive life the way the literati did. They imitated the mountain adept with her love of privacy and love of travel. Many took to a life of public daring: they were political activists, avant-garde thinkers, and iconoclasts who challenged traditional pieties. Even a woman like Wang Wei, who despised her entrance into the district, had a kind of freedom derived from her status as geisha. As a woman of the education district, Wang could travel on her own, and did so—it was something she loved to do. "I am by nature addicted to mountains and waters," she said.[9] Wang traveled all over Hunan, wrote poetry about her travels, and is credited with editing the travel compilations, *Records of Famous Mountains*.[10] Wang Wei was both a furious servant, abased by life in the district, and yet an aloof emblem of freedom. The role of geisha countenanced such extremes.

This leap, however, from sexual humiliation to independence, or from privation to consequence, may seem absurd. To a modern observer the geisha is irrevocably contaminated by her life of sexual alliances. In traditional China, however, the geisha was a complex figure with ambiguous status, for though she was damned as immoral from one perspective, yet within an elite, male subculture the geisha was sanctioned and accepted. She was a *ji*, a female performer of popular arts of the theater. More than simply a stage performer, a *ji* had an entree to literati life. Although from our western vantage point it might seem as if the geisha was an ostracized figure—a prostitute excluded from decorous society—since at least the medieval period the lives of the geisha and literati intersected.[11]

Since the Tang Dynasty (618–907), the geisha was the doyenne of the gathering of male elites; she was the chatelaine of the public event, functioning as hostess when men of the government held convocations outside of the Court for the celebratory side of official life. Nor were these gatherings insignificant events in the life of the literati. The artistic gathering, with its elaborate games of poetry and drinking, had always been important. Since at least the early medieval period, men gathered to cap each other's rhymes, to display their calligraphy, or to recall lines from the Classics; some of the gatherings lasted for days, and some few gatherings became famous for centuries. They became the standard, the hallmark of great literati moments, helping to define the literati as a class. Clearly these gatherings were not trivial social events; art was competitive sport at these occasions—good poetic composition indicated a measure of artistic readiness in the participant. The banquet games served as a continual ritual of evaluation, as a source of accreditation for membership in the elite. The geisha participated fully in these events. A wife was by social requirement minimally educated; training in poetry was for the geisha—she was the woman who capped the line of poetry or knew the right citation. At these banquets the geishas were poet performers, near equals for a specific time in a circumscribed world.

When geisha halls were established in the early Ming, the formal aspects of the geisha's role were maintained. The early Ming Emperor Tai Zu created the geisha compound of Nanjing for the purpose of hosting public functions;[12] the Emperor charged the geisha halls with "assisting in banquets for persons of rank."[13] These banquets were not seedy or vulgar; the geishas of the sixteen houses of the Compound were listed as entertainment officers.[14] Officials and geishas were in fact forbidden to have sex.[15] The role as banquet organizer continued throughout the Ming. One geisha operated an extensive banqueting facility and was known for holding performances at the banquets and for managing large numbers of often difficult guests.[16] Another geisha utilized her geisha house for artistic gatherings; her establishment was more studio than banquet hall. The poet Yu Huai described the social gathering he held at her house: "Every time I invited my comrades for a literary gathering I would arrange to hold it at the house of Tenth Lady. Each friend would hire one of her intelligent assistants to attend them at the inkstone and mat: they would grind the ink in the inkstones and burn incense."[17] At all these gatherings, the geisha served as the woman of the public realm; the industry of these women was the public, artistic entertainment of the masculine elite, not whoring.

The geisha of these "artistic gatherings," however, was more than a hostess, for her role was not limited to public reception. Historically and during the Ming, the geisha was a stage performer. Not just an entertainer, a mere "singer" or "songstress," she was trained and skilled in the arts of the musical theater. True, her arts were often popular arts and she was known more as a performer than as a creator; but her competency as a performer was valued. Western translators have typically minimized her skills; since they first encountered her, they have relegated her to a linguistic no-man's land, characterizing her more as a whore than trained artist. They have used terms that vary from diminishing to evasive; if she is not called prostitute, she is called "singing girl" or, better yet, a "sing-song girl"—all conveying the impression of a cross between chanteuse and street waif. These women, however, were not practitioners of revue, skits, or folk songs; neither were they chorus girls, music hall singers, or streetwalkers. The famous geishas were artists trained in *xiju*—opera. They were known for the types of roles they played, for like all actors and vocalists, they specialized, often performing selections of the major arias, and some were known for performance of single operas. Their work required this specialization; their repertoire was complex and difficult, and no vocalist or actress could achieve brilliance in the entire corpus of spoken or musical theater. One actress was famous for her portrayal of the maid-matchmaker, Hong Niang, in the "West Chamber Dream."[18] Another geisha was a diva famous for decades for her tragic roles. The literatus Yu Huai invited her to perform at his estate when she had been long established as a performer. He commented on her personal style as well as on her performance:

> She was direct and elegant with none of those affectations of applied makeup and gesturing sleeves. By practice and custom she had acquired a specialization in opera. When she took the stage she dared equally to the roles of young male lead as well as to the ingenue. When I first met her it was late in her life; I invited her to my home that she might perform the play, "A Tale of Thorn Hairpins"; she assumed the part of the major role of Wang Shipeng. When the time came for the two scenes "Sacrificing at the River" and "Mother's Visit," she performed those heartrending, tear-soaked lines; her voice and her sobs rushed against each other in a torrent. We were overwhelmed as we watched: even fellow veterans of the Pear Garden training sighed at her unmatchable performance.[19]

This geisha—without makeup or gesturing sleeves—is here both an individual and a musician. Some few paintings suggest these same qualities in geishas. Wu Wei, in his famous illustration of a Tang anecdote, is thought to have used a Nanjing contemporary as his model. His geisha portrait of a thoughtful, focused woman of slightly masculine bearing has no echoes in that vapid, pidgin term "sing-song girl"[20] (see Color Plate 3).

Hence the best term for this woman is not "prostitute" but, in fact, "geisha." The Ming word for geisha, *ji*, like the Japanese term *gei-sha*, conveyed artist, not whore. The word *ji* specifically means "female artist or performer"; the expression *gei-sha* means "person of the arts." *Ji* is related to words meaning ingenuity, talent, and ability. Like the Japanese geisha, the Chinese geisha was trained in theatrical, musical and literary composition, and performance. Other Ming terms used for the geisha indicate her specialization: geishas were labeled poet-geishas (*shi ji*) or song-geishas (*ge ji*), and some were known as actresses (*you*). The geisha was in a basic and important sense a woman of the theater.

Of course, the geisha class, like the merchant class, encompassed an enormous spectrum of practices and practitioners; many geishas were paid for single sexual encounters, and even the most elite and artistic of the geishas had intimate relations with a series of partners. Notions of sexual contamination, however, should not prevent a fair assessment of the geisha as a skilled theatrical performer; whether she had no sexual partners or many, she was still an artist who was judged by high standards long established by other performers and by connoisseurs. She was not a mere courtesan, and she was certainly not a "sing-song girl."

If the geisha was more than a street performer, the literatus was more than a civil servant. In the late Ming, especially in the South, the literati became men of the hermitage, of the romantic, and of the intimate.[21] They claimed to worship leisure and elegance and imitated the "carefree man" as opposed to the pious man. "I admire this man secretly for his 'self contentment,'" said Yuan Hongdao.[22] They championed *xian qing*—idle feelings: "If you can equip yourself with idle feelings and the eyes of wisdom, everything you see will form part of a picture," said Li Yu.[23] Words such as "fascination" (*qu*) and the "childlike heart" (*tong xin*) were new mottoes. Above all, the literati praised passion—*qing*—above even the values of loyalty and piety. These men now took intimate and affective life to a level of high importance and reconfigured their private estates as new centers. An artful life in the contained domestic spaces became the goal of life, and the Empire now rotated on a changed axis.

This class of very wealthy—often unemployed—intellectuals became the "new men" of the literati class. These men of the South spent their energies on the private, not public, life, staying home to work at a life of private passion and a life devoted to the arts, calling themselves "urban recluses," attending obsessively to "things close at hand." The educated Southerners turned their backs on government service; the *jinshi*—the sign of achievement for elites, the advanced degree accorded successful examination candidates—became less important.[24] Wealth was a factor in these developments. Wealthy estates and idle sons were supported by a prodigious economy; Imperial employment became less vital. Indeed, "the new prosperity challenged old ideas about the good life."[25] One Qing scholar looked back on the idle pleasures of the Ming elite and observed that many explicitly disdained official employment; he complained that the cream of society held neither title nor official employment.[26] These gentlemen of the South, he noted, referred to themselves rather as "students," or "recluses," as if employment was beneath their dignity.[27] Many critics were appalled by these "new men," especially the sober critics from the Qing era; they said these "students" and "recluses" were the "great shame of the literati class."[28] Despite the apparently small focus of the obsessions of the literati, however, their goals were ambitious. These men did not use the term "recluse" lightly; the world of the hermitage had serious intent. The garden setting, the literary and scholarly arts, even the accoutrements of reclusive life all had resonance; for the literati did not just attend to the daily and trivial, they elevated them, investing them with cultic, if not religious, overtones.

This shift in masculine priorities created a new landscape for the geisha. The woman of the arts became chief counselor on the artful life, central focus of the affective life. Geishas were more than silent partners in the idealized landscape; they were heroic, grandly symbolic of the values of the private life. Geishas were the romantic exemplars that fit the romanticism of the age.[29] "If you are deep in *qing*," said Feng Menglong, "you can surmount difficulty, you can display brilliance in the arts, or you can explode with anger."[30] Geishas understood true passion; there was something brave and quixotic in them, and only they were "free and unrestrained" (*fengliu fangdan*). They were the true "cavaliers of *qing*" and made fine "*ying xiong*," heroes; or they displayed true "*hao*"—magnanimity or grandeur of spirit. "That air of shining magnificence and the qualities of generosity and bravado are not sustained so much in men as they are in women," asserted Feng.[31] Geishas appeared as guardians of the passionate; they were the ultimate judges of the worthy or extraordinary act. "When *qing* is not achieved, and moral daring does not surge up," Feng warned, "then the event will not be remarkable, and such lack of *qing* is what women find ridiculous."[32] In his famous anthology of stories about *qing*, Feng Menglong wrote of bravado, heroism, and defiance—all carried out for *qing*. One of his chapters is exclusively devoted to "heroes of love"; half of these heroes are geishas. Geishas were the appropriate partners in this reconfiguration of elite culture. Later observers damned these exercises in romanticism as self-indulgent; but the results in the Ming were significant. Through such theories of the romantic and the heroic, the literati and geisha—as well as the literati and the companionate wife—redefined private life, mystifying the affective just as the Confucian mystified the lineage.

W. H. Auden has written, "Opera is the sustained expression of those moments when we say, 'I feel like singing.'"[33] By extension, the creation of utopias are "extensions of those moments when we say 'What if . . . .'" They are life "in the subjunctive mode."[34] In the late Ming, the literati and geisha attempted life in the subjunctive mode; they sought to create a cultic utopia in "things close at hand." Together, they created an alliance of passionate aesthetes, attempting to sustain a romanticized subculture, to construct a world of perfect gesture and perfect feeling. They manufactured a second world separated from the actual world—a "green world," to use the Renaissance term. These women and men, behind the walls of estates, cultivated ideal landscapes, seeking to create "ecologies of perfection."[35] Nor were these constructs a private vision limited to the small landscapes of some few geishas and poets; this was a collective revision of life. Literatus and geisha received wide-scale acclaim from the urban observer, achieving celebrity and status; the ecologies of perfection became a widely practiced, ad hoc cult.

Mates in Excellence

In these ecologies of perfection, a perfected domestic life was the grand ideal, and the private hermitage the new sacred space. In these mystified places, there appeared new icons. Instead of the filial son and pious daughter, there were the passionate and sensitive aesthetes. Now in some circles the geisha-literatus dyad supplanted the old exemplars. The glamorous term for such a couple was *jia ou*, "mates in excellence"; it implied the match of two who were devoted to the artful life. *Ou* means an equal matching or pairing, and *jia* refers to a refined life as well as a life of achieved excellence. Another term for the mating of these two icons was "the man of talent and the woman of excellence" (*cai zi jia ren*). The expression implies a love match of the woman and man of artistic talents and sensibilities. This alliance was not the pairing of a dominant male and passive female, but rather of two comparable and complementary figures. "Whether they are paired in virtue, talent, or appearance," Feng Menglong determined, "they must be mates to one another, and then they are equal matches."[36]

If the two "mates in excellence" were idealized, then still more so was their life together. In these new mythologies, conjugal life became a cult, the rules of which were simple: private life is an art, one of the higher ones. If the rules of the cult were simple, however, the rituals were not, for it is difficult to imagine the extremes to which the practices would go; the goal of romantic life was nothing less than perfection. Like the literatus who made his yard a cosmic replica, the mates in excellence made their marriage an affective utopia; they intended to elevate the common to the "the lands of the immortals" or to life "above the mundane," and to locate in domestic life a sense of the transcendent.

Together the two mates created a theater of the romantic; their intimate life was configured as spectacle, with the mates cast as both protagonists and audience. Each gesture had great significance; small communications became elaborate productions, marked by the properly nuanced tone and simple but elegant props. Intimate life was a continuous display of studied but apparently artless gestures that conveyed charm and sensitivity. Yu Huai, one writer of the late Ming, describes the manner of saving the record of a love affair. What may seem like a simple matter was to him a question of elaborate requirements; you clearly did not just transcribe the details in your journal. Paper, ink, script, and literary style—even storage, aroma, and wrapping—had to be obsessively right.

> For a record of this affair, you must use a slip of paper that is ice-like silver in color, and draw on it raven-black thread-lines; then with small seal characters you should compose the record in the poetic genre of the "Goddess Lo"—*fu* style. Then you wrap the poetic record in a ribbon shaped like a phoenix among the clouds, store it in a kraken-dragon box, and finally steam it all through with incense. Then, when you hold it you will be confused and lost from the deep aroma of it.[37]

All this, of course, sets up the perfect moment when you may read it, which Yu Huai does allow you to do: "In the breeze-clear moonlight, among the white blossoms of the red bean— the blossoms of longing—you may open it."[38]

Domestic life for such men and women had a quality of the mythic. In these descriptions, there is a sense of constant self-reflection and self-regard; consort and literatus are being seen and being studied. "On the occasion of our walk, the glorious setting with the throngs of observers shone forth brilliantly; the scene has become myth ever since";[39] or again: "As I think back on her now, her image surges up before me as elegant as a painting."[40]

Even the erotic was transformed, as the mates in excellence altered the connotations of intimacy, recreating the tactile and sensual as refined and effete. The scholar-official Mao Xiang recorded just such an idealized relationship with his concubine Dong Xiaowan; he wrote of the preoccupations of the two as they pass the evening together. Their night—as he described it, in any case—was not a night of sexual pleasure but a night of refined, even esoteric, attractions. Indeed, Mao's text is not an erotic text at all. These mates in excellence are concerned rather with the details that constitute their perfected landscape: the space itself, the carpets and curtains, the incense selected and the burners used, the look of the embers, the aroma created, and, finally, the overall atmosphere of the scene.

> Then on winter nights we would have a jade curtain draped on all four sides of a small room, and the carpets piled thickly on top of each other; then we would burn two or three crimson candles, each one two feet long. . . . Then we would arrange a few incense burners—of various sizes—of the Xuande reign period and light them. The fire among the ashes was like molten gold or an amber-colored jade. Then we carefully stirred the living embers of the burners and placed some fine ground pebbles over an inch-high level of the embers, and selected the right incense to burn there. We passed half the night, as one stick of incense hardened. The rock of incense neither scorched, nor dissipated, but gradually thickened into a resin. The aroma that arose was of a pure sweetness, and the crystallized hot incense seemed to have within it the smell of plum blossoms halfway opened. . . . I remember that together we would sit in stillness to contemplate this aroma and the way it permeated the air of the room.[41]

The tenor of their interlude is, of course, insular and private. This is not a simple romanticism. In the obsessive attention to minutiae of the room, there is rather a sense of love displaced; the erotic has become the esoteric.

If the customs of these perfectionists were complex, however, they were never made explicit. The Confucian codes were far more helpful: where you stood, where you sat, what utensils and what tone of voice—they prescribed every action of pious domestic life. For the domestic aesthete, however, you were on your own. The problem was as subtle as the definition of style; no gesture was fixed, and variety according to moment was essential. Shades of meaning depended on a thousand variables. Hence the importance of taste, for clearly this was not a project for ordinary wives and pedestrian husbands; all these baroque convolutions had an implied warning label: Do not try this with the untrained. The perfectly conducted love could only be achieved by the male aesthete and the female artist. One did not sit and compose the perfect love poem on the perfect paper with the perfect tea, etc. etc., with just anyone, for one might slip up and, as Feng Menglong warned, "the affair would not be extraordinary (*qi*)."[42] This, of course, is where the geisha came in. In the precious atmosphere of a highly cultivated domestic life, she became the authority, counselor, sage of the subtleties of the aesthete's life, instructing the literati on the details. One scholar has called these men of the South "useless men,"[43] but these women were not. For example, Dong Xiaowan, the geisha who married Mao Xiang, became an important source on domestic aestheticism. Of course, she had all the prerequisites. She was established as a poet when she worked as a geisha;[44] as a woman of the arts she was versed in the world of the intimate; once married to Mao Xiang, despite his age and status, she appears to have become his teacher on matters of taste.

In the portrayal of his marriage to her, Mao Xiang describes a lecture he received from her on the properties of various types of incense. She lists six kinds, describing the plants from which they derive, mentioning the appearance of the leaves, the trunk, where they are grown, and how and by whom they are gathered. She lists for him how the root of the plant may look, its coloration and shape, and even how it may be carved by the artisan. Then we learn how it is burned; how it is transformed into incense; and, finally, what the aroma is like—whether vulgar or superior, rancid and scorching—and what it resembles—whether "a cluster of roses saturated with genial dew," or "aloes wood wafted by winds," or wine in a "jade goblet," and so on. Her language is elaborate, her knowledge esoteric. Nor is she patronized for her knowledge; Mao suggests that he is the student in this discussion. "My elegant consort would sit quietly with me in her own room; then she would meticulously rank the qualities of the best aromatics."[45] She is the local expert, the source on the intimate and affective life, the retainer of the vast oral tradition on a life of *qing*. If the literatus wrote books on incense, furnishings, fabrics, and precious stones, the geisha was one of his sources.

These southern preoccupations may seem too arcane for any but the initiated; there would hardly seem to be a wider audience for such private obsessions. Surprisingly, however, these icons had an enthusiastic public. Qing Emperors had their portraits painted as southern romantics; perhaps they play acted the aesthete when weary of Court matters.[46] The geisha Gu Mei, after marriage to Imperial Attendant Gong Zhilu, had great renown as a cultivated woman. She received scholars and artists, awarded her paintings to devotees, and gave famous literati parties. Her birthday party in Nanjing was held at a luxurious estate decorated in hanging lanterns; hundreds of guests were entertained with theatrical performances. After her death, the rather austere-looking Gu Mei was renamed Lady Xu, and she was distinguished in death with a famously elaborate funeral[47] (see Color Plate 4). Even the broader public followed the fortunes of the man of talent and woman of excellence. Their romantic attachments were circulated in classical tales, and then were quickly adapted into vulgar sources.[48] The public seemed to love these figures; you could achieve some real renown as a mate in excellence, in fact, and become very famous for being very sensitive. At times, there was even an urban audience to applaud you. The artist and intellectual Mao Xiang depicted an episode of adoration in which he and his mate in excellence were celebrated, as their private excursion became theater for the masses. On a jaunt with his stunning match, Dong

Xiaowan, the two caused a sensation among the holiday hikers, drawing the attention of the hoi polloi who followed along after them.

> We had tied our boat up to the bank at that time. My noble consort was wearing a gown made from a piece of western fabric. . . . It was very thin—like a cicada's wing, and of a snowy whiteness. The gown had a pink lining and in it she looked like the famed beauty Zhang Lihua who wore the rainbow skirt. After we disembarked from our boat, we climbed up Gold Hill, and saw five dragon boats fighting the waves in the waters below. Thousands of other travelers followed behind the two of us, pointing us out as a pair of transcendents. As we circled up the mountain, wherever the two of us stopped, the dragon boats would vie with each other to stay near us, circling and circling, refusing to leave.[49]

Clearly, the exclusive nature of their rapport did not preclude the attention of "thousands" of observers. Rather, mates in excellence together elevated the art of the intimate and simultaneously garnered public attention as icons of the artful life. Geishas enjoyed no small part of this public acclaim, and the enthusiasm of "thousands of other travelers" gave them a status that was denied them through clan and decorum.

The status of "transcendent" accorded by an adoring public would seem, however, exaggeration. When Ming intellectuals called their mates River Consorts or Divine Women, we might safely assume the suggestion of divine status to be a linguistic conceit; romantic enthusiasm is one thing, deification another. One scholar has asserted, however, that there may indeed be cultic overtones to the woman of excellence, that these female icons did have an iconography, that the glamorous epithet "Divine Woman" had deep cultural resonance. Rolf Stein in his *Worlds in Miniature* asserts that the woman of excellence portrayed as a divinity is not arbitrary, that she has a legitimate claim to divine status. For Stein, the gorgeous woman of the garden is not simply an erotic or artful icon; rather she is the avatar of female divinities of fertility, and, conversely, the garden is her precinct. In the ancient lore of both China and Vietnam, divine women ruled fertile places. The goddess Thien-y A-na of Vietnam was the goddess of floods, of rains, and of aromatic woods and was the goddess of lush landscapes and gardens. In Chinese myth, Holy Mothers and female mountain spirits inhabited great parks and governed the magical events that sustained the lush life of the garden and the cosmos it encapsulated; they governed fertility, restoration, rebirth, and beginnings. Gardens, growth, power, and sacred women were all linked. "The abundance of vegetation in a propitious site (mountain and rivers, trees and stones), connected with a blessed world of immortals—all the themes of fertility, power, and endurance go along with the image of the vessel . . . that holds an inexhaustible drink and with the Holy Mothers."[50] Although the geisha may seem a far cry from a Holy Mother, her place in the cosmic gardens of southern estates irrevocably suggested these mythic echoes. Nor was the literatus simply her master; in the sacred garden, he was more visitor than owner. Indeed, when the literatus ordered his groves of bamboo, planted his rows of peonies and chrysanthemums, or created the rocky settings to look like mountains, he imitated the god of fertility; but a woman was looking over his shoulder. He was in her world. Gorgeous, manufactured landscapes with their cosmological overtones called for the presence of the fertile, sacred female. The garden is a female image, not a male, evoking from myth not a literate man but a fertile woman. The literati nimbly adopted these magical sites, making the garden a sign of masculine culture.

There are many stories of women and goddesses in the contained garden in Ming literature. In the novel *Jin Ping Mei*, the concubine Lady of the Vase is essentially the woman of the garden and of fertility—her name means vessel or container; she is the concubine whose property becomes the garden of the master of the house, she is consistently associated with wealth and increase, and she is one of the two women on the estate to deliver a child.[51] Perhaps Stein is right; the literatus-gardener of the Ming, like the garden aesthete of Vietnam, took a feminine folklore and made it his. Whether he converted the tradition or invented it, however, the literati relied on the idealized women; the "mates in excellence" were the icons in the hermitage garden, essential players in the romance of affective life.

Geisha–Recluses, Warriors, and Artists

In the late Ming the geisha did more than remain in the hermitage garden, however; she did not simply join the literatus as mate in excellence in pursuit of the perfected moment, limiting her intelligence to the esoterica of daily life. Rather, the geisha imitated the literatus, becoming a pseudo-literatus herself. She exploited her life in the studios of these great estates and adapted to it, successfully colonizing some of the spaces of elite life. Like the urban recluse in his perfect study, she became a member of the "untrammeled class" and took on some of the features of this complex persona. Geishas were especially adept at assuming three aspects of literati life. First of all, geishas made brilliant recluses; many imitated the itinerant recluses and kept travel journals based on their trips to famous gardens and famous mountains. Some of these geisha-recluses bought property and moved out of the district, refused marriage, and established themselves as hermit-artists in their own studios. If reclusiveness did not suit, however, some became defiant iconoclasts or political activists, members themselves of the late Ming avant-garde. These geishas claimed to be "knights errant"; they mocked convention and called themselves "heroes of love." Finally, some geishas commanded that basic preserve of the literatus—his studio; these women became important authors or great artists; they authored volumes of poetry, edited collections of literature, or supported themselves as painters. It may seem anomalous for the geisha to demonstrate such independence; but in the Ming, independence was thought to mark the characters of these statused and artistic geishas. Their risky lives were based on precarious sources of power, but geishas did become emblems of boldness and originality. It is one of the ironies of the Ming, in fact, that the category of woman whose life seems most clearly to represent subservience came to represent autonomy.

Recluses

As recluses, geishas were as solitary and proud as any male recluse. Geisha-recluses loved mountains and mountain travel, wore clothes of a monastic simplicity, and preferred the pristine, simple, and well-ordered studio. The retiring and quiet life of the recluse was natural to them. Nor was this surprising. Members of the untrammeled class were typically misanthropic as well as arcane and learned in their interests; geishas were no different. Geisha Fan was "austere and tranquil, very restrained in her tastes and preferences. All such objects as clothes, jewelry, flutes—not to mention the gorgeous and glamorous—she rejected out of hand. Typically she burned incense and brewed tea; she would sit facing her alchemical stove with books of scripture; or she closed her doors, faced burning incense and painted landscapes."[52] Dong Xiaowan, the concubine of Mao Xiang, was well known for her reclusive style. "She was inward looking and self-sufficient; she found flirtations unbearable. She longed for the mountains and moved to a river to live in a small rustic hut with a bamboo fence."[53] Geisha Jiang lived in seclusion and never ventured into the bustle of the city.[54] Like their male counterpart, the urban recluse, these women could be eccentric; one geisha, like the untrammeled men of the South, washed the trees and wiped the bamboos of her garden day and night.[55]

This love of seclusion did not necessarily conflict with their roles as mates; as spouses of scholar-officials, they were not only partners in the artful life but also partners in the life of scholarship. Work in the studio centered on books: on bibliography, editing, redacting, and interpretation. High officials, themselves well trained in poetry and history, worked alongside the geisha-consort;[56] together they composed, interpreted, edited, copied, and memorized.[57] The geisha was, in fact, the necessary complement to the refined urban recluse, the woman of learning a match for the man of learning. The geisha Gu was a famous woman of the education district. She was established first as a geisha, but married as a concubine a distinguished official; the husband and concubine "became together elegant recluses."[58] One long-familiar term for a geisha of high status was, in fact, "a book reviser,"[59] and one contemporary scholar has asserted that the best term for the learned mate of the recluse is "poet-collaborator." [60] Mao Xiang described the geisha-wife Dong Xiaowan as a partner dedicated to research and literary projects:

> Dong Bai spent the days assisting me in meticulous redaction for collating and transcription, as well as in the careful establishing of the correct versions. We would spend not just the day, but the entire night sitting face to face, forgetting even to speak. When it came to poetry, there was nothing she didn't understand. She could produce insightful analysis for interpreting passages. . . . Her own books lay stacked all around her by day and at night there would be tens of volumes of Tang poetry gathered around her amidst her pillow and coverlet.[61]

The bookish life of the hermit seemed to suit the geisha well. Reclusiveness was at the heart of the role of the geisha; geishas were essentially artists, and art demanded privacy, whether the artist was male or female. In the Ming, her love of solitude was a mark of her artistic nature. "Poetry wells up within solitude," remarked the poet-geisha Liu Shi.[62] If solitude was natural, however, so too was complete rejection of men. It is another irony of the Ming geisha that the powerful woman announced her status by imitating the eremitic. The final step for these geishas was the same as for any recluse-artist: complete withdrawal from contact with the common.[63] Many geishas refused completely to associate with others; they took vows never to be married[64] or became nuns or adepts. Some became Daoist Priestesses; many others became devoted to Buddhism. Others became increasingly reclusive until—although they remained as geishas—they no longer received men. The final conclusion to the biographies of many of these reclusive geishas is the simple statement: "They no longer saw guests" (*bu jian yi ke*).[65]

Warriors

Geishas could not be limited, however. If the untrammeled class meant flamboyance for men, it meant the same for a geisha; if the literatus could be insulting, eccentric, and impulsive, so could the geisha. Both male and female eccentrics cultivated the style of the extraordinary; both found common behavior only common. The geishas took to the showiness of the unfettered class with apparent ease. In Confucian lore, the first wife was so constrained by ritual and space that one name for her was *nei ren*—person of the inner apartments. The geisha as *ji*—a performer and public figure—was expected to use grand gestures and public display. Indeed, some flaunted their identities as they transformed their private lives into performance. The role of geisha also gave them a limited social freedom; they appeared in public the way few other women ever appeared. These flamboyant geishas called themselves "female knights errant" (*xia nü*), although they never took up a sword nor practiced esoteric arts. Rather they took the name to indicate their natures. Like the knight errant or woman warrior, these geishas had a grandeur to them; they were stamped with a quixotic valor; they supported dangerous political causes; they were aloof and impulsive, and expressed in their lives a risky brilliance.

One of the most common features of the warrior-geisha was a life of public defiance. Male eccentrics could be famous for their grand displays or arrogant acts; people loved to collect stories of eccentric acts by eccentric men. The warrior-geisha was equally discussed and had her own following. Indeed, her renown was part of her capital. There were unofficial rankings: who was the most outrageous, the most passionate, the most defiant, the most brilliant in the arts. How did this geisha reject a callow suitor, how did that one accept a worthy one? Geisha life was a life of performance and display, always in the public eye. One typical display for the geisha was to parade astride a horse. On horseback the geisha had superiority; mounted on the animal associated with the military, she looked the part of the aloof warrior. In the cities of both North and South, horseback outings were small tableaus for an adoring public, and the colorful rides of the geisha were a repeated spectacle of the springtime.

> Out at the Gallery of the Wind in the Pines, we had a gathering of our society. Finally, when the two geishas, Snow Robe and Eyebrow Birth, had both finished drinking, they mounted their horses and rode back into the city linked side by side. In their red makeup and with their halcyon sleeves, they rode along brandishing their whips, making their horses leap and frisk; all sorts of people gathered along the road to watch. It was a stunning sight during that happy time of great peace.[66]

If the geisha on horseback suggested defiance, however, it also suggested escape; geishas were seen in these settings as free of the confines of the house, the district, and even the city. Unlike the extreme exemplars of the inner apartments, they could travel. One poet of the Qing describes a geisha leaping out over the confines of the city boundaries:

The Beginning of Spring by the City Wall, by Sa Tianxi

> A courtly geisha of the capital rides out on her white horse—
> the green silk reins in her hands.
> She wears a short jacket with narrow sleeves;
> Her silver stirrups glisten.
> At the Imperial Moat she lets her horse drink,
> But doesn't turn him back.
> She's eager to see the lushness in the willow trees beyond;
> She sets him bounding out over the wall.[67]

The geisha was not limited, however, to colorful displays suitable for short anecdote. Some of the warrior-geishas were deeply defiant and despised convention. Like the eccentrics and recluses of Ming lore, these women had "courage, resoluteness and independence of spirit." [68] They were willful, proud, with a great sense of personal dignity.[69] When the geisha Kou Baimen was married to Marshal Bao, a man of vast wealth, he kept her in rooms of phenomenal luxury; she served as a symbol of his wealth and his passionate nature. At the collapse of the Ming, however, the master of the house surrendered in the cataclysmic final days, and geisha Kou requested that she be released. The woman purchased her freedom, and, we are told, "then departed. Clad in her short jacket, attended by one servant, she mounted her horse, and rode back home on her own. Once home, she claimed the status of knight errant, constructed a garden studio and either received her own guests as she pleased or went out and about with literati and poets"[70] (see Figure 2.2).

Not only resolute, geisha-warriors were also passionate. They often took on the persona of the grand romantic, becoming cavaliers in the tradition of romantic knights. These women actively sought partners; they demanded lovers or demanded marriage. Feng said that a geisha "could select her own mate"[71] and thereby "leap over the rituals of society."[72] Geishas were aggressive; there are many surprising women in Ming fiction and history who are unmistakably the suitors—"reckless and unrestrained," as Feng call them, in pursuing a lover. Even Dong Xiaowan, the effete tutor of her aesthete lover, was an unrelenting suitor of Mao Xiang. In Mao's account of the courtship, Dong requests that she become his concubine and then demands it. She "swears by the flowing the river" that she will not return to geisha life again. Once married to Mao Xiang she asserts how pleased she is that "my oath to pursue you for the past year was not in error."[73]

If the geisha-knight was a romantic, however, she was a doomed romantic. Her role in the Ming was informed by a sense of the tragic. She was a figure of noble tragedy, of futile devotion; there is something of the martyr in these women. Often the geisha is too good for the man she loves; her affair ends in disaster, the negligible male rejecting the noble geisha; and suicide is her resolution to the affair.[74] The love affairs themselves were not necessarily joyous, for even devoted lovers were not, in the conventional sense, "happy." In the West, lovers may be expected to live happily ever after, but in the Ming they were not, for the fragility of love and the vulnerability of these women was part of the lore. There is a sense in the stories of love and courtship that separation—by death or tragedy—is the normal conclusion for an affair. Love is by definition a short-lived moment, intense but evanescent; a truly great passion takes place in the context of sadness. This romantic pessimism, however, was not solely a feature of the lore of the geisha; rather it tapped into a deep vein of tragic romanticism in the culture. From this perspective on the heroic, failure was glorified, greatness was visited on those who fail, and romance was tinged with a bitter knowledge of eventual separation. Whether the hero of the event was a rejected statesman or a geisha of the education district, the heroic implied the tragic. Many of these accounts of geishas are intensely nostalgic, characterized by pathos—seeming to anticipate, with an almost perverse relish, the bitter conclusion of the affair. Like warriors who die for a cause, these women were the knights errant who died for their love; a great love almost required it.

Beyond love affairs, geishas were romantic in the sense of the grandly heroic. They were cavaliers of great causes, quixotic in style, figures of doomed magnificence like the male warriors. Warrior-geishas, in fact, mimicked the masculine, calling themselves *di*, younger brother, and wearing men's clothes.[75] One Ming writer described a musician-geisha who was known as a warrior type. "By nature she was magnanimous and extravagant, and imitated the knight errant. She traveled with famous literati and eventually closed her door to guests. Then she traveled with her friends and treated them all as brothers and sisters."[76] Like male romantics the geisha was often allied with political causes, and many were known as great patriots after the fall of the Ming dynasty, supporting the doomed cause of Ming loyalism.[77]

Figure 2.2 *A Portrait of the Geisha Kou Baimen*, by Fan Qi and Wu Hong. Qing Dynasty. Note the dominance of the landscape in the painting, in particular the large, gnarled tree. This image is geisha as recluse: a human figure disappearing into the uncultivated landscape (Nanjing Museum).

One woman of the late Ming typified this colorful warrior-geisha: the famous artist Xue Susu. In her life we see encapsulated many of the features of these dramatic women of the geisha class. Xue, like many of the geishas of high status, was a painter; one of her scrolls has been ranked as "the most accomplished work of its kind in the whole of the Ming period." Scholars have claimed her brushwork is "vigorous and forceful," calling her a "master of technique"[78] (see Figure 2.1). Xue was established as a mate in excellence as well; she lived at different times with some of the most important intellectuals of the late Ming.[79]

Besides her painting, Xue was famous for her flamboyantly defiant romanticism; she was one of the most charismatic women of the Ming. One intellectual thought she was extraordinary: "Xue Susu has a spirit that is heroic. She values herself highly, and does not receive common people, but only the learned and intelligent"[80]; and another noted that she deliberately took her name from a famous female warrior of the past.[81] As a knight errant, she loved martial causes. Xue challenged one of her lovers to fund and organize an attack on the Japanese, the perennial invaders of the Chinese coast. Her lover demurred; he was unwilling to risk his money or his safety. Xue was outraged: disgusted with his hesitation, she summarily cast him off as her lover and, we are told, "rode off on her quick steed."[82]

Nothing demonstrates the charismatic nature of these women more than the exceptional sport to which Xue Susu dedicated herself. Xue was an expert in mounted archery, and she loved to prove it (see the frontispiece). Qian Qianyi tells us that "as a child Xue Susu lived in Beijing for a time; and out in the suburbs she practiced the arts of the mounted archer."[83] The geisha then continued her training and eventually became famous for her exhibitions. When she lived with a military officer in the "barbarian regions," the local natives were much taken with her and circulated a picture of her. Xue achieved a sort of cult status, attracting fans from among the local population. When she finally returned to civilization, her renown as an archer increased, and she attracted crowds of observers to watch her displays. On one of the many playing fields of Hangzhou, she practiced her sport before an eager public. As in the case of Dong Xiaowan, Xue's personal life became a form of theater for the urban citizen. Of course, both these women were *ji*—performers; and the transition from a brilliant professional performer to a woman who constantly performs was not surprising, nor was the attention of the masses. If urban citizens of the very rich southern cities could spend their copious supplies of disposable income at the great entertainment centers, they certainly had the leisure and inclination to watch a famous "warrior-geisha" enjoy her fame. The thrill of enjoying her performance was captured by the poet Lu Bi:

The Song of Watching Susu Shoot the Arrows

As the wine grows sweet we ask her now to perform the arrow-shoot.
With her hair tied back and her single-layer shirt, she hesitates now before the shot.
The fine bindings and her red sleeves exposed now to show her armlet and glove.
She tips her head to measure the shot; and beneath her cloudlike tresses now,
Both her shoulders square back.[84]

Artists

The dazzling aspects of these women should not disguise, however, the high seriousness of many of their lives. Geishas were not simply the subjects of colorful exemplars of *qing*, nor simply icons of the artful life. Rather, they directed their passion to self-expression, becoming disciplined and prolific artists. Geishas became poets and chroniclers in their own right, articulate women who spoke for themselves about themselves. They produced books of poetry, books of essays, as well as notes of their scholarship; they exchanged letters that were published and wrote personal journals that were printed up. There was a minor industry of geisha authors.[85] The scholar Qian Qianyi listed in his collection of poet-biographies 118 female poets of the Ming, many of whom were geishas. The command of the word is not surprising, however, for the geisha lived a literary life. Along with the "man of talent," this "woman of excellence" devoted herself to poetry and essay; she could hardly have neglected such skills. In the urbane culture of the southern cities, brilliance in composition was the surest mark of the truly "untrammeled"; this was a bookish world where noteworthy men and glamorous women spoke naturally to each other—and to their enamored public—through the written word.

Of course, often the geisha survived through alliances with elites; coming from low origins, geishas belonged essentially to the silent margins of elite life—to that class of maids, entertainers, and concubines that served and observed. But access to the male elite gave them occasion to colonize it, to become honorary men in the world of the hermitage. And some geishas made good use of the privilege, devoting their wealth, their status, and their time in the hermitage to become authors and artists. They took up the writing brush, signed their names, and stepped out of the shadows of anonymity, usurping finally that essential space of the intellectual—the writing table. Trained from childhood to express themselves in public, geishas in the late Ming expressed themselves in print.

One geisha stands out as a particularly brilliant colonist of elite life: Liu Shi, a woman known for her charismatic style as well as for her curriculum vitae. At the age of twenty-two, Liu Shi married out of the geisha class into elite respectability. She became the concubine of the very important senior official, Qian Qianyi. From 1640 to 1664, the two epitomized a kind of fragile glamour that characterized the late Ming and early Qing South. More than a study in social ambition, her life was that of an artist, full of paradox and contradictions—for Liu was not only a successful mate in excellence, she was also a serious scholar, painter, and writer, producing works that hold up to criticism today.[86] It is just these paradoxes in Liu's life, however, that illuminate the nature of the geishas as a class and set in relief their astonishing successes.

As with many famous artists of the education district, Liu Shi was both consort of the rich and a great poet. As consort, she was the archetypal woman of excellence: beautiful, romantic, committed to affairs, pursued by many, and very proud. Liu was famous for her looks, said to be "one of the three great beauties of the South" and a "romantic beauty of the Empire";[87] she was a brilliant beauty as well, a regular guest at literati parties.[88] Part of her charm was a sort of public charm: wealthy admirers pursued her, attempted to collect her; she complained of her many impertinent suitors, some of whom she offended with her refusals.

Liu lived the life of a great beauty. Her affairs were perfected dramas of *qing*. She had a series of love affairs that firmly fit the ideal of "the man of talent and woman of excellence." Liu Shi and her partner would set up house together, often on a boat or in a mountain retreat, and devote themselves to poetry and painting. The mates she chose matched her well; they were major figures of the day, important intellectuals and officials. At the age of seventeen, Liu had her first long-term affair with Tang Shuda, a wealthy artist and intellectual, not much older than Liu herself; they were said to be deeply in love. Her later affairs were with other

famous writers and officials: she allied herself with Song Yuanwen, Chen Zilong, Wang Ranming, and finally with Qian Qianyi. Nor was she in these affairs the passive object of adoration. As geisha she was clearly "steeped in *qing*," quixotic and aggressive, rather than coy.

Like Xue Susu, Liu played the part of the romantic gallant. In one lush episode, a rejected
lover begs for her attentions. One winter night he stands on the shore by her boat where she
is living and pleads with her. Angry with him, she ignores him. He refuses to be abandoned,
however, and plunges into the cold river and stands there attendant. Liu takes pity on him and
takes him into her bed.[89] She is full of passion, but she is also full of anger. Like all warrior-
geishas, Liu Shi is famous for her sense of personal dignity. In another famous episode, Liu
ends her affair with the official Song Yuanwen, her lover for more than a year. Liu, accused
of being an "unaffiliated geisha," is threatened with banishment and sends for Song to ask
for his help—probably hoping for an offer of marriage. The two meet in an infamous encounter. When Liu asks her lover for a solution, Song produces some mealymouthed objections, apparently concerned about how his mother would react to an alliance with a geisha.
Liu berates him, smashes her lute, and throws him out.

The culmination of her role as consort is her affair with Qian Qianyi, high official of the
late Ming. Like all of the highly statused geishas, Liu clearly wants more than a limited relationship: she wants marriage. There was an expectation in the late Ming that a geisha of
real accomplishment would marry a man of wealth and literary fame. This she finally
achieves with the official, Qian Qianyi. After a painful break with her lover Wang Ranming,
Liu sets off to accomplish a meeting. Her strategy is a particularly bold one. In the late fall
of 1640 Liu Shi dresses up as a man, presents herself to Qian Qianyi (see Figure 2.3), and
asks his opinion of her poetry. According to the lore of the event, for a moment Qian Qianyi
believes the ruse; he thinks the poems are indeed written by a man.[90] After the meeting, Liu
returns to her boat for a month; but by the end of the year Liu joins Qian on his estate. Once
there, Liu lives and works in her own hermitage that Qian builds for her, the "According to
the Sutra Studio." The next year, the two vow loyalty to each other in a famous banquet on
the river, and Liu becomes Qian's wife. In the first decade of the Qing the two mates in excellence even occupy the grandly expansive Suzhou estate, the Humble Administrator's Garden. The marriage lasts for twenty-four years until Qian's death.

The high drama and obvious sensuality of her life, her very obvious commitment to
qing, and her social rank as professional geisha, however, should not detract from her authority as a writer, for despite Qian's ranking her as "one of the three great beauties," she
was also a disciplined poet and scholar. Not that her sexuality was in conflict with her role
as artist. Each of her monogamous affairs was seen as a great romance, not as a cynical,
mercenary alliance. Many of these affairs provided inspiration for her poems, and mates
in excellence often assisted one another in writing and editing. Art was, in fact, the goal
of their lives; together they were poet-collaborators, or painters, essayists, or scholars.
Four of Liu's works were published with the assistance of her several lovers.[91] Indeed,
Liu's ruse of dressing as a man to meet with Qian Qianyi looks as much like an artist seeking patronage as a woman seeking a lover.

Liu was famous as both visual artist and as poet.[92] There are large numbers of references
to her in journals, local histories, and biographies.[93] A prolific writer, she published four collections of poetry before she was twenty-two, including the *Yuanyang lou ci* (Songs from the
Chamber of Mandarin Ducks) and the *Hu shang cao* (Poems Drafted by the Lake), and her

河東君初訪半野堂小景

清余秋室繪河東君初訪半野堂小景

**Figure 2.3   The Lady East-of-the-River first visits the Half Wilderness Hall.
Portrait of the geisha Liu Shi dressed as a man on her visit to Qian Qianyi.
The image was likely not to have been a life portrait but rather a reflection of
the legend surrounding her (Chen Yinke, _Liu Rushi biezhan_, frontispiece).**

more informal, more intimate collection *Chi tu qijue* (Notes and Poems). After her marriage to Qian Qianyi, the two composed and published poetry, finishing the *Dongshan chouhe ji* (The Wine Pledge at the Eastern Hill) together. As an editor, Liu helped define the tradition of female poets by compiling an important collection of female writers. Qian then included her compilation in his larger anthology, *Historical Anthology of Poetry.*

Like the male poets of the Ming, Liu Shi lived a writer's life in all its aspects. For her, as well as for men, poetry was a constant enterprise. Composition was for every occasion, in solitude or in company. Liu wrote spontaneously and frequently on all the many topics and occasions that men wrote on: travel, solitude, festivals, and friendship; the seasons, food, banquets, and separations. The female mate in excellence with her years of literary training expressed herself naturally in verse. Liu Shi was not a shadow poet, a mimic dependent on the men she accompanied. Like male intellectuals, she had a level of independence; a great traveler, Liu Shi bought a house and a boat that she used to journey in all over the South and was known as "the woman who traveled all over Wu and Yue." [94] This followed a tradition in which all intellectuals and artists traveled. The folklore of the educated class glorified tourism; rural journeys suggested the esoteric adept and the refined recluse. In her own boat, Liu frequently toured during the holidays; for example, early in 1639, Liu traveled on both the Cold Food[95] and Qing Ming[96] festivals, each trip taking several weeks. West Lake was a favorite place for her to visit and easy to get to in her boat. Even more popular than river travel, however, was mountain travel. Although the urban adepts brought the mountain to their ecologies of perfection, they also loved traveling into the mountains. Liu journeyed to most of the sacred mountains, and to many of the less important ones of the South as well.[97]

Despite being independent, Liu loved contact with other writers. She was part of a network of women, especially women writers, and was a friend of Xue Susu[98] and maintained contact with her sister, another geisha author. She even had contact with the artistic first wives of respectable families who were themselves poets.[99]

These successes did not eliminate the insecurities of her life, however. Although Liu Shi prospered as the brilliant artist and the deft artisan of a romantic life, she was also the most precarious of women, with only a tentative grasp on security and status. Well traveled, well known, and widely read, she was also essentially marginal. Whatever stability she achieved as geisha-celebrity did not fully equal the protections offered a woman by orthodox society. In the change of season or of hour, she could become suddenly extraneous to the man she courted, transformed into a pathetic image of feminine dependence. Even a marriage could not fully protect her from her origins; she was still vulnerable, the ambiguity of her status as geisha never resolved. Like the daughters of Master Tie who "descended into the district," Liu Shi was one step away from extreme degradation.

Many features of her life reflect her fragile status; her childhood and teen years were riddled with episodes bordering on the sordid. We know little of her early childhood, virtually nothing of her family backround. She changed her name, as geishas often did, from Yang to Liu, which reflected a desire not to shame any relatives; as such, it is the perfect expression of the very precarious nature of her connection to society. We know also that she had a sister who was a geisha.[100] Yet other than this, she was a woman with an obscure background and an insignificant past. We learn more of her, however, when she reached puberty—that is, when she drew the attention of men. In her early teens, she served as a maid or concubine to the family of Zhou Wenan, a former prime minister. Her first foray into elite society was only a mixed success, however, for she was slandered by someone in the household. She was accused of having an affair with one of the servants and was threatened with summary expulsion from the estate. Fortunately, she was protected by the matron of the house; Zhou's mother liked the young girl and prevented her from being cast out to survive on her own.[101] Her next position was with a well-established geisha, "Buddha" Xu. After this she began her affair with Tang Shuda. This period allowed her to acquire fame and some stability, yet she was often exposed to risk. At one point she was accused of being a *liu ji* (unaffiliated geisha) and was threatened with banishment "in order to correct the behavior of officials."[102] (The banishment of geishas was apparently a punishment intended indirectly to control the conduct of male elites.) If Liu was subject to attacks from the law, she was also subject to financial crises. At another juncture, she acquired significant debts and was threatened with imprisonment for nonpayment.

After a series of love affairs, Liu ended her days in apparent stability. Yet even her marriage to Qian Qianyi provided only limited shelter. Although her marriage was celebrated as one of the most famous alliances of mates in excellence, of two lovers who were equals in the arts, there was nonetheless the taint of exploitation. When Liu Shi married the great man, she was twenty-two and he was fifty-nine. When Qian Qianyi died, Liu and their daughter were treated ruthlessly by other members of the clan. She was, after all, just a geisha-wife; the ecology of perfection was Qian's dream, not theirs. The clan was intent on forcing out these pretenders to clan status and money. This was no idle threat, and Liu and her daughter could easily have ended up penniless. To prevent such treatment, Liu took the course established for centuries. To underscore her virtue and the plight of her child, she assumed the role of the virtuous wife. In 1664, in order to shame her predatory relatives, to draw attention to their threats, and to prove her virtue as a woman, she suicided. Her tragic plan succeeded; her daughter was given shelter by the clan. But her suicide underscores her marginality. Her brilliance, creativity, daring, and ideals could not exempt her from her status as outsider. It was only through imitation of the filial woman that she achieved—through death—the protection of the clan.

The very precariousness of her life gave her a particular authority on the late Ming, on its ideals, on its romanticism and on its impermanence. Like the men she loved, she studied the world around her and, like them, personally encapsulated their ideals and failures. Unlike them, however, she was never a detached observer, an aloof elite luxuriating in tragic romanticism. Liu Shi rather restated the tropes of the solitary traveler, the abandoned lover, or the devout ascetic to express harsh personal realities. Her angst was hardly existential; poetic laments were home truths, not conventions, in her hands; and, indeed, the complaints of the literati can pale in comparison to Liu Shi's lines. She was a passionate narrator of a passionate life, living a life of quixotic heroism, a life exposed to constant risk; but she was a woman who earned through her own recklessness the authority to describe the dangers of a vulnerable life.

In one collection of poetic journal notes, Liu narrated the events of her life. More personal than the regulated verse and elaborate rhyme-prose she usually wrote, these are often bitter narrations of her loves and needs. There are few texts from the Ming that have such a harshly personal tone. In notes written in the year 1640, she described an especially harrowing period—her failing affair with Wang Janming and then her failed affair with Chen Zilong. These disappointments reflected more, however, than the despair of lost love; they left her vulnerable to the attentions of belligerent suitors, exposed to the possibility of a lifetime as a public performer, and—always lurking in the wings—subject to a life of financial desperation. Her *Notes and Poems* from this particular period are full of "the bitterness of this terrible time."[103]

The entries for these notes were written in the summer and fall of 1640, just before her alliance with Qian Qianyi began. In the summer of that year, Liu was twenty-two years old and becoming unmarriageable. One earlier affair—with Chen Zilong—had ended in disappointment, and her current affair with the educated and well-off Wang Janming was her next hope.[104] Over the course of three years from 1637 to 1640, Liu and Wang traveled together—the man of talent and the geisha-poet—to famous mountains and gardens of the South. By boat, they toured West Lake and journeyed along the famous waterways that connected the southern cities. In the summer of 1640, however, Wang Janming was withdrawing from the affair, and Liu was helpless to re-engage him. Seeking to re-establish the affair, she wrote to him to request a face-to-face meeting and then followed him to his hometown. She wrote a letter asking him to meet her at a well-known lodge, Rainbow Pavilion, in Wujiang. The Pavilion was often used by geishas and intellectuals; it was accessible by boat and an easy location for women to travel to. After sending the letter, Liu went to the Pavilion and spent several days there in humiliating expectation of Wang, who never arrived. During the days of a rainy autumn squall she wrote of waiting to hear from him:

> Yesterday I risked the rain and left the mountain by Shengci Garrison.
> In the morning I again risked the rain and disembarked from my boat.
> It used to be said, "When you make a pair of shoes you resolve a tattered destiny."
> How I've come to know of this!
> Tomorrow morning I'll anchor my boat for a day, hire a cart and take a turn around the Lodge. . . .
> I am waiting for you.[105]

Wang Janming, however, had returned home and sent a letter to tell her he had family problems he must take care of. But they both knew that this refusal to see her was a refusal to pursue the affair. The request for a face-to-face meeting was, in all likelihood, a demand that he marry her, and Wang Janming opted for avoidance. This was bitter news for Liu, for she needed the patronage and protection of concubinage. The life of the aging geisha was tolerable to some; they could earn a living as teachers of music and poetry or become attendants in the geisha houses. But for Liu Shi this would have meant a life in the public eye that suited her less and less. Her entries in these months clearly reflect her sense of failure and her deepening despair. In the late fall she described her vigil as she waited to hear from Wang:

> I returned to Shengci; by the bridge surrounded by fog, there was a flute blowing.
> I listened to the soughing wind in the moonlit kiosk and heard the precious zither and jade-mounted panpipes.
> The painted eaves are laced now with spiderwebs.
> Each day I look off into the icy chill and gaze into that lightly tenuous beauty. . . .
> The traces of my own progress now abide in the smoky waters below the bridge.[106]

Once she knew Wang had refused her, Liu sank deeper into hopelessness. She returned back to her home, now without any sense of hope for her future. In retreat from all connections to the mates in excellence of her past, she recalled only her failures. In the next lines she describes her break with Wang and a similar failure with the great official and poet Chen Zilong. Alone in her mountain retreat Liu catalogues her misery:

> I have already arrived by the bank of the lake, though
> I know that my Master has still kept within his former precincts. . . .
> My dark thoughts are bitterly painful, harrying me into the present.
> Recently I heard that my Master had already returned. . . .
> It is the mountains that have a glorious beauty, but except for my alchemist's stove and my
> Chan meditation pallet, there is just the wind in the pines by the bank of cassias. . . .
> I lean on the pillow all grass filled.
> I understand nothing.[107]

Conclusion

In the late Ming, geisha life provided a life for the unaffiliated woman. A woman without essential social or clan support could prosper; she could own property, live in comfortable circumstance, enjoy stability and status. Like so many arrivistes in the southern economy, geishas acquired currency; they were the personal entertainers of a class that paid dearly for entertainment, becoming entrepreneurs in this very entrepreneurial world. Yu Huai described just how prosperous such a woman could become. The compound of one geisha—Lady Li— was magnificent: "Lady Li was by nature a bold woman-warrior type and she had the air of a distinguished man. Her towers, courtyards, halls and chambers were decorated and gorgeous. She had over ten attendants all garbed in silk gauze with long trains. When she set out the wine for her grander banquets she had an orchestra of lute, zither and panpipes."[108] A geisha could become a woman of means; and despite an existence in the moral no-man's land of the demimonde, she could transform herself. Of course, the geisha was always subject to the dangers of a status system based on indirect sources of power; she could be abased in an instant. The poet-collaborator, for all her achievements, existed in an impossible position of weakness; she was somewhere between being an authority on beauty and a mere object of beauty. But as transitory as their power was, it gave them a voice within the culture; the "transcendent" gardens and idealized affairs provided a stage for the geisha. In these new subcultures of experiment, the geisha became a necessary woman. These women who had "descended into the district" and were desperate to be "removed from the registration lists" acquired a limited authority. Not content to rely on their new status for trivial favors, they achieved a modicum of importance as they exploited their position. These geishas became, on their own, successful artists, reclusive intellectuals, members of the southern avant-garde, famous for their summary rejection of the social constraints that limited every other woman of the Ming.

3

Grannies

Once in a while, four times so far for me, my mother brings out the metal tube that holds her medical diploma.

"Shaman," The Woman Warrior: Memoirs of a Girlhood Among Ghosts
Maxine Hong Kingston[1]

In traditional China, especially in the Ming, you could get arrested for being a granny; you could also achieve high office or acquire a royal title. The word "granny" may conjure up to a modern reader the image of a harmless old biddy, but in the Ming no one thought a granny was harmless. "Don't ever let the three grannies pass before your hall," warned one household adage. "Don't invite in, for any reason, a nun, a monk, an adept, a wet-nurse, or a granny money-lender."[2] Grannies were dangerous visitors; they caused discord and disaffection, and intimacy with them risked disaster. Indeed, it was their public status and private intimacy that worried officials, for the wizened old herbalist, the cackling matchmaker, the benign wet-nurse had access to the intimate that gave these women a worrisome authority: grannies needed to be controlled. These moralists were not naive. Grannies did have power; they governed biology, the world of *yin*, the realm of the body, of fertility, and of childbirth. In a culture that worshiped the lineage and considered childbirth and fertility the essential link to the ancestors, the agent of fertility—the granny—had real expertise. Men took care of the execution of laws, the administration of government, and the education of other men—the realm of the public—but grannies were in charge of governing the private.

In the Ming, grannies assumed multiple roles. They constituted an informal bureaucracy that supervised life's transitions. Matchmaking, fertility, birth, nurturing, and, finally, illness and death all called for the visit of a granny. Granny matchmakers legitimized marriages; granny doctors cured the sick; granny-midwives attended births; young "grannies" served as wet-nurses; and in magistrates' handbooks we learn of a woman who worked as a coroner's assistant. Some granny-jobs involved the religious, such as a shamaness, adept, or nun; and some were more mundane: broker, merchant, or herb seller. Grannies could have very formal

Figure 3.1 *Gossips in the Late Qing* **(Luther Theological Seminary Archives).**

roles and social status of a very public sort. One young female healer was known in Beijing; "her knowledge was equal to that of male physicians."[3] The Court maintained a list of granny work; the Palace in Beijing listed three officially: doctor, midwife, and wet-nurse.

Even in their formal roles, however, grannies were also intimates. Grannies were, in fact, grannylike; they were someone to invite into the "back apartments" in times of private need; hence the term "granny," *po*, which suggests an elder auntie, a favorite grandmother, a familiar relative. Her other epithets connoted the familiar as well; Old Grandma (*lao po*) was one of her more common names, as was Old Sis (*lao jie*), Old Lady (*lao niang*), Old Mum (*lao ma*), and Old Auntie (*lao sou*). But the paradoxical meanings in the term "granny"—her formal and yet familiar identities—only reflect her role. Grannies occupied the border between the private and public (see Figure 3.1).

In translating such terms, however, we are caught by the limitations of English; in the twentieth century the terms for granny-healers are as few as the women themselves. The few words still in use have become now as degraded as the status of the village granny. In the West, the expression "gossip" once designated a very important granny: "gossip" is derived from "god-syb"—the woman (or man) who witnessed the christening of a child as god-parent. Now the word "granny" is, in English, tinged by ageism and sexism, and words such as Beldame, Good-mother, Goodwife, Goody, Gammer, Grandame, which designated the women who bridged the formal and the intimate, have gone out of use. Still, I will rely on the term "granny" for *po*, as it is the best word to catch that mix of intimate and formal that describes the Chinese *po* (see Color Plate 5).

The most pervasive—and probably the most ancient—of all grannies was the shamaness. She was very much part of the popular setting, seen in the "back alleys of the capital" and in rural areas. One intellectual of the Ming described the granny-shaman at work. "Nowadays shamanism is especially prevalent in the southern regions, especially far down in Fujian and Guangzhou. . . . When there is illness in a wealthy household the women have great respect and reverence for the shaman. . . . They come to the house and sound gongs and drums and ring bells without cease in the courtyard."[4] Not that this intellectual approved: he went on to note that, with such treatment, the dying increase day by day: "It is a disaster that they are not forbidden," he chides. Such disapproval is not surprising. The granny-shaman was the most damned of grannies. The educated official was worried about most grannies, but he was violently opposed to the shaman. In the Ming, in many parts of the Empire, shamanism was illegal.

Such damnation was not, however, always the case. In prehistorical times, the shamaness was the essential healer—at the center, not the margins, of life. She was part of a class of great priestesses, with powers that rivaled the powers of any priest class of later periods. Considering her fate in later dynasties—her isolation and condemnation—her great authority in the ancient period may seem surprising; but her transition to marginal parallels the transition of many religious leaders from central to outcast. Originally, during the Shang era, the shamaness summoned the rain and governed "seasonal purification," as one ancient text tells us. Her method was dance; she performed the shamanistic step of Yu, a step named after an ancient god of floods. The dance was part of a sacred drama in which the shamaness chanted spells, babbled incoherently, and achieved a state of ecstatic madness. "The shaman is a woman," affirms one ancient dictionary, "who serves the invisible and brings down the spirits by dancing"; and through this divine possession she "causes the gods to descend into her."[5]

These sacred dramas, however, were by no means benign, for rainmaking magic was exorcistic. The shamaness was burned in a fire, or exposed naked to the heat of the sun. The drought was thus driven out, and the forces of nature compelled to rain. Women were the logical choice for seeking water: rain was the extreme example of the *yin* principle, and so the *yin* of a powerful woman was, by sympathetic magic, used to compel *yin*.

As the guardian of the rain, the shamaness was the guardian of the earth's fertility as well, for she ensured through ritual the seasonal flow of water and seasonal growth of life. Even the language bears this out. In the earliest of texts, the words "shamaness," "dance," and "fertility" were all one and the same. Similarly, words echoing the core idea of fertility were related phonetically to "shamaness"—words such as "fertile," "mother," "mound," "membrane," "ovary," and "receptacle."[6] Myths of the archaic period repeated these associations. Deities of fertility were female. The goddess Nü Gua was a snail woman who created mankind from the slime through which she moved. Even the dragon, later made masculine to suit the mythology of the Court, was originally female.[7] She was the overarching symbol of the rain; curved, watery, snakelike, and powerful, she both commanded the water and was herself the element water. The term "dragon lady" was, in this ancient world, redundant. Water, fertility, rainmakers, and dragons were all feminine; and the shamaness was, as Edward Schafer said, the "rightful rainmaker."[8] Nor were her powers used only in public ritual. Within the cult of the family, the shaman in some regions led the rites. In the Han period an ancient practice was reported from the area of Shandong, where the eldest daughter was forbidden to marry and remained instead at home, where she carried out the family rites within her household; this daughter was referred to as the "child of the shaman."[9]

The priest class changed, however; the shamaness was set aside, and she was systematically scoured from Court ritual. As early as the ancient period of the Han, her magic was made suspect and she was supplanted by men. Her ancient practices of ritual exposure and rainmaking were taken over by male officials, and the performance of women in the role of shamaness was labeled "licentious." Female magicians became, by definition, heterodox. In the ancient and medieval periods, officials boasted of their efforts to cleanse the Empire of such profanity. The famous "Judge Dee" of the Tang set out to destroy the influence of shamanism; over fifteen hundred shrines to local magicians were destroyed by the detective-judge.[10] By the time of the Ming, shamanism, like European witchcraft, had gone underground. Still the shamaness practiced her arts, as she does today; but her influence moved from central to peripheral. The shamaness became only a feature of popular life, disdained by officials and intellectuals. As the aforementioned intellectual tells us, "They delude the masses . . . and claim to cure illness to advance their own greed" and survive in rural areas away from the capital[11]—namely, away from the North, away from the Court, away from the male elite.

Orthodoxies of a masculine hierarchy notwithstanding, human fertility remained a female preserve. Cosmic polarities could not be rewritten completely; *yin* and *yang* still inscribed the universe, and the alliance of the female with the all-important facts of menstruation, fecundity, conception, childbirth, and nursing held true. Issues related to fertility dominated, with the lineage still the focus of the culture. Hence all the manifestations of the principle of *yin*, its connection to water and the natural world, to fertility and childbirth, and even to cosmic polarities and metaphysical principles—these were still accepted. Even though the shamaness herself was forced to practice the art of rainmaking and of healing outside the powerful center, for women and men of the Ming—whether in the Court, in the households of the gentry, or in the populated cities—there needed to be a shaman substitute. Here we find the granny. She stepped in as a latter-day "child of the shaman," a much diminished governor of the *yin*. Her magic was degraded, she was relegated to the margins of elite culture; but she was yet the guardian of fertility, with all the metaphysical significance this guardianship implied.

Ming Grannies: Women's Work

The pious women in the estates of the educated had one set of rules, but the women called grannies clearly had another. Their roles as caretakers of the world of *yin* gave them authority as well as intimacy with the wealthy. They had a certain freedom; they moved in and out of the households and through the streets of the cities of the Ming—if not at will, at least as necessity required. Their roles as caretakers also gave them income and social stature, not to mention a legitimacy and even a mystique. Of course all this independence was dangerous. In the words of many patriarchs, the freedom to travel was nothing but trouble. One magistrate of the early Qing reviled the granny for her freedom to enter the homes of the elite, but his criticisms show just how much access to the world at large these women had:

> Female intermediaries such as match-makers, procuresses, female healers, midwives, shamanesses, or Buddhist or Daoist nuns, often act as go-betweens for people indulging in sensual debauchery. Many innocent women from good families are enticed by these female ruffians to engage in licentious acts. . . . Midwives should not perform any other service than taking care of delivery. Procuresses and shamanesses are parasites on the community. They should be banned and driven away. When these measures are taken, good social customs can be preserved.[12]

The good magistrate knew full well that the granny was essential in a household but could do the one thing the devout wife could not: she could leave. His complaints were typical and never fully heeded, for the granny continued to move easily through the streets of China.

The granny-matchmaker was a case in point. Her tasks took her all over the city and included many important junctures in Ming courtship. A family would first consult a granny go-between to find a suitable bride or groom. Her job was to serve as the official busybody of the town; she had to know the available youth of a community. Then if one side was interested but another unwilling, she might also need her powers of persuasion to induce a reluctant family that the match proposed was satisfactory. Often matchmakers traveled in pairs, working the interests of a family together. The matchmaker did more, however, than seek out mates. Once the match was arranged, she traveled back and forth between the prospective families. The ceremonial arrival of the bride at the home of the groom was preceded by weeks of ritual visits, consultations, and exchanges of cards and gifts. It was the granny who selected the dates for the important exchange of numerological information about the birth dates of the bride and groom. It was the granny who took the information to the adept for his pronouncement. The granny also escorted the exchange of gifts between the two families. These rites were finally concluded by the ceremony at the groom's house, and the matchmaker was also present for these often-grand ceremonies when the bride was received into the wedding chamber.[13]

The matchmaker had access to the underside of life as well. The granny known as the *ao po* served within the Yamen offices of civic administration. She assisted in the examination of corpses and handled the body at the direction of the local magistrate. If a crime was suspected, the *ao po* turned the body or lifted a limb to expose any indications of one.[14] This sordid world may seem an ugly place for a granny, but the job indicates how pervasive these women were. Granny work also provided remuneration; some women could be well rewarded. The granny-herbalist was especially known for making money. In the Ming, she was the first choice for house calls, and in Ming fiction, hardly an illness is cured without her help. A good herbalist tended to specialize in certain concoctions. One granny, we are told, used the placenta and umbilical cord for fertility drugs. The wealthy of the Ming paid great sums of cash for these potions.[15]

There were grannies, too, who could travel where few ordinary citizens ever set foot; these grannies ministered to the women of the Forbidden City.[16] The Palace grannies, drawn from the population of female healers throughout Beijing were in many ways no different from the population of women that worked in estates and households all over the Empire. The access these women had to the Forbidden City, however, gave them unusual status and unusual freedom, making them the most powerful of grannies. To many they were infamous; they reaped immense power out of their intimate Palace connections, and used the power cruelly. Infamous or benign, there is no arguing that their knowledge of the private gave them currency in the Imperial.

There were as many as nine thousand women within the Palace walls; in addition to the Imperial harem, there were daughters and aristocratic companions as well as attendants and maids. In this city of women, grannies were essential. There were three types of grannies who ministered to the women of the Palace: physicians, midwives, and wet-nurses. All three of these women governed the *yin* worlds of healing and reproduction, but each granny had somewhat different sources of power. The physician-granny was known for her expertise. Her chief fields were gynecology, pharmacology, and sphygmology (pulse reading) (see Figure 3.2), although

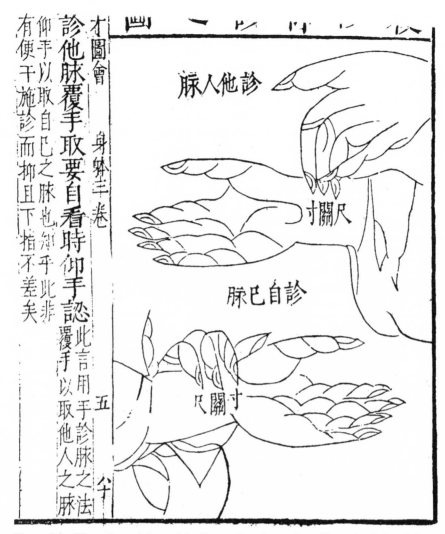

Figure 3.2   The pulse points used in diagnostic sphygmology (*San cai tuhui*, vol. 2, "Shenti").

we know that these physicians could also treat any and all illnesses suffered by the Palace women. Compared to the lowly herbalist and banished shamaness, the granny-doctor was accorded the most honor by male historians. The term for her was close to the term for a male physician. A male physician was called *yi ren*—doctor; the granny was called *yi po*—physician-granny—or *yi fu*—physician-matron. Both men and women practiced the same arts, yet clearly the physician-granny was a rival to her male counterpart for the position of Palace healer. One intellectual of the late Ming was eager to point out the competition. In his description of a female physician—a sphygmologist—who worked within the Palace, he noted her relative competency: "The first time I visited the Yamen area of Wanping I met with one of the women selected for the Palace as granny of medicine. She was barely fifteen or sixteen years old. I tested her on the profession of medicine. Her responses were all in good order; in fact, she could not have been surpassed by the great specialists in pharmacology and sphygmology."[17]

Although the female physician competed with male doctors, she was not an honorary man. She was not trained at the Imperial medical college; rather she received training under an apprentice system. Her affiliation, too, was with other Palace grannies, not with male physicians, for ultimately she was one of the women who governed the world of *yin*.

The job of Imperial granny conferred social status to those chosen; and clearly service to the Palace aristocrats enhanced their importance outside the Palace, for these women were much in demand outside the Forbidden City. In the case of our second granny, the granny-midwife, we see how these women could capitalize on their Imperial appointment to increase their custom outside the Palace.

> Among these midwives there was one who was well known; when she was employed in and about the Palace she was coifed and adorned in the style of Palace women. Thus did she distinguish herself from her midwife comrades outside the Palace. And so it generally happened that ordinary women outside of the Palace preferred to employ the Palace midwife whenever they could, because they set special store in her prestige.[18]

If matrons of medicine had expertise and midwives had special prestige, the wet-nurse could have great status. Her power was not derived, however, from technical knowledge, but rather through her role as surrogate mother. The granny-wet-nurse cared for the children of the Palace, one of whom might be a future Emperor. It was important that the royal wet-nurse satisfy the royal women who employed her. She had to come from a relatively humble but stable social background; wet-nurses were drawn largely from the class of military wives that populated Beijing: "The wives should be between the ages of fifteen and twenty. They must have a husband, and be proper in appearance. They must have had three children, male or female . . . and be fairly humble, always proper, none of them gorgeous empire-topplers."[19] The Imperial mother-to-be first reviewed several candidates. Then, at the birth of the child, a few wet-nurse were sent in and tried for a month, and one was finally kept on. Occasionally, the wet-nurse selected "did not suit the Imperial Predictions," and a desperate, last-minute search took place to find a replacement.[20] Once selected, the Palace wet-nurse became a royal family member by decree. So despite humble beginnings, she became a royal relative; and since family connection was no small issue in a culture that worshiped the family, a wet-nurse's role was a true mark of status. As surrogate mother, she could acquire the full trappings of Imperial motherhood.

The first sign of her status was permanence; in contrast to other women who served the Palace, the wet-nurse was appointed for her entire life, and she had access to the Palace long after the Imperial child grew up. "The wet-nurse serves the child she nurses for the rest of her life, and receives abundant Imperial favors: never again does she have to manage for herself."[21] As Imperial wet-nurse, she also had great social status. "Glorify her too with a name of distinction." And her stature remained great, even in death: "After the wet-nurse passes away, they bury her with lavish ceremony."[22]

Nor were her rewards vaguely defined. The granny-wet-nurse was set for life: she had an income, a house, and an allotment of food and goods. "Every day, each of the women is provided with eight *he* of rice, four catties of meat, and payments for her daily support," lists the account. "And annually she is provided with a supply of goods, coal, vessels, and utensils. This is provided by the Yamen Office. The approximate yearly cost is over four hundred in silver."[23] Just in case the Yamen officers were unsure of how to spend the four hundred in cash, the Board of Rites provided a list. This detailed account serves us today as a useful report of what constituted the necessities of life in sixteenth-century Ming Beijing. The Yamen provided the wet-nurse with money in both silver and paper, as well as daily supplies of coal and peat. They sent her brushes, ink, candles, grass mats, crockery bowls and plates, as well as cooking pans, brooms, bamboo poles, wooden boxes, and even iron pipes. Tea leaves and fabric for household linen were all included, as were iron ladles, nails, iron implements, wooden tables, and wooden implements. Daily utensils such as knives and basins and buckets used for washing, for wells, and for toilets were dispatched. Then there were also luxuries, such as porcelainware, lanterns, pedestals, and bamboo screens.

All these supplies, however, were not what made the office of wet-nurse so powerful. She was powerful for her granny-nature. The wet-nurse became—as granny—an intimate and a family member. She then was due not simply goods and titles but also piety: she could be due the reverence due all mothers and fathers. At that point, the granny crossed the line from tolerated and necessary outsider to intimate kin at the family altars. The powerful filial affections of an Imperial child could transform the woman of a "fairly humble sort" into a powerful member of the Court. The wet-nurse was thus the most dangerous of all the grannies. Of course, in the orthodox sources that we depend on, the only wet-nurses we learn much of are the disruptive ones.[24] The beneficial grannies are lost to history. But even in the accounts of the dangerous grannies we do learn that the wet-nurse could dominate the Inner Courtyard through her control of the world of *yin*.

In the late Ming, one of the most infamous of these powerful nurses was Lady Ke. She was wet-nurse to the infant Emperor Xi Zong early in the seventeenth century. Nurse Ke was a granny who wreaked empirewide havoc. She and her ally, the eunuch Wei Zhongxian, waged a vicious and terrible struggle, one that damaged beyond retrieval the late Ming government. Nurse Ke was, like other wet-nurses, of "humble but stable" origins; she was the wife of a soldier. But her power increased as the power of the child she tended diminished. The Emperor Xi Zong was a fifteen-year-old boy when he assumed the throne, a boy much happier with his hobbies—carpentry was his favorite—than he was with ruling an empire. His audiences with his officials became ritualized beyond any real content, and the unofficial intimates of the Palace ruled in his stead. Mistress Ke herself was given the right to award appointments, titles, and emoluments—a privilege that in 1623 was made perpetual. She took swift advantage of her position by appointing her own relatives to important positions. Of course the Emperor was warned of her influence, but his response reveals his weakness as well as Lady Ke's power: "When [my own mother], the Illustrious Progenitor, was young, it was my wet-nurse Ke who protected me."[25] The wet-nurse received the loyalty due a real mother, who indeed she virtually was.

Politics was not, however, the sole issue. The wet-nurse, like the shamaness of ancient times, was a cosmic rainmaker. Her influence was not merely in the area of the natural and the rational but also in the world of the supernatural. Thus the literati who reviled wet-nurse Ke castigated her not simply for her political meddling, but also for the cosmic reverberations she set in motion. Her *yin* nature, her watery powers, invited *yin* forces into the Palace, it was thought. Lady Ke was an aspect, claimed one official, of the "dark *yin*"; and, he raged, "it is the *yin* force that overturns destiny." Naturally, the literati claimed only the literati could re-establish the proper cosmic polarities. "The Middle Kingdom and the literati represent the *yang* force: thus the prospering of the Middle Kingdom derives from the employment of the literati," he counseled.[26] Wet-nurse Ke was allied not with the *yang* world of order, but with the dark world of disorder. By the metaphysical principles of *yin* and *yang*, Lady Ke was, he claimed, connected to the chaos of the barbarian Manchus.[27]

Nurse Ke was, for a while, a successful tactician. She waged with her eunuch ally a vicious struggle against the literati, annihilating the members of a reform party. After her violent death, she was attacked as one of the most destructive political forces of the late Ming. But ultimately her power did not derive from her role as politician, her alliance with eunuchs, nor her intrigues, but from her intimacy as wet-nurse to the Emperor.

Granny Control

The world of male officialdom, however, was not to be challenged, at least not by the granny. These officials set their considerable energies at granny control. Shen Bang, one worried observer of Ming Palace life, had much to say on the subject, intoning on the dangers of grannies let loose in the Palace: "Political disruption does not depend on men at arms . . . for power can be drained by one's intimates and favorites."[28] History had provided shocking examples. In the ancient period, the Han Court had been rocked by plots circulated, according to Shen, by wet-nurses and female healers. He recalled that during the Jianyuan period (140–134 B.C.), there were cases of infamous grannies attacking the Empire. This case was indeed famous, as were other cases throughout the Han. Female physicians and wet-nurses were implicated in plots against the Emperor himself, and it was claimed that grannies had used imprecation, spells, and poisoning based on witchcraft to attack the royal family. The plot reached even into the highest circles: an empress and a crown prince committed suicide after the plot was exposed.[29] Down even into the Song, grannies were trouble. One scholar related, "During the time of Emperor Xiao Zong of the Song, certain women from outside the Palace were granted permission to enter on the basis of their medical profession to serve within two Palaces. These women, however, became implicated in internal strife. They relied on Imperial favor and received gifts amounting to hundreds and thousands in cash."[30]

Bribery, assassination, witchcraft, political intrigue: from the literati perspective, grannies were clearly dangerous. If the literati had anything to say about it, the grannies would never gain a foothold. There would be no repetition of granny-calamities in the Ming. So the healers and nursemaids who entered the Palace were watched: what they wore, whom they saw, how long they stayed, and the reasons for their entrance. "The severity of our domestic arrangements," boasted one bureaucrat, "surpasses all those of the ancients."[31] To ensure this "severity," the Ming bureaucrat created an office designed specifically for granny watching. This office registered, inspected, selected, and, when necessary, punished the generations of wet-nurses, doctors, and midwives that entered the Forbidden City. The office was called the Lodge of Ritual and Ceremony.

The Lodge was located near the women of the Palace; it was convenient. The women of the Forbidden City were housed in the northeastern part of the Forbidden City called the "Eastern Palaces" (*dong gong*); the women of Beijing who served the Palace came directly from the Lodge through the eastern gate of the gigantic Imperial compound. Although the Lodge was both close and convenient, it was nonetheless a well-designed impediment, for the main task of the Lodge was to granny watch. The Lodge looked at everything: clothing, hair styles, health, behavior, decorum, family backround, marital status—the bureau considered it all. Of the many issues pertaining to the Palace granny, however, the most important was the length of stay; the granny, once in, could be hard to remove. As a new entrant into this life of isolation, the doctor, midwife, and wet-nurse introduced some worldly and knowing companionship. One contemporary told of a physician-granny who cultivated a dangerous intimacy with the Empress herself. His version is steeped in the prejudice of his class. He was a *yang* literatus bound to be suspicious of a granny's companionship, but his account tells us much about attempts to regulate the power of the Beijing granny.

> The Empress, the Compassionate Sage, had for a long time suffered from an eye ailment. She had tried various cures and yet continued to suffer. In 1553 there was a Matron of Medicine, the woman Peng. Those who had access to the Empress recommended the woman. Miss Peng was, however, merely skilled in the arts of chitchat and jokes, and could relate miscellaneous trivial matters of the marketplaces and city walls. She greatly pleased the Compassionate Sage, the Empress, who then had her remain within the Palace. Now woman Peng was already far along in her pregnancy, and her belly was big. The female servants of the Palace all encouraged the Empress to request that Peng immediately leave; but the Empress was dilatory and could not bear to expel her. Finally one day Peng gave birth to a boy right before the throne of the Empress. . . . His highness, the Emperor, was enraged. He sent an order to have the woman Peng executed. But because the Empress tried to save her, twisting and turning with repeated ploys, his highness found it difficult to carry out the execution. Rather, he commuted the death sentence and sent an order to the Lodge of Ritual and Ceremony that she be punished with thirty strokes and then expelled.[32]

We will probably never know how skillful Doctor Peng actually was; this account by a Beijing courtier is too biased to reveal the physician's skill with any accuracy. The account does, however, show us that the granny had access to the highest levels of the aristocracy, and that the literati did everything it could to prevent it.

In addition to the Lodge of Ritual and Ceremony, there was a chain of offices that intensely supervised and governed the Lodge. Shen Bang, an observer of Ming China, described the chain of command. "The Lodge of Ritual and Ceremony is a bit north of the Gate of Eastern Peace. It is also known as the Bureau of Nursing Children, and is attached to the Polychrome Damask Guard and affiliated with the Inspectorate of the Bureau of Governing Ritual. There is a superintendent's lodge as well as the attached lodge; and both are under the regulation of the Polychrome Damask Guard."[33] The Polychrome Damask Guard sounds flowery enough to be insignificant. In fact, it was the Imperial police force. It had considerable power in the capital, and was in turn watched by eunuchs of the Palace. Ultimately, the Lodge of Ritual and Ceremony was governed by one of the major branches in the Imperial government, the Bureau of Rites. This Bureau administered the Imperial examinations, reviewed official promotions, and monitored as well the pervasive and all-important issues of Court ritual. The three types of grannies were thus locked into a structured, explicitly laid-out system of regulation that was intended to give them few opportunities for prolonged intimacies.

The Lodge that governed the granny was not of great rank or import, for the Lodge of Ritual and Ceremony was part office, part warehouse. The Lodge was part of a network of lodges (*fang*) that were spread throughout the city; they were used to maintain goods, animals, and people to be used by the Palace. There were lodges for goats, for medications, for geese and pigeons, for flowering plants, and for horses. In this stratum, the three types of grannies occupied a middle ground somewhere between livestock and professional healers, with the Lodge serving as buffer between the pristine world of Palace women and the world outside their walls.

Warnings, rules, and punishments notwithstanding, however, every period had its Doctor Peng, and every household its necessary granny; they were too useful. But it was not just the practicalities they knew that made them important; it was the metaphysical principles they governed. Their power was not just of the moment and of the condition; it was connected to the overarching principles of the universe. Like the ancient shamaness, the granny governed aspects of the feminine that implied aspects of the *yin*—fertility, childbirth, breast feeding, child care—these aspects may have been deeply alien to the patriarchs and bureaucrats, but they were acknowledged to be of great and potentially ominous significance.

Granny Lore

The whole story on grannies was not written in the books of stern household counsel, however, nor in the dynastic accounts of the Court, nor even in the private journals of the literati. Grannies roamed as well in the world of popular stories, folk tales, and folk songs. These collections of the noncanonical and often obscene, touched by the vulgarity of popular entertainment, tell of a different sort of granny. She is hardly the reviewed, regulated, and chastised candidate of the Lodge of Ritual and Ceremony, but rather the intrusive and authoritative granny of the streets. These grannies are freer, they talk back, they are irreverent, sexual, and very funny. If Freud's commonplace is right—that "permanent subjugation of the human instincts is the basis of civilization"—grannies of folklore constantly test how permanent such subjugation is, or is not.

Probably the best way to learn about one of these outrageous grannies is to meet one; the infamous Granny Wang is just the candidate. She is the chief troublemaker for the novel *Jin Ping Mei*, but her ilk run all through the folklore and fiction of the Ming. This granny, like the Palace grannies, earns a living as healer. Unlike those employees of the aristocracy, however, Granny Wang is not a specialist. She is a jack-of-all-trades, a social parasite who lives off the city she inhabits. She is certainly more vulgar than the Palace grannies, but so are all the characters in these vernacular tales. This granny's primary employment is the tea shop she owns; but, as she is quick to point out, tea is not her chief means of livelihood. "Although I sell tea here, in fact, I'm like a ghost employed to sound the night watch. I have actually sold tea," she strains to recall. "In fact, it was three months ago in the third month, and it was snowing. But actually," she continues, "I make my way by various opportunities."[34] Some of her various opportunities are the same opportunities relied upon by the Palace granny; others are more questionable. Wang tells her story.

> I've had no old man since I've been thirty-six. He left me with a little boy, but no way to earn a living. So I set to work to ply the matchmaker's art of persuasion with people. After that, I made some clothes to sell to people in their homes, and then I was a midwife giving a squeeze to the middle to receive the little one. Also, I managed to play Madame Ma and make some introductions. I can do acupuncture and cure the sick as well, and also I can do certain handiwork.[35]

Granny Wang's list is clearly that of an opportunist; she relies on a city of women to provide her with a living. Granny Wang, however, is more than an urban parasite; for despite the ignominious list of "various opportunities," this granny, like all grannies, suggests an arche-type. The granny in Ming literature is a classic trickster and a comic hero. She speaks, like Falstaff and Reynard the Fox, with the voice of instinct; and in her knowing asides, in her quality of omniscience and in her wicked, satirical voice, she reveals a mythic authority. Her authority is based on her alliance with the base; from midwifery to matchmaking, seamstress to acupuncturist, she intercedes in the realms of the physical. She is especially concerned with sexuality; so that with her tricks and mischief—her "various opportunities"—she sug-gests a fertility spirit. Ultimately what she evokes is her ancestress, the shaman-rainmaker. The ring of authority, long since denied the shamaness, seems once again conferred on the granny of folklore, as if that banished rainmaker took a left turn into popular culture, by-passing all the legitimizing and regulating suffered by the granny in hegemonic texts written by and for a masculine elite.

Playing the role of archetypal trickster, the grannies of literature are troublemakers. Though they function in orthodox texts as arrangers of marriages, in folklore they arrange sex, a role that often pits them against the domestic. The granny is a homewrecker, an agent of illicit passion and marital discord. If something can go wrong, it will, largely through her assistance. She is the incarnation of the domestic world upended. In literature she is the matchmaker of the absurd alliance, a mis-matchmaker. Nor is she apologetic; as the agent of sexual misadventure, she is thrilled with her power to disrupt. Granny Wang of *Jin Ping Mei* is the essential granny-trickster; she is the oil that greases the nefarious events. When the lord of the estate Ximen Qing needs Golden Lotus, Granny Wang plots the liaison. When the two lovers need poison to kill the husband, Granny Wang finds it. As the story proceeds and as events require, she acquires a fertility drug, an abortion medication, and a plot for another li-aison. She is the first choice for the lovesick and needy of the novel, and the catalyst for the disruption of home.

Indeed, the extreme members of these grannies are not simply agents of the erotic, they are eroticism itself. Like Panurge in Rabelais, they are all sexuality, all energy. One infamous granny of the late Ming initiates an affair by climbing in bed with a young and very innocent bride. After the granny herself has aroused the woman, the lovesick suitor sneaks in and fin-ishes the encounter.[36] This granny, like all grannies, has the polymorphous sexuality of the god Eros. The only issue with these grannies is sexual satisfaction. They are amoral, not im-moral, as they advance the needs of the libido; the more vulgar the text, the more sexual the granny.

Feng Menglong compiled an unusual collection of Ming poems, called *The Mountain Songs*. Feng claimed his songs were transcribed in the villages and back streets of cities: gen-uine folk songs, he asserted. These poems covered a great range of subjects taken from the vulgar and the mundane: barnyard sounds, boatmen's chants, children's songs, love songs of the marketplaces—this is a popular collection of songs from very common situations. When the granny appears in this source she is both crude and libidinous; she assists affairs and has affairs. She is bawdy, sexual, and comical. No trace of romanticism colors her portrait, and the contrast with the Palace granny is extreme. Though the two types of grannies share a con-cern with the erotic and physical, the granny of folk song is a parody of romance. One poem tells of a granny determined to find a mate:

> The grandma of eighty was wanting a husband;
> She sought him, she wracked her brain, and berated all her neighbors.[37]

The granny in folk song is also obscene. Like all the base characters in this base collection, the granny is oblivious to decorum. Of course, love in marginal texts often becomes indecorous, as nonelite literature is the perfect place for chaotic thoughts.

Old Sis

Now our Old Sis went off to hunt a man.
Hunting here, hunting there, she got herself a little one.
She used this plan; she used that plot.
She tracked him; she won him.
Off with the skirt!
Off with the pants!
She held him tight and down they went.
Now this Old Sis, she said to him:
"Ah, m'boy! I feel as if my scab's submerged in nice, cold water, and I've rid myself of some old itch!"
Under the rays of the shining moon, even an empty lantern seems to show a bit of light.[38]

Their grandmotherly age notwithstanding, grannies of folk songs are sexual women; and ultimately the one and only concern of the folklore granny is eros. Such concerns do not earn them contempt; rather, these women have in literature a type of power. The source of the power is knowledge of the appetites, knowing that love is unpredictable and overwhelming, that it can strike the innocent bride or distinguished official and make each one need her. She assumes that human nature is both romantic and idealized, but also base. She can see right into the chaos of desire, an ability she has had for centuries. With her unerring ear for the truth of human nature beneath the required decorum, she has an unshakable sense of her own legitimacy. She has obviously seen more than the young and untested, and much more than any man. In a culture that yields to women low status and a precarious economic existence, grannies in Ming literature have a miraculous contempt for the lord of the estate. The feeling is, of course, mutual. A very uneasy truce existed between the ruling male and the unruly granny.

Nowhere is this dynamic more apparent than in the portrayal of our earlier granny, Granny Wang of *Jin Ping Mei*. In the novel, powerful men seek her help, and when they ask, they discover their lack of power. Ximen Qing, the ruthless parvenu of the book, needs Granny Wang. He has fallen in love with Golden Lotus, the young wife of the insignificant Wu Da. He cannot, however, accomplish the affair alone, for love affairs, both legitimate and illicit, require the services of a granny. Ximen turns to the granny, the neighbor of Golden Lotus, as his obvious choice to bring off the affair. Granny Wang is, of course, pleased to seize one of the more profitable of the "various opportunities." Now she has a man in her power, and a wealthy one at that. The encounter between the ruling lord and the resourceful granny occurs after Ximen's encounter with Golden Lotus. We see him as he turns for assistance to the capable Granny Wang.

"If you'd like to do some matchmaking," Ximen Qing requested, "I have a rather personal matter which, if you handled, I'd be very, very grateful."

"Oh, I think you must be toying with me," said the granny. "If your Lady of the house should hear about this, I'd really be in disgrace."

"Oh, my wife is of kind temperament. I actually have several at home, but none that actually suits me just right. If you have one, suggest her to me. Even if you know of one that's been married before I wouldn't mind, just so long as I find that she suits me."

Granny Wang replied, "Well, I did hear of one a few days ago; but I doubt you'd care for her."

But Ximen Qing replied, "If she's a good one, you and I can come to terms and I'd be truly grateful!"

"Well, she's an exceptionally handsome type, but may be a bit old for you," the granny said.

"Well," Ximen Qing said, "people say that to marry an older woman makes a marriage in which feelings grow; so if there's one or two years' difference, I don't care. But how old is she?"

"Well, this particular woman was born in the year *ding hai*, which was the Year of the Pig. Now I guess," said the granny, "that would just make her ninety-three years old!"

"You crazy old granny! You make your crazy faces just to get a laugh at my expense!" Ximen Qing laughed aloud. He then smiled as he got up, and he took himself off.[39]

Granny Wang clearly knows she has Ximen Qing in her clutches and strings him along for a laugh at his expense; when the ruling male requires her services he can do little besides serve as her straight man. This granny loves to play, and Ximen Qing is her entertainment; like a cat with her prey she enjoys diversion with her meal. Not that the meal is pretty: grannies have a sordid, ugly side. Allied with the trickster and the persuader is the hustler and con artist. Grannies are often predators with a nose for the smell of human frailty. Granny Wang is a typical example: a hard-core cynic, shrewd, knowing, and manipulative. Like many hustlers she is tinged with icy malevolence; beneath the cheerful vulgarity and "crazy faces" is a cold, still center. Granny Wang shows us the icy ambition beneath the humor. When Ximen Qing turns to the granny for assistance, she knows instantly just how vulnerable he is. After Ximen Qing's first request for the granny's help, he remains by Lotus's door.

> Now as Granny Wang caught sight of the lovesick Ximen Qing, she said to herself, "Why, this brush circles round and sweeps his path clear; so don't you know, all I've got to do is smear a bit of candy on his nose that he can't quite get off! This boy has made something off of everyone in the county. But now I'll have him into this old granny's grasp just to provide me some income, and help me earn a few strings of love-cash!"[40]

The granny is a paradox: ugly because she knows the ugly, yet witty, resourceful, clever, and dominant. Such a paradox may seem a strange feature of a Ming granny, yet the same paradox characterizes many men and women of the trickster type. In her resourcefulness, in her command of the realms of possibilities and opportunities, in her ability to survive the long brawl of life, she is a female comic hero. Robert Torrance in *The Comic Hero* notes that these characters are shifting sorts of heroes, paragons of "multiplicity and craft" in the "unremitting contest with fortune and misfortune."[41] The characters are men—and women—of disguises and excuses, men—and women—who know "every nook and cranny of 'seems.'"[42] Tragic heroes have great principles; comic heroes rule uncertainty and change. Granny Wang may seem an unlikely hero, but like all comic heroes, she has the same slippery abilities. And like all comic heroes, she has one gift in particular, one skill of heroic proportions: the use of language. Comic heroes are famous for their virtuosity with words—their power of speech is all they have. Reynard the Fox and Br'er Rabbit survive on little else. The Ming granny is a member of their guild. She dazzles her prey with words; whether devising seductions or persuading a naive bride, she is the advocate, the artist of oral persuasion, the true comedian, actor, and wit. Granny Liu of one story says of herself, "I'm a woman Sui He, and a female Lu Jia; I can talk an *arhat* into dreaming of love, or Chang E into being homesick."[43] Granny Wang of *Jin Ping Mei* is compared to the great sophists of ancient times:

> With her lance-sharp speech, her fine rhetoric, she persuades the Six States.
> And with her sword-like tongue, she talks into submission the Three Qi.[44]

Grannies are great talkers; they argue, list, ridicule, expose, and overwhelm. The subject of all this verbiage is love, although this alliance of sex and language is not surprising. Riddles, imprecations, secret words, and even babble are the typical codes of the erotic. The trickster who governs the realm of the sensual often governs name-magic. Grannies, like many tricksters, are great namers. Like the ancient shamaness who babbled in her state of divine possession, grannies too unleash great speeches with long lists containing the endless possibilities of love, from disaster to achievement. There are the sobering threats, the happy assurances, and the frightening eventualities. Grannies spellbind. Their plans are not just articulated, they are displayed like a magic show, full of drama and suspense and, above all, timing.

When finally we see Granny Wang called on by Ximen Qing, she steps to the role like the professional she is. She tells Ximen Qing, "You cannot seduce a woman without the Five Necessities," and lays out for him the five skills necessary for seduction. She also tells him, "She will come into your power with the ten plans."[45] She proceeds then to explain them carefully, step by step, dramatizing the potential failures to enhance the tension (see Figure 3.3). And as she talks, she clearly has Ximen Qing on a hook. Of course, the ten plans, all carefully laid out, prove to work. Liu Sima, in another story, discusses the desires of a geisha to become a wife. She tells her of the "eight types of getting out"[46] and explains them in meticulous detail. When the author of *Jin Ping Mei* tells us that Granny Wang can match the great persuaders from the Warring States period, the famous advocates of the competing philosophies, he is making a very conventional and apt comparison. The grannies are the mistresses of codes, lists, threats, and promises: language in full battle array.

With Granny Wang, Ximen Qing finds a woman who knows about his needs more than he can possibly imagine. This granny is fully prepared to facilitate his desires. Through her jokes, her mockery, and her near perfect timing, she will first reduce him to buffoon and supplicant—that is, to who he really is—and then accommodate what he wants. She has both the power and the knowledge to play with him. The granny knows the darkest aspects of the "dark *yin*," and she knows how essential to men and women this chaos of love can fully be.

Not surprisingly, when the author praises Granny Wang in an expansive poem, he credits her with the ability to persuade anyone of anything. She has the skills, claims the poet, to stir up trouble among the gods and the saints. Even the archetypal puritan, the Martyred Woman, is vulnerable to the granny's magic.

> Mustering her arguments head to tail,
> She excites the Martyred Woman to painful thoughts of a lover.
> Now the warm, then the cold,
> She manipulates Chang E to steal from her mate.
> This granny, absolutely so practiced in the skills of love;
> So knowing in the matters of wind and moon,
> Ready at the public gate she sharpens now her sparring skills.[47]

Despite official contempt expressed for her vulgarity and troublemaking, she is the essential catalyst; and men such as Ximen Qing rely fully on her unconventionality, or rather her anti-conventionality. Since she lives outside of the constraints of elite custom, she is free to ignore them.

We are looking at more, however, than a literary convention useful to Ming fiction. For if the Ming storyteller needed her, so did the mythmakers. The literary trickster is virtually never absent from myth, for her vulgarity and troublemaking belie a complex set of values

Figure 3.3 Illustration from the Ming erotic novel *Jin Ping Mei*. Granny Wang arrays her battle plans for Ximen Qing: the "ten plans" that will be used to seduce her neighbor Pan Jinlian (*Jin Ping Mei ci hua*, *juan* 2).

and themes. Grannies impart knowledge, knowledge that the innocent protagonist must acquire. She is a comedian, but it is comedy with the purpose of all comedy from Aristophanes to Beckett: to name the unnamable. If wit is the voice of the unconscious, Wang's jokes are the voice of desire. The chief role of Granny Wang is the same as that played by the grannies of the Palace—to acquaint her audience with a knowledge of the instinctual. What the granny knows is the simple fact that man and woman are made of flesh. It is not a profound truth, just one that is consistently denied by the decorous. It is certainly not the only thing for a character in literature to learn, but it is one of the first things, and it is the necessity of this knowledge that allows a plot to happen. Thus the granny's role is not comic relief from the main action of a story but is at the heart of the action of the story, for like all comics, she is one of the few who can name the truth. Fiction and plays are plotless without them. These literary mischief makers are thus as ubiquitous as they are necessary; in Ming fiction, the initiator is usually the granny.

Some version of the granny-catalyst is found in all storytelling. In the theater of the Ming, these granny-tricksters are often young women, maids, and confidantes, who run messages for the lovesick or urge their mistresses to meet a lover. One famous mischief maker of the Ming play *The Lute* complains about the ascetic life that her mistress leads: "While in your service, if a man happens by, you don't even let me raise my eyes. The other day was so fine—flowers red, willows green—it would have moved the heart of a dog or cat, but you weren't moved a bit."[48] Her mistress is too puritanical and too boring. "Sounds of music and rhyme appall her; her only wish is to sit and sew." Like all tricksters, this woman has better plans. "Well then I'll leave you and go serve somebody else, and carry love messages back and forth for her, and get a chance to have some fun myself."[49] These women are true initiators, necessary devices inserted into the drama to motivate a plot into action and a hero out of stasis.

If Ming audiences expected a troublemaker, so did readers of other tales. Agents of eroticism and misbehavior are everywhere in literature, although they often vary to suit the conventions of the culture. In elite literatures of Europe, these figures are typically men. Often they are social parasites, "entertainers, cooks, masters of ceremonies or masters of revels like Falstaff," as Northrop Frye has observed.[50] Each literature has its variant: the tricky slave (*dolorosus servus*) in Renaissance comedy, the scheming valet in British, and, in Spanish drama, the *gracioso*. This male granny is brought in, says Frye, "to oil the machinery of the well-made play. . . . He is very useful to a comic dramatist because he acts from pure love of mischief, and can set a comic action going with the minimum of motivation."[51] Like the granny, the *gracioso* and his ilk are at heart allied with the wicked. The trickster of Elizabethan comedy developed, Frye points out, from the "vice" or "iniquity" of medieval drama.

Popular literature, however, seems to prefer that these troublemakers be women. In Arabic shadow plays, Spanish love poetry, and Spanish romantic drama, the crone Celestina stirs up the lovesick. She is a matchmaker much like the granny of Ming literature; and, like the granny, she is a fertility spirit, for her origins lie in the god Eros, messenger of love. She has at her disposal the expected tricks of the trade: cosmetics to enhance beauty, a laboratory to concoct love potions, fertility drugs, and magic spells. Her persona is both witch and matchmaker, and she arranges magic as easily as marriage.

But if the Arabic matchmaker is useful as a "vice," she also symbolizes the same earthy physicality as the Ming granny. Indeed, one Arabic granny conveys a complete portrayal of the world of *yin*. This matchmaker even evokes the shamaness of ancient China, for her name also implies all aspects of fertility. This matchmaker is Umm Rasid, and her name, Umm, means mother. She is often depicted as a mother in paintings and shadow-play figures, appearing as a pregnant hag. Like Granny Wang, Umm Rasid tells her own history. Like the granny of the Ming, she represents through her own life all aspects of the *yin*: "I was a lesbian as a child, a sodomite as a young girl, an adulterer as a mature woman, and a matchmaker as an old woman."[52]

Grannies were the expelled gods of fertility; they ruled the realm of physiology, a realm that was essential to the survival of Ming life. Childbirth and child care were the obviously vital links in the continuity of the culture. The great array of filial rituals and filial education existed largely to help sustain the forces linking the child to the parent and the parent to the past. Reproduction was ultimately the essential matrix of the lineage; and in this kingdom of the physical and the biological, the grannies ruled. Of course, official dicta consigned them to the heterodox, the treasonous, and the vulgar; but even in this position at the margins of society, as part of "the dark *yin*," they came through myth and folk tale to assume their authority.

One simple folktale epitomizes the spectrum of granny lore, catching the humor, the power and the confidence of this woman, situating her in the realm of fruition and fertility that she so competently governs:

> There was once, during the Tang Dynasty, a man named Li Guanming. Li possessed an apricot tree; but the tree produced no fruit. He summoned the matchmaker, and she said to him with a smile, "Come spring, I'll arrange a marriage for this apricot." Then, in the deep of winter, she appeared with some wine and, proceeding to the tree, she bound a woman's skirt around it. When spring came, the tree bore countless fruit.[53]

4

Warriors and Mystics

The Queen Mother of the West chanted again for the Son of Heaven:

> I'm going off to that western land,
> Where I reside in wild places,
> With tigers and leopards I form a pride;
> Together with crows and magpies I share the same dwelling place,
> Fortune and destiny can not be transcended,
> I am the thearch's daugher. . .

Mu Tianzi zhuan, Suzanne Cahill trans.[1]

Female mystics and female warriors look, at first glance, to be honorary men. Their ascetic mien seems borrowed, their magic derivative; men must be the proper practitioners of the crafty sciences, the ones appropriately skilled in martial arts, in inner alchemy, and in the arts of longevity. Ming observers did not agree, however. "When going into battle," warned one general from a great epic novel, "be extra careful of Taoist priests, of Buddhist monks, and of women. They always command magic arts."[2] They "always command magic arts" because they have a historical claim to them; neither general nor official was surprised to find a woman brandishing a sword. Nor was a woman's divinity awarded to her by a religious male elite. Although many women are classified as Daoist, Buddhist, or Confucian, their basic marks of feminine sanctity seem to be outside such classifications; sacred women do not require masculine, text-based affiliations. Conversely, there is constant overlap of female sacred traits. Female warriors, Daoist mystics, and even water goddesses can all begin their sacred courses as filial daughters; and chaste women suicides can become shamanlike drought deities. The skills and traits seem, in fact, to be more primal than religious categories suggest. One female warrior claimed, "I trace my skills to the arts of the Dark Maiden,"[3] and anthropologists agree. There seems to be an ancient, preliterate configuration of feminine sanctity informing their thaumaturgic powers. Sacred women, whatever the school, inherit a constellation of traits: magic travel, horrific self-sacrifice, divine lan-

Figure 4.1   The Furry Woman, an adept who was once from an aristocratic family. During the disorder after the fall of Qin, she withdrew to the mountains and could be seen from time to time. She felt neither cold nor hot, and her body was so light she could fly (*Youxiang lie xian quan zhuan, juan* 2).

guage, and affiliation with the agency of water. Whether Daoist or Buddhist, these women mimic the shamaness.[4] If there is not some ur-language of feminine sanctity located in ancient shamanism, there is at least a sense that sacred women owed their emblems of power not to masculine religious culture, but to their own.

If sanctity was natural to the feminine, it did not always sit happily in the eyes of the community; sacred women were often considered the most dangerous of women. We have seen how grannies could rattle the structures of palace and home, but a mystic with divine authority or a warrior with faithful adherents could summon thousands of worshipers and alarm the government. "Tan Yang Zi," said one man of the mystic he worshiped, "perceived the indistinct sound of the music of the immortals."[5] When she died, he claimed, "There were a hundred thousand people, some worshiping, some kneeling, some weeping and calling out to her."[6] Such support worried people; officials charged female mystics with sorcery or treason. "They are everywhere," fumed one intellectual, "endlessly deluding the masses, causing disaster."[7] Warriors and mystics could be branded loathsome or divine.

The Transcendent Maid Yu suffered just such extremes. This strange woman was a famous Daoist who gathered adherents and performed miraculous acts. She was known for her skills in the arts of longevity; it was said she no longer needed food or drink. Her fame, however, earned her the attention of a local official who was eager to prove her a fraud. "The magistrate Cao Ximin was a man of stern character who heard what others had related about the woman's marvels, so he went personally to investigate the case. When he saw her, her appearance was like that of a hoary ancient."[8] As a man of "stern character," Cao naturally refused to believe in this mystic—it was in fact his job to be doubtful of such women and reports of their "marvels." Officer Cao devised a challenge. Since her arts of longevity meant she no longer "consumed the five grains," he tested her skills and her authority by requesting she drink: "May I present you with a cup of tea," he said. Forced by Cao to violate her abstinence, she hesitated. "It has been a long time since I have had anything to drink." Cao, however, persevered: "Then may I urge you to take a sip," he said.[9] The mystic dealt easily with the challenge: "After a sip, the Transcendent Maid extended her two hands—white as jade they were. And from the fingernails of all her ten fingers the tea drained out onto the ground. The color of the tea appeared unchanged. Cao Ximin ordered his aid to collect the liquid from the ground and ordered him to taste it. It was as fragrant as when first poured."[10]

We can imagine the magistrate returning to his office, disgruntled, aggrieved—the story of the undigested tea already part of the woman's renown; but his job and even his own "stern character" left him few options. Both Cao Ximin and the adept played out roles cast for them for centuries. Magistrates could only regard the adept with suspicion; she was solitary, badly domesticated, and known to communicate with the gods. Nor was the adept tolerant of the magistrate. Her life was devoted to acquiring sacred texts, to sacred flights to supernatural worlds, and to the intensely private discipline of achieving longevity (see Figure 4.1).

The primary problem for Cao Ximin and other "men of stern character" was the religious adept's popularity. They were everywhere, of every variety, and people flocked to them. The Ming was an age of faith, and the sign of the times was the ascendancy of the adept. Religious teachers of all sorts—monks, nuns, adepts, even local shamanesses—commanded support. City dwellers, aristocrats, officials, eunuchs—virtually anyone could search for a religious teacher. When these teachers appeared, they could collect masses of worshipers: "When Master Zibo came to the capital," an artist recounted in his journal, "a lot of famous people and many eunuchs were overwhelmed and went to him like pilgrims to the Buddhist festival on the sacred mountain."[11] The Emperor himself subscribed to these enthusiasms. The famous Ming adept "Dirty Zhang" inspired an Imperial search throughout the realm; the Emperor was determined to find him and discover his secret arts.

All of this meant that adepts like the Transcendent Maid Yu had potential for great support. Worshipers from the Imperial Palace as well as local adherents were ready to believe and ready to donate. And adepts were not women of myth and story; they lived, taught, and attracted followers in this elaborate patronage system that sheltered them in specific and substantial ways. There was no surer sign of this religious support than the sight of the temples themselves; an estimated one thousand temples in Beijing were devoted to the cults of a variety of deities and sacred teachers. These temples, big and small, housed religious personnel of monks and nuns whose population was estimated at 31,000.[12] These temple complexes were not a minor part of city life. Temple activity thrived: religious teachers gave lectures; meetings were held at them; and the troublesome women warriors typically took refuge in them. The famous Daoist Monastery of the White Cloud in Beijing was filled with people on important holidays: "Men and women from the city visit the temple, as well as performers and musicians, all in their jewels and silks, all of them block the road and parade to the temple without end," one Grand Secretary observed.[13]

All this enthusiasm, of course, meant money. Adepts needed concrete forms of support, not just devotion. Places of worship required upkeep, monies for feast days and special ceremonies as well as for the constant refurbishing of their often palatial furnishings and decorations. Disciples and initiates also required support, and if a cult thrived, the support was necessary for generations. Resources of both the private and public were thus given over to religion; patronage thrived on a massive scale. Women of the Palace were especially lavish in their contributions; but the Emperor, aristocratic families—women and men included—the official class, villagers and eunuchs all contributed.[14]

The chief source of support was, of course, Imperial, for if the Emperor favored an adept he often established her in the capital. In the city of Kaifeng there was a famous pair of adepts, a brother and sister team—sibling magicians—who could summon the rain. During the Yongle period (1402–1423), Adept Jiao and her brother became famous enough to be "favored with" an Imperial summons. They were brought to live in Beijing within the huge complex of the Imperial Palace itself, where the Emperor built a temple for the woman, the Temple of Arcane Truth.[15]

For some women, however, Imperial patronage meant not only a lifetime of support but also support for generations after. One woman in the Ming became, in effect, an institution. It is rare for us to get a glimpse of the specifics of how these women were transformed from adept to cult icon, but in one case the history is preserved. Early in the Ming, a child was given to a nunnery in Shanxi; in the conditions of poverty and unrest this was probably not uncommon. What was unusual was that as the child grew up she became a local religious teacher, well known in the province as Nun Lu. She would have remained insignificant, but local rebellion drew the Emperor's gaze. A popular uprising brought the Imperial armies, led by the Emperor himself. During the military expedition to Shanxi the Emperor discovered that this local adept had a substantial following; and when the Emperor led his troops to the province to attack the locals, Nun Lu confronted him and warned him against continuing. He was impressed with her dire warnings as well as her "marks of sanctity"—and perhaps he noted as well the size of her local following—so he withdrew his attack. But the Emperor, true to the tenor of the times, saw the adept as more than a local leader. He saw her as a talisman of religious authority, and so he elevated the woman from local magician to Imperial religious teacher. Like the brother and sister magicians of Kaifeng, she was changed from provincial magician to Imperial adept. The Emperor brought her back to the capital, established a temple for her, and, as one scholar notes, "benefited her with his Imperial Presence many times." The temple, well known, was located in the Shuntian district; besides the official name for it—Temple of the Preservation of the Light—it was also called the Temple of the Illuminate Maiden.[16]

Her cult and her temple lasted more than her lifetime, however, for Imperial patronage could be very sustaining. Government patronage was substantial and long term, and provincial adepts who became Imperial visionaries were solidly protected, and lands and structures maintained for them. One hundred years after her temple was established one visitor noted that the complex was still in fine repair. "The buildings are still solid," he said, "and the sacred images and the wall hangings still beautiful."[17] These compounds were maintained even when it meant sacrificing the practical needs of local citizens, and if local residents came into conflict with the temple, the temple came first. During the history of the temple there were encroachments. When the Female Monk Woman Yang, a latter-day worshiper of Nun Lu, lived in the temple, nearby farmers began to use the temple lands. These lands, however, were used to support the operation of the temple, so the Emperor stepped in and warned the nearby farmers off. "From now on if any occupy these lands," read the Imperial proclamation, "damage or destroy the buildings and thereby do injury to her teachings, or dare ultimately to disobey My Command, I will subject them to the law."[18]

Nun Lu and her adherents were thus declared to be more important than the farmers and townspeople nearby. An adept brought magic and even legitimacy to the realm; a farmer only fed himself. The temple continued to exist at whatever the cost, and continued to shelter the women of faith who followed the teachings of Nun Lu. Our visitor who earlier saw the handsome appointments of the temple also saw the nuns who inhabited the site. The nuns, he noted, "nowadays refrain from shorn heads, but wrap their heads in turbans, and go about in the black square-cut jackets of Buddhist monks."[19] They continued under the protection of Imperial support, and the needs of the ordinary citizen were a pale second.

In this atmosphere of devotion and royal commitment, adepts could and did come from everywhere, for adept status was not limited to a few isolated eccentrics; they were a growth industry. You could find an adept or mystic in any part of the Empire—rural areas, mountainous regions, villages, towns, and especially Beijing. They could be supported anywhere. Tan Yang Zi, the mystic who attracted one hundred thousand mourners at her death, lived in the sophisticated and wealthy southern city of Suzhou; the sister and brother who summoned the rain were from Kaifeng. Rural areas could easily produce a mystic or a warrior, and of course the typical place for mystics and warriors was in the mountains. One scholar told of a small monastic community with one adept and her two disciples; the three women led ascetic lives of simple farming as they studied to become transcendents.[20] Adepts also came from all walks of life. In the hagiographies of the Ming, there were high-born women as well as farmers and geishas who assumed religious life. The nun Wise Truth came originally from an official family;[21] the reclusive woman Sun had once been a farmer;[22] and Lady Qiang, who became an adept, was originally an aristocrat.

Of course there were always grumblings about adepts; nor were such complaints without reason. Money, effort, work, and people were all required to support religion. In the late Ming in particular, as temple projects continued unabated, official buildings were literally in ruins, and offices for local city administrations were collapsing. Even in the district closest to the Palace, the district with a magnificent collection of temples, the public offices were a disaster. "Where there was once a great hall," Shen Bang recorded, "now there is no hall at all." The noise of the shopkeepers traveled right into the civil offices, he complained.[23] Officials often wondered why there were so many temples: "Why is it," one minister pointedly remarked, "when only one altar was needed for sacrificing to heaven and earth, and only one temple required for the ancestors, we must have a thousand Buddhist temples?"[24] Just as worrisome was the popularity of these teachers and adepts. The scholar Zhou Chen complained that adherents of both Buddhism and Daoism were everywhere. "Loafers from their native villages flock to (the abbots) . . . and offer their services, and the young men . . . dress as monks, complete with staffs and alms-bowl. Sometimes they form groups and perform religious ceremonies. . . . Thus an abbot often has several score in his service and an ordinary monk may have three to five loafers under him."[25] The most often heard complaint was leveled at the system of tax exemptions. A large amount of lands were devoted to religious communities; temples were often temple farms, which were maintained to support a population of monks and nuns. These lands could not be taxed, privately farmed, or otherwise used.[26] This removal of lands from public use and from the tax lists was one of the major fiscal problems at the end of the Ming. The temple to honor Nun Lu may have had devoted supporters, but it also robbed the locals of an income, and ministers, magistrates, and tax officials complained loudly.

The main problem with these adepts, however, was not economic but rather religious. Magistrates like Cao Ximin were more worried about the orthodoxy of these women than about their incomes. Local officials were specifically charged with maintaining religious order, and they were ever wary that a woman's communication with the gods might be demoniac, or their skills in magic heretical. The official class was on guard. They did more, however, than lead investigations. The Ming legal code outlawed sorcery and heresy, and punishments were explicit. Official castigation could thus be swift and venomous. One writer described Tan Yang Zi herself as possessed of a demon, and in 1581 the Imperial Censorate accused her of heresy and sorcery—charges that were ultimately dropped, but charges nonetheless.[27] Thus when Cao Ximin visited the Transcendent Maid, he came armed with the knowledge that the Ming legal code did not take kindly to women and magic.

If mystics were subject to suspicion, women warriors were subject to attack. Daoist or Buddhist adepts could be dangerous with their sorcery, but warrior-adepts were more dangerous still; they could be guilty of sorcery in the service of politics—treason. Their skills in the Dao were especially suspect, for when they did not confine themselves to the arts of abstinence and longevity, they excelled at and were infamous for more dramatic forms of magic. Their magic arts varied: some controlled the arts of flying swords, others could manipulate the weather, some could summon armies out of paper cutouts. But the essential skill of the warrior was spirit wandering (see Figure 4.2). Warrior-adepts even claimed a patron

Figure 4.2   Red Thread, Tang Dynasty warrior-adept known for her ability to travel thousands of miles by spirit wandering (*Wu Youru huabao*, vol. 1, "One Hundred Beauties Past and Present").

saint, a goddess who transmitted esoteric skills to the worthy. The Primal Woman of the Nine Heavens supplied secret texts, talismans, and knowledge to the warrior. Feminine discourse with the divine could thus be used in warfare and in rebellion; both female and male warriors came dangerously close to resembling the leaders of millenarian political movements. Of course, warnings proliferated, and some sober analysts tried to denigrate them. "They are like sword swallowers in the marketplace," one intellectual said, "practiced merely in tricks of illusion."[28] But most, including the Emperor himself, took them seriously.

This means that for every Nun Lu who was brought to the capital to be worshipped, there were others who were banned. One warrior rebel was pursued for decades by the Imperial army. The woman warrior Tang Saier was an infamous knight errant of the Ming. She led an insurrection during the reign of the Yong Le Emperor. In the early part of the fifteenth century, she and her band of soldiers captured several walled cities and stockades in the rich and important province of Shandong. What made her so potent as a rebel, however, was her adept status. Like the mystics she resembled, she could command esoteric skills; she was called "Buddha Mother" by her followers. She learned her military secrets through ominous transmission of a sacred text; and in the same cave where she found the sacred text, she found also her talisman, a magical sword. Like all warriors, she could command magic; she could create soldiers out of paper cutouts. When she was captured, the weapons of the enemy could not touch her. When finally the Emperor sought to eliminate Tang Saier, he looked for her where any adept would likely be hidden. In his exhaustive search to capture the woman he commanded all the Buddhist and Daoist nuns in the province of Shandong to be rounded up and brought to the capital for questioning. She was never caught, however, and the historical account of this rebellious adept concludes the way these accounts usually conclude: "We have no idea where she went."[29] Tang Saier walked a fine line. She was a charismatic leader, a saint who gathered an army; yet she risked official condemnation and Imperial rebuke.

If Emperors took a jaundiced look at such adepts, fathers and mothers were at least as troubled. Accounts of adepts are filled with dubious relatives and accusing husbands. When women demonstrated esoteric skills and changed from daughter to adept, parents worried, accused and forbade; they didn't like it. Few wanted to see a daughter or wife respond to the calling of adepthood. The official Cao Ximin had, in fact, many cohorts—figures of enforcement, men and women worried about a girl's adept tendencies. All their objections, however, simply show how ambivalent society was, and how alien the mystic was in the context of home. To some families these women were deeply different—clearly not the bride waiting for a mate, nor the daughter caring for her parents—and alien to the collective. This communal mistrust could delay the adept, force her to take a crooked path to adept status. Challenged and rechallenged, her life became a tug of war between the life of the visionary and the obligations of the community.

One adept from the Song period illustrates this uneasy progress. This adept began life as a filial daughter, then grew up to become a loyal wife. Early in her life, however, she discovered the calling of the arts of the Dao; like Tan Yang Zi and the Transcendent Maid, she was confronted with skeptics. Her challenges came from both within and without her family; her life became a series of tests. Before her final escape she was challenged by her parents, her husband, and a Daoist priest. They accused her of being a "female demon" and a "creature of illusion." Only after a strange series of challenges and counter-challenges did she achieve the status of adept, at which time she renounced them all to live as a recluse.

This adept is known only as "the Daughter of Jiao Sanshi." Her early life is a story of secret practices and suppressed skills.

> Master Jiao Sanshi was a man of Fangzhou. His house was next to the academy of Scholar Yong. Now master Jiao had a daughter who had been born during a period of family mourning and who also, from a very young age, loved books. Each day she listened secretly to all the students reading next door; and after listening to them she would chant the texts to herself from memory. Her father was himself dedicated to the study of the recipes of Daoist texts, and put these arts into practice. So when the daughter was sure her father was out, she practiced her gramarye in secret.[30]

What was acceptable in the father was clearly not acceptable in the daughter. Though the daughter had inherited her father's talents and inclinations, she had not inherited his prerogatives; her skills had to be practiced in secret, her career forced to go underground. Nor did maturity and adulthood bring her the chance for transcendence; where the father left off, the community continued. True to the exigencies of the culture, the daughter married and conformed to the needs of family and community; she suppressed her adept nature in favor of marriage.

Eventually, her life took the necessary strange turns. Her husband Shi Hua, a merchant, was forced to go off and work in faraway Guizhou. Whereupon the wife, in a strange combination of filial devotion and Daoist magic, performed an apparent death. Using the technique of sending the soul after death, the daughter "died" at the home of her parents in order to send her soul to live with her husband. Her "death," however, was discovered. A neighbor of the devoted couple caught on—he learned of the earlier death and yet saw his neighbor happily ensconced—and reported on all this to the parents. Daughter Jiao was then confronted with this monstrous and unexplainable event—how she could be dead in her parents' town, and alive and married in Guizhou? She simply explained: "It was not a true death."

Everyone now suspected trouble. Adepts can send their spirits walking abroad, but so can demons. A woman operating magic without benefit of clergy was clearly dangerous, and all were quick to accuse her of being a malign ghost. "This sister of mourning is bad luck," they counseled the husband. "Drive the demon out." Hostilities were now in the open. The woman's "gramarye" was unwelcome in the family and had to be assessed. Was she demon or mystic? The husband needed to know. To test this "sister of mourning," he called in a specialist.

> Husband Hua then thought up a test. The next day he invited a priest to examine rigorously his wife's essential being. After arriving, the priest wrote up a magic talisman to ward off demonic influence, but before he had even finished, the wife wrote one that defeated his. The priest again wrote a talisman, this time of the Officer of Demonic Exorcism, but again she completed one— of the Primal Woman of the Nine Heavens—which again defeated his. The priest did not display another one. Instead he brandished his sword and said, "What are you!—some female demon or creature of illusion?!!"[31]

Having defeated the chief arbiter of religious orthodoxy, the daughter then explained herself:

> She replied: "As a child growing up I read my father's books of magic, and so [using these techniques] I journeyed in a dream to the Nine Heavens where the Primal Woman transmitted to me her techniques of returning to life and of returning the soul. So when I returned to man to dwell in this world of illusion, I often had a mystic sense of oneness. So, although I never violated the prohibitions of man and earth, yet I did pass through to the Vastness many times. So how can anyone who respects the true gods defeat these methods I use?" The priest was without a response and could only withdraw.[32]

With the daughter's victory over the priest, and her skills finally revealed, we might expect her apotheosis to be near; but once again the demands of the community win out. The daughter of Jiao continues in her marriage. Not until later does she rediscover her adepthood, to abandon the hearth and became a recluse. The story ends as the young woman flees to the mountains for a life of seclusion. "After that the woman was back with her family as before. Then some years later, the whole household traveled together to what had been the daughter's 'grave site,' and her mother pointed it out to her. At that the daughter gave out a laugh. Suddenly she simply took herself off, far away to the mountains. And from then on, she was never seen again."[33]

Her disappearance marked the final apotheosis of the adept, for it could only be achieved when she was cut off completely from family and community. But the community did try its best; from the start it opposed her—it cannot be faulted. It blocked her training and questioned her skills; like the dubious Cao Ximin, the relatives of the adept kept a worried eye on the strange woman, and if they didn't "drive the demon out," at least they drove the adept out.

Rebels such as Tang Saier, the Transcendent Maid, and the strange adept of the Jiao family, however, could never be thoroughly scourged. Neither family disapproval nor official regulation could ever eradicate them, for despite the disapproval of some intellectuals, they were an established part of Ming religious life. The adept was not a marginal practitioner of sleight of hand; she traced her techniques to the gods, summoned the gods, and served as a conduit for the gods. Thus, when the daughter Jiao defended her techniques—"How can anyone who respects the true gods defeat these methods I use?"—she was accurate. Her methods were deeply revered.

The ambivalence of family and community could be overlooked with one important sign, however: Imperial attention. The sanction of the Court gave instant legitimacy, and the Emperor was, in turn, well aware of the usefulness of a female adept. Her "love of the Dao" could prove very practical for a dynastic ideologue. The adept could receive dynastic talismans, a sign that divine legitimacy was shifting. One sure sign of her authority was her influence over weather. Like the Court rain makers of ancient times, these adepts could summon the natural world. The powerful warrior-adepts looked often like latter-day shamanesses; storms, earthquakes, strange weather followed them. They were domesticated lightning rods, conduits for heavenly power. Since the Emperor himself was chief agent of heavenly power—literally, the Son of Heaven—the adept mirrored his power. True, the adepts were a risk. But ironically, what made them dangerous also made them useful. Of course, you had to prosecute the ones who allied with your enemies, but the loyal ones were essential to any well-run dynasty; no one knew this better than the Emperor.

In the last years of the Yuan dynasty, when the Ming was establishing its legitimacy, the founding Emperor called on the powers of an adept. She was known simply as Woman Liu.[34] This adept was not banished, like Tang Saier, nor allowed to disappear, like Daughter Jiao; rather she was put to use in the service of the new dynasty, where her skills in the crafty sciences made her important in the violent transition from the Yuan to the Ming in the year 1368. Ultimately, in reward for her achievements as warrior-adept, she was given a title. The first Emperor of the Ming, in the first year of his rule, in recognition of both her and, more importantly, of his own legitimacy, enfeoffed her as "Matron of Subtle Divinity." Her story, however, is not a story of aristocratic connections. Woman Liu, like all the women we have looked at, derived her power from the magical. Her rise to political prominence was thus based on the power she brought to the Emperor, not the power he brought to her. Her life was, in turn, a story of magical co-option, a story of how her powers were borrowed to establish the new dynasty.

Like all adepts and mystics, Woman Liu showed early signs of her supernatural connections: "When she was born there were numinous and strange signs. When she was an infant, bandits attacked her family. But when they struck at her, she was untouched, nor could they hurt her with their swords. The bandits dashed off in terror."[35] Of course, Woman Liu was a scholar of the esoteric. "As she grew up she was fond of the Dao and knew the arts of the Apocryphal Texts of Daoism."[36] Later in her career as adept, she found a secret text, "a scroll of talismans and diagrams," given to her by an old man who said, "With this scroll the Ming will command an army of six gods and demons."[37]

What made her especially important, however, was her connection to divine knowledge of the political realm; she knew where the mandate would reside. As a young woman she defied the loyalties of even her father and grandfather because of her knowledge. "Woman Liu's ancestors were from Sichuan. . . . Her grandfather Liu Bingzheng and father Liu Zhen both served in the Yuan government. Her grandfather planned to resist the Ming army, but Woman Liu told him, 'The Mandate of Heaven is with the Ming.'"[38] Adepts had access to this type of political knowledge, and Woman Liu thus became part of dynastic folklore. The first Ming Emperor, however, got more than the adept's declaration. As befits a moment as earthshaking as the change of dynasty, he also got an adept who controlled the forces of nature. Of course, such control was not unusual for these women; woman Liu, however, could hardly make a move without involving the weather.

After the adept left her family, she took a journey. Traveling up river, the woman found that "the waters surged and roiled for an entire day and night, and there appeared an eerie light." When she stopped by a cliff—"Tigerhead outcropping"—and received the secret scroll of talismanic magic, the weather again participated. "That night wind and thunder uprooted trees, birds and beasts hid themselves away, and the brush and trees crashed about."[39] Like the shaman who summoned the forces of *yin* for the fertility of the earth, this adept was a catalyst for dramatic storms. Yet these were mere flurries of nature. When she finally accomplished her destiny as dynastic soldier, she brought forth wild demonstrations of natural power, a display of appropriately apocalyptic violence. To aid the Ming general in the final years of the Yuan era, the Woman Liu called up an earthquake. As the Ming armies were losing in battle, "suddenly the skies darkened and a flock of ducks rose up. The woman appeared in a great robe, on a horse soaring in the sky. There was an earthquake on Mount Pili and the cascading rocks stirred up the sand. General Deng took advantage of it and pacified the area of Mayang."[40] Like some ancient king who called on the shamaness, the Emperor adopted an adept who controlled the wildest forces of nature. Just as other Emperors recognized Nun Lu and Maiden Jiao, he rewarded her with a title in recognition of her powers; Woman Liu, in turn, became a talisman, and her powers reflected on the greater glory of the Emperor and his line.

Hence it is not surprising that Nun Lu, Adept Jiao, and other adepts—male and female— were brought to the capital to live happily ever after as symbols. For it was not just to consult with Nun Lu that the Emperor brought her to the Court, nor was it just to summon the rain that the Emperor brought the Kaifeng adepts to Beijing. These adepts served as signs of dynastic legitimacy. Not just passive icons of the divine, they were living catalysts who could induce by sympathetic magic the blessings of the gods. The city of Beijing was thus their appropriate destination, the place where the *axis mundi* connected the secular and divine worlds. Local adepts were brought to the capital that their magic might rest in the appropriate center; the profane space of man was thus made sacred.

The thousand temples, criticized by some officials, were clearly essential. Like so much divine costume on the body politic, they enhanced Imperial power, creating a divine aura that sanctioned the new dynasty. One observer noted the incredible splendor of the temples. "I have traveled about to see these buildings . . . their halls and altars, and hangings and banners like billows of clouds and falling stars. At one temple, the Temple of the Thousand Ages, the throne of the Buddha cost a thousand pieces of gold."[41] Our observer, however, was not just a dazzled tourist; he decoded intelligently the symbolism of all this physical glory. "Whenever I consider the Buddhist temples, monasteries, Daoist monasteries and abbeys, the sacred halls and the temples of this Wanping district of the capital, I sigh at the . . . authority of the sage kings, their boundless generosity, and their flourishing stability."[42] The intellectual knew that religion and politics were of a piece, with religion used to reveal the "authority . . . and flourishing stability" of the Imperial house. If religious architecture symbolized power, it also symbolized the eternal. When another observer saw a magnificent Chan temple, he too touted the elaboration of riches, "the splendor of its halls, the magnificence of its images, the expansiveness of its groves, and the wealth of its fields and gardens." He too interpreted such majesty as a link to the eternal. "Thus may this Chan temple of Eternal Peace from now on into the future, in splendor and glory, last as long as the mountain itself."[43] The capital needed clear manifestations of the apotheosis of the dynastic inheritors. These temples were not just edifices; they were symbols of a political structure that would "last as long as the mountain itself." Acquiring adepts thus served the sacred mission of dynastic legitimacy. They were important characters in the sacred theater of Imperial power. Like all adepts, Woman Liu was the symbol of raw nature tamed and regulated, drawn into the circle of Imperial power—made useful, finally, as a controlled conduit for the divine.

The adept did not always perform her assigned role, however, and efforts to co-opt her did not always succeed. These women made excellent talismans but poor pets. The problem was control. Sacred women socialized poorly and were not so easy to domesticate; in fact they tended to wander. In their temperaments, instincts, behavior, desires, talents, teachings, and mythology, they were not part of the confined space of the village. Rather, they were the proper residents of undomesticated and alien space. Such exotic space had its own folklore; the remote and the wild places of earth were configured as magical. Mountain cliffs, cloud-filled peaks, torrential river gorges were numinous; craggy, uncivilized ground had potent energies and sheltered powerful beings. The altar of the city god had authority to the city dweller, but the uncontained landscape of the mountain had power for the adept. In this lore of exotic space the *axis mundi* reached the earth not in the capital, among the city and the walls of civilization, but in the mountains. Sacred ground was uncontained ground, and adepts were resolutely of this antihome. Clearly it was no accident that Woman Liu seemed to carry the storm wherever she went. As we saw in her description: "The waters surged and roiled for an entire day and night, and there appeared an eerie light"; and "That night wind and thunder uprooted trees, birds and beasts hid themselves away, and the brush and trees crashed about." Woman Liu was the exotic space she bore with her. So too did the Daughter Jiao "travel to the vastness" many times; and when she finally disappeared, she took herself off to the mountains. These women were saints of alien ground; the quintessential act of the adept was exotic travel. The mystic and the warrior were primarily sacred travelers to the strange. They were not only prone to travel, they needed to travel; and no matter what the communal niceties, whether established for them in home, palace, or temple, they tended to leave, to take to the mountains or to the the air, to reclaim their native habitats.

Daoism in particular, relied on the exotic journey as the sign of religious power, and all the adepts we have looked at controlled exotic space. The adepts journeyed into the cosmos, among the stars, to the regions of the palaces of the gods. Such flights were called "pacing the void," "star-stepping," or the "pace of Yu."[44] These were well-charted flights whose patterns were laid down for centuries in the Daoist collection of sacred literature. Such practices were of course esoteric, but they were preserved specifically in the canon: the daughter of Jiao Sanshi acquired her ability to "travel to the Vastness" in her father's Daoist library.

The means of travel varied; meditation, ritual, and alchemy were used, all requiring years of discipline (see Figure 4.3). Some techniques enabled the adept to travel out of body to supernatural realms. Other techniques, however, took the adept on inward trips to a sacred world in microcosm. By the techniques of "inner alchemy"—physiological microcosmology, as Suzanne Cahill terms it—the mystic created in her own body the sacred space of the exotic. The technique of inner travel had many methods. One is described as a type of cosmic mimicry: a process of creating a miniature cosmos, drawing the stars she travels then into her person. According to this method, the adept lies down on the bed at night "on a diagram of the Big Dipper laid out . . . with its bowl like a canopy,"[45] recites the names of the stars of the Big Dipper, visualizes them in her own mind, and prays. If successful, the adept brings these stars down into her body. Like Tan Yang Zi, who had the "steam of the former heavens" circulating through her system, the sublime embryonic essences of the stars will exist in her own now exotic inner space. Eventually these essences of the cosmic outer space will "build up, in the course of time, an immortal body which will ascend to heaven in broad daylight."[46] Thus, like the shaman who brought nature with her, and like the Nun who seemed to carry the storm with her, the adept becomes the cosmos and thereby transforms the most familiar of all spaces—her own body—into exotic space.

Such travel would seem to be a very exotic event, available only to the few, seen only in obscure settings—relegated solely to the mountain retreat and the inner sanctum of the temple. The sacred travel of these adepts, however, could be performed anywhere, for they brought exotic space with them; this exotic space was a space that coexisted in and among the domestic—or at least it could. The mystic Tan Yang Zi, who had left thousands of worshipers "weeping and calling out" at her death, left an account of her sacred travels. This well-known visionary of the Ming had an industrious follower, the official Wang Shizhen, who transcribed her account. In his biography of the adept, he called Tan Yang Zi "My Master." In his worshipful account he described the adept's spirit journeys.

Tan Yang Zi's journeys took place while she remained at home. Since she was confined to the sedate life of a gentry family, her method was inner alchemy; like the daughter of Jiao Sanshi, she traveled to the vastness within the walls of her own room. In such a context, however, there were practicalities to manage. Thus she asked her father's help to keep her undisturbed, to remain by her side as she took her inward flight. "Don't go out. Stay for a while and look after me. As the daylight fades and my face becomes red, and the breathing from my mouth and nose becomes faint, this will mean that my spirit is departing. Take care that no one from the household spies on me."[47]

Figure 4.3 The Woman of Great *Yin*. The adept seen at her alchemical stove.
She was famous for her studies of inner alchemy and attained transcendence
after completing the preparation (*Youxiang lie xian quan zhuan, juan* 2).

After leaving her instructions, the mystic then began her meditation, and we are told: "At noon her spirit did depart. Her father held his breath and guarded her, protecting her while he waited. In the late afternoon, an icy sound like chimes came from the void."[48] Finally, the journey completed, Tan Yang Zi tells her father what she saw: "My Master [Tan Yang Zi] then woke up. She smiled and said to her father, 'Luckily nothing went wrong. In an instant I traveled hundreds of thousands of *li*. I beheld all sorts of things; mountains, rivers, grasses and trees, dragons and snakes, the nests of birds and bees. And all of them are spirits that reside within my body.'"[49] Even in the context of family, in the confines of the gentry estate, next to her own watching father, one adept travels. Nor was her travel wondered at, for clearly her sacred journey was not an eccentric gesture. Rather it had the mythology of two thousand years of sacred travel informing it—which made it easy for her to command even her own father: "Don't go out"—and he obeyed. Even the most filial of daughters could summon the power to travel to exotic space.

Tan Yang Zi, of course, had obvious forebears, for the power of these untamed spaces traces its origins to the lore of shamanism, where the potentiating nature of these dangerous places first appeared. In this lore, the shaman is a medium who seeks out the demonic in just such exotic spaces in order to control them. Nor are these creatures demons of illness, or war, or grief, or any other abstraction. They are demons of specific places; her ritual communication with the gods, her chief act of transcendence, is often seen as a journey to their habitats. Shamanistic literature reads, in fact, like road maps: which strange creature is met at which juncture.[50] One early text—purported to be a shamaness's guide book—reads like a Michelin guide to supernatural creatures. *The Classic of Mountains and Seas* is both a verbal map of exotic space and a described progress through the space. Although the title is invariably translated as "Classic," the word *jing* also suggests a "journey through" Mountains and Seas. "Go eastward three hundred *li* to Mount Dai. There is much water there, . . . and you will find a fish within. This creature lives in a mound, has a snake tail and wings, with feathers below its shoulder. . . . If you eat this creature, you will not suffer from swellings."[51] Remote and wild lands are magical lands, and shamanistic travel expresses the attempt to control these places. Nor is this power of the alien landscape limited to shamanism; it has permeated other areas of Chinese folklore as well, for the magical journey in exotic space is one of the most potent themes in Chinese iconography.[52] The cosmic journey of poets, the Imperial journey to the sacred mountains, and the Imperial progress through the realm—all show traces of the strange journey of the shaman. The worship of the five sacred mountains of China and the love of pilgrimage, and even the fascination with landscapes in miniature, are all informed as well by the myth of exotic space.[53] So when the mystic and the warrior are commanded to settle down in the confined spaces of the Forbidden City itself, it looks like a temporary arrangement.

In the lore of the family in traditional China, women were the minor deities of the confined space. They were so emblematic of that space that if they exited, a ritual rupture occurred. If traditional myth constructed the feminine as the archetypal sex of community, however, it also constructed in adepts and warriors a feminine countertradition in which women could be solitary travelers, exploring and naming that clearly alien space. It was a dangerous space, but a space that gave power to those who survived it. Women, to the extent they mimicked the shamaness, belonged there.

Few tales exist to tell in detail of women who chose the adept's life. One story, however, from the late Ming does give us the history of a woman who, barred from the stability of the communal, found the option of the adept open to her. Her story is contained in a collection of short fiction from the early 1600s. The author of the story was Ling Mengchu, an intellectual of the late Ming who wrote in this collection about the religious leaders and adepts of his era. Fascinated with her not only as an adept but also as a woman, Ling details how the woman—Madame Wei—was forced to choose the life of an adept.[54]

In the story of Madam Wei we first see the obvious features of the type. As with most adepts, her skills were not idiosyncratic talents, they were teachings handed down from generations past to her. Like all adepts, her natural place of residence was the monastery, where a nun passed on to her the secrets of the esoteric teachings; the arts were traced originally to the gods. Like Woman Liu and Tang Saier, who received their talismanic texts, Madame Wei also received an ancient gramarye. Madame Wei tells us:

> These arts of war did not begin in the Tang nor were they cut off in the Song. These arts derived from the time when the Yellow Emperor received the military talisman from the Primal Woman of the Nine Heavens. But the Yellow Emperor felt these arts were extraordinarily strange and was afraid that mankind might use them wantonly. So the Lord on High created stringent prohibitions, not daring to let them be proclaimed about. Rather he trained one or two people of devout faith to receive these arts through oral transmission and learn them by heart. So the arts were not lost to posterity, yet neither were they spread about.[55]

If Madame Wei was a religious initiate, she was also a recluse. Like the daughter of the Jiao family she took to the mountains, inhabiting a cave in a wildly remote cliff. In one sighting, she appeared suddenly from out of the forest, in a mountain trail, high up at a wayfarer's inn. She appeared the way these sojourners typically appear: unnamed and aloof. The locals viewed her as an outcast:

> Just as the scholar was eating he saw a woman . . . approach the front of the wine shop. When he raised his head to look at her Cheng saw that she was about thirty years old. Her face was coolly composed and her style reserved. She had an obvious air of martial valor to her, and indeed she seemed poignantly heroic in her style. Now as all the patrons in the restaurant craned round to look at her, they wagged and nodded their heads. They all sat there staring at her and discussing her, and they made barbaric comments and foolish remarks. Only the scholar sat quietly without saying anything. The woman was aware of it all.[56]

In the rest of her story we learn how the woman became the outcast, how she moved from the communal to the solitary. It was a progress predicated on three failures: first she was married to a man who abandoned her; then she was barred from accompanying her natal family; and, finally, she was threatened by the men of her spouse's family. Her story, however, is not simply a tale of failure and social isolation; rather, we see that as her life in the community deteriorates, her life as an adept develops. Madam Wei tells how she abandoned the family for the mountain, how she was transformed from, as she put it, "a woman alone" to a solitary adept:

> Originally I came from Chang'an. My parents were poor, and we moved to Pingliang to live and make our way by handicrafts. After my father passed away, my mother and I lived alone. The years passed and I was married to a young Master Zheng, of a family in our home village. My mother then herself remarried and went away. Now my husband Master Zheng was feckless and self-involved, and he delighted in the warrior-wandering; often I reproved him for his absences, and in the end we could see no longer eye to eye. Thus he cast me aside and set off with his band of rootless friends to seek for glory in the border lands. I have heard not one thing from him since.[57]

Left alone in the household of her husband's family, she sinks further into danger; she falls prey to her eager brother-in-law. "Now then, my husband's elder brother was not a good man; he made suggestive remarks to me which I repulsed with a stern manner. One day, however, he crept into my bedroom, near even to my bed."[58]

Madame Wei now appears lost, destined to become the victim of the predatory male; she has more in store for her than mere abandonment, however, for this is a different typology. The female in this folklore is informed by sacred travelers, not by chaste victims. In this mythology, abandonment and escape are not a penalty. When the brother-in-law sneaked into her room, she rewrote the event by exploiting the lore of the warrior-adept. Madam Wei recounts her response when the man approaches her bed in the night: "I drew my sword from the head of the bed and struck him; and when I injured him he fled. After that I considered my situation. I was a woman alone, without a husband with whom to live. Beyond that, I could not with ease remain with a brother-in-law whom I had injured. I could no longer live like this."[59] Although most men would hesitate to approach a woman with a broadsword by her bed, brother-in-law Zheng did not, conveniently providing his sister-in-law with the motivation to change from wife to warrior. With relative ease, she assumed the warrior-adept's role and joined the tribe familiar to Cao Ximin and all the other dubious observers, the obvious hallmark of which was her sword.

The next day Madam Wei continued her new life in her new place; she left the home and village to search for Nun Zhao and enter the exotic space of the adept.

> There had been since I was a young girl a certain Daoist woman Zhao who had always cared for me. She had herself a command of sacred esoteric arts, and she told me she could pass them on to me. But because my father and mother were still alive, I could not go off on my own. Now, however, I could seek to be taken under her guidance and I could leave my brother-in-law's house. The next day I went to see Adept Zhao. She took me in and was happy to have me there. But when she spoke to me she said: "We cannot live here. On my mountain there is a retreat. We will go there." She led me then way up to the mountaintops, where, among the peaks, there was a simple rush hut. It was there she taught me the recipes and magic arts of the Dao."[60]

It is an exaggeration to claim that Madame Wei became a purely solitary woman. In her mountain aerie she first lived with Nun Zhao, then later took on two disciples. She did, however, in a small subculture of adept women, become a woman of solitary space. Like Crazy Old Zhang and that strange collection of male outcasts so admired by the Ming, Madame Wei found a proper space outside of settled life; and the story of Madame Wei is no simple story of an escape from the conjugal; rather, it is a story of an escape that is deeply legitimate, shored up by centuries of religious belief, an escape that is constructed as a calling.

The solitary nature of this clan of warriors might seem to limit their popularity—what sort of folk hero could be so unlovable, so clearly an alien? But as anyone who has taken a glance at Chinese popular culture knows, warriors fascinate.[61] Theater, opera, folk tales, novels, movies, television shows, cartoons, illustrated books, classical tales, new year's prints, paper cutouts, decks of cards, and puppet shows depict them. Women warriors have even migrated out of China to the West, into translated tales, American literary fiction, American-made films, and American-made cartoons: solitary, proud, aloof, and a growth industry. Female warriors are a staple of popular texts and popular iconography; more than any of the women we have looked at they inform popular constructs of the feminine.

In traditional China, warrior-adepts do more than go off wandering. They command military expeditions and are famous for battle strategies; they avenge Imperial honor and save dynasties. The woman Qin Liangyu was raised in a Confucian family. At the end of the Ming during the uprising of Li Zicheng, she led a military command to defend the decaying dynasty. Her troops numbered several thousand and she was responsible for the recapture of several important military posts (see Figure 4.4).[62] Some warriors, however, were all brains: great strategists like the Qiao sisters, who studied the ancient texts of warfare; their status as great beauties of the kingdom did not prevent their devising a plan to aid the kingdom of Wu. Many women warriors were out upon the battlefield, often riding horseback, and some are not Han Chinese (see Color Plate 6), the aura of the exotic perhaps justifying their colorful autonomy. Like male knights, female knights were often found in times of trouble: the ends of dynasties produced bands of loyalists who struggled on in the wilds. The end of the Han, the end of the Song and of the Ming all produced famous warrior women.[63] Often they formed their own clans (see Color Plate 7); the women of the Yang clan even formed a battle array that defeated the barbarians. Like male warriors, female warriors were dedicated to the variety of martial arts skills, which included an impressive repertory of death: besides the common flat sword, there was the curved dagger sword, flying knives and darts, bow and arrow, whips, lasso-ropes, and numchuks (see Color Plate 8). Female warriors were typically aided by the esoteric and were the equal of any male warrior because of their knowledge of the crafty sciences (see Figure 4.5). They had the power of flight—Red Thread could cover thousands of miles in a night—and the power to disappear and transform; they had the power of superbreath that sent the enemy flying, as well as the power to create armies out of cutouts; they knew of magic drugs and powerful medications. These women were the baroque versions of the mystics and transcendents of religious lore.

In addition to their superhero-like powers, they also had a kind of literary superpower: the power to replicate. Like the hairs of Monkey and the paper cutouts of Tang Saier, warriors created a kind of *matière* of themselves, beginning as a single episode, then multiplying into many, increasing again by combining with other legends, forming and reforming until they became folk epics. The Ming warrior Tang Saier became the heroine of a Qing dynasty novel, the *Unofficial History of the Female Transcendent*; eighteenth-century intellectuals transformed her into an exemplar of a dynastic loyalist and created out of her obscure life a two-volume novel with repeated episodes of swordplay and expeditions.[64] One of the most popular of the warrior archetypes is Lady White. Although an ethnographer might properly categorize her as a snake demon, she shed her demon identity and became more of a popular warrior. In her earliest versions she was pure evil; by the time of the Ming she was ambiguous—half benign woman, half demon. Her portrait in Ming fiction details her love of her husband and her eventual capture under the Pagoda of Thunder Peak. As she continued to evolve in popular sources, however, the warrior trickster dominated, and she took on the features of a "Monkey," the hero of *Journey to the West*. She is a thief; like a female Prometheus she steals the drug of immortality from the gods. This episode is one of the most popular of the tale, as she shows off her warrior skills against heavenly guardians. Her battle with the Monk Fa Hai is another battle scene, and now the monk is more the villain than he appeared in earlier versions. She became in the many versions of her tale a full-fledged comic hero: a trickster outcast, a

Figure 4.4   Qin Liangyu led thousands of troops at the end of the Ming, defending several walled cities against the rebel Li Zicheng (*Wu Youru huabao,* vol. 1, "One Hundred Beauties Past and Present").

Figure 4.5 "An Interesting Encounter in Jiang Hu" is the title of this anecdote. A young woman from a martial arts family is married off to an itinerant martial arts performer. After the wedding, the husband tests his wife's martial arts skills and is suitably impressed. The bride's parents are in the background. The author of the anecdote concludes that the man got an excellent bargain: a coperformer in martial arts and a good home (*Wu Youru huabao*, vol. 2, "Anecdotes of Past and Present").

master of disguises and transformations, retold in an amalgamation of episodes. She is not a figure of elite literature; no source has ever been established as the canonical version.[65] Rather she is replayed to popular audiences. Yet as is the case of many epics in the making, she exists very persistently in a healthy variety of retellings: in novels, in opera, in films, as well as in television, woodblock prints, and even cartoons.

Is it possible that such grand myths have a place among earthbound women? Fieldwork on this question is, of course, impossible, but if Late Imperial sources on daily life can be believed, the woman warrior has had some ordinary incarnations, women who, though not warriors, demonstrated—sometimes only briefly—their traits. In the latter part of the nineteenth century, during the late Qing, one famous author and editor mimicked the warrior's daring. Qiu Jin was a revolutionary politician who edited a newspaper and wrote extensively on women's rights. She was ultimately executed for her radical politics, most especially for the publication of her revolutionary views of women. Despite the forward-looking nature of her reforms, however, she took a name that was ancient, a name that called up two thousand years of cultural history: she called herself the Woman Warrior of Mirror Lake.[66] With this epithet, Qiu Jin became the adopted descendant of a lineage of sacred women, an ambitious child bearing the exotic hallmarks of the adept.

If a radical politician could assume the warrior manner, what of the truly ordinary woman? One Qing-era illustrated magazine, *Dian shizahi huabao*, has anecdotes from the streets of Qing cities. Even in this mundane source, we read examples of ordinary women in a warrior mode. Fourth Sister was just a woman of Beijing who walked daily to the market district. She was thirty years old, proper and attractive, but drew, unfortunately, the attention of four laborers. They were infatuated and pursued her with vile words and suggestive remarks. Even after she looked down and hurried along, they pursued her. Finally she turned on them: "You louts! How do you think a woman like myself can stand all this?"[67] They, of course, laughed at her show of mettle; at which point she gave the ringleader an icy, direct stare, whipped up her umbrella, and jabbed the man in the breast (see Figure 4.6). The illustration of the anecdote strongly resembles the pictures of the warrior swordswomen; Fourth Sister assumed the pose for the necessary moment to rid herself of their impertinence.

Even the most base of women could look like an adept, or at least share some of their properties of flight and height. The same illustrated magazine described two female thieves who were the most marginal of urban characters: nameless, without family or home; they lived in an abandoned temple during the day. At night, however, they stole about like Red Thread. "In

Figure 4.6   The woman with the umbrella: in the classic stance of the warrior, Fourth Sister has just pierced the young man in the breast (*Wu Youru huabao*, vol. 2, "Anecdotes of Past and Present").

the quiet time of deep night, they would fly about the eaves and roam on rooftops, steal into homes and use their acrobatic skills; and they couldn't be caught." It took a band of militia to ambush them, but not before they "fled over the rooftops with their loot on their backs, twisting and threading their way, moving as if they were flying; the men in pursuit could not get near them" (see Figure 4.7).[68] Of course, these two thieves were women of no particular status, yet the magazine accorded them a romantic portrait. Despite the likely sordid aspects of their lives, they had the esoteric skills of the adept, held that ambigious position of the warrior, and belonged, like the other women of exotic space, beyond gravity.

Figure 4.7 **"Two Women Become Thieves." The two thieves being pursued by the militia with their loot on their backs (*Wu Youru huabao*, vol. 3, "Customs").**

5

Predators

> To every wight comanded was silence,
> And that the knyght sholde telle in audience,
> What thyng that worldly wommen loven best.
> This knyght ne stood nat stille as doth a best,
> But to his questioun anon answerde
> With manly voys, that al the court it herde:
> "My lige lady, generally," quod he,
> "Wommen desiren to have sovereynetee
> As wel over hir housbond as hir love,
> And for to been in maistrie hym above."
>
> *The Canterbury Tales*,
> "The Wife of Bath" (III, 1031–1040)

In the spectrum of feminine archetypes, there are absurd extremes. There are the "dark" women of mountain retreats, with their uncanny powers, icy strangeness, and love of solitude; these women despise social connections and hide themselves away to work. Then there are the grannies: earthy, offensive, practical, and, above all, gregarious. Now add to this mix of conflicting archetypes the female predator. She is the furious opposite of the icy adept and contrasts nastily with the playful granny. The predator is a social deviant, epitomizing the darkest of human desires; she is willful and overwhelming, atavistic in her impulses, vindictive and cruel when thwarted. She has great destructive powers, powers sufficient to bring down families and dynasties; she is eros, but it is eros without a trace of the romantic, eros configured as animal instinct, both base and lethal. In this lore a woman is barely human, a subspecies, a type of primitive, resembling lower animals such as snakes, eels, and snails (see Figure 5.1). Nor is she a solitary character in the theater of the erotic; she is paired always with her natural victim: the innocent male. In this branch of folklore, men are creatures of the mind and the spirit, of social order and self-sacrifice. The female, by contrast, is the eroticized sex, the sex more needy of gratification, the sex more likely to create crisis, the sex least likely to succeed. All this may seem to be so much nonsense, ideological

Figure 5.1   Half-woman, half-tiger
(*San cai tuhui, juan* 3).

fluff offered up by the village scold; but, as Gore Vidal remarked, there is no position so absurd that you cannot get a great many people to assume it.[1] Many people did assume it, and the ramifications for the characterization of women were far ranging and deep.

The female predator was most infamously found in politics; she is the sexual adventuress who gains access to the Imperial realm through intimacy and then destroys the body politic she finds. This woman is one of the regular *dramatis personae* in the accounts of empires, as conventional a figure as the Emperor or his minister. Unlike her male counterparts in Court, however, she was emblematic of disorder, not order. She was the predictable cause of fin de siècle chaos, suitable for all dynasties; like an ominous punctuation mark, she announced the downfall of a Court. The Dynastic Histories, the official compilations of Chinese history since the Han dynasty, stockpiled this stock character, labeling her with an unofficial yet official epithet: "state toppler" (*qing guo*) or "city toppler" (*qing cheng*).

Typically, she was a consort without heir (*fei*), but she might be an empress. The opening homily of *Jin Ping Mei* provides a pedigree of her ilk.[2] The hectoring storyteller begins his list with Bao Si of the Spring and Autumn Period and continues through a series of femmes fatales who caused the decay of the kingdoms of Chen, Sui, and Tang. It is not surprising that the narrator begins his tale of seduction with Bao Si; her childlike delight in the joys of political chaos were legendary. The infamous Bao Si lived in the ancient period in the feudal kingdom of the Zhou; she was the consort of the besotted ruler. The problem with Bao Si, however, was her ennui; she was not content with simple pleasures, but preferred the grand spectacle of blazing bonfires. The Zhou king accommodated her by lighting the military bonfires of the great watchtowers along the kingdom wall. Unfortunately, the fires were supposed to warn the kingdom of approaching troops, so that the feudal lords could come to the aid of their king. Of course, when danger came and the bonfires were lit in earnest, the vassal armies didn't come. One dynasty down, many more to go.

The state toppler, however, was more than a bad omen, more than a sign of disorder; for in her archetype was expressed a set of perceptions on the nature of civilization, on the nature of chaos, and on the nature of the feminine. In the lore of the state toppler, an eroticized woman is a form of social rot, a decay introduced by the unsuspecting male. She is architectural in her powers, a cultural earthquake expressing the deepest instability of a culture. As her epithet suggests, the erotic woman assumes a fantastic scale; she is larger than life, or rather, larger than Empire, growing huge like Alice. The words "state" and "city" both suggest a contained civilized space, and her function—to topple—means to place aslant, to tip over, like a child with her toys, the solid world of masculine kingdoms. The state toppler is anti-*civitas*, antipolity, and anarchic.

This stock villain, this obvious scapegoat for political failure, may seem a transparent conceit, a device invented by the scholarly few of the Bureau of History; but the crude convenience of the role did not diminish its currency. Indeed, historians did not invent the creature. Their bleak assumption was sewn deep into the culture; it reflected what was seen, known, tested, and proven. Imperial Edicts, Dynastic Histories, private journals, Household Instructions, moral treatises, popular-advice books, homilies in plays, and vernacular fiction all advertised the power of the predator. The late Ming was an age of tedious advice, and, for those anxious guardians of social restraint, predators were all around. These women lurked not only in the crumbling Palaces of weak-minded royals, they could set aslant any place of reason and order. Any civilized place could be their habitat; city, village, family altar—look and you will find—indeed, home is where the predator was.

Popular-advice books were especially wary of her. These texts, known as "goodness books" or *shan shu*, were improvement books, self-help texts with a focus on morality. Far from marginal texts, these books tell us much about widespread ideas. They began in the Song, and readers clamored for them in the Ming. As more books generally reached more people in the Ming, private tutors were no longer the only source of ethics, canon, and text; now this new, more accessible canon—these "goodness books"—offered the finest in deadening monitions. You could go to any bookstall and—along with a treatise on gardening, or an illustrated calligraphy manual, or a popular novel about martial arts—get some pablum on how to establish good karma. The text of these books is hardly riveting; they consist of nothing but injunctions and warnings, black and white, conservative, conventional wisdom, useful for conditioning a broad range of people within a hierarchical society. The conventional mind, however, rarely avoids the juicy exemplar. There were, consequently, many predators in their pages. The *shan shu* held a spotlight to their image, exposing them, arming the worthy against them.

One such compendium is invitingly called *Meritorious Deeds at No Cost to You*; it counsels the ways to attain merit through good deeds. There is advice on business, on family relationships, on child rearing, on farming practices, on official duties; the author opines on most aspects of daily life, although on eroticism and women he is especially grave. The author advises:

> Do not stir up your mind with lewd and wanton thoughts.
> Do not make remarks about feminine sexuality.
> Do not disport yourself with lewd friends.
> Do not allow yourself to be overcome by personal desires, and therefore treat others unjustly.
> Restrain others from arranging lewd theatrical performances.
> Do not keep too many concubines.
> Do not encourage the spread of immoral and lewd books.[3]

The gist of these adages is, of course, puritanical, with sex singled out as the root of a man's troubles, and with women the chief agency of sex.

The Ming predator, however, was not just widely known. Wise counselors also infused the predator with ominous import, giving her a mythic resonance. Common rhetoric was often, on the subject of women, high-mimetic. Of course, free advice is often both vulgar and hegemonic, both ordinary and of high importance. Advice givers always seem to be able to convert, with the use of high diction, the obvious adage into a kind of ideological truth for all time. The feral female was no exception; the predator was both a troublemaker and a monster. Novels in the Ming provided great assortments of such paradigms; they were a virtual antibible of nasty women. Mimicking the marketplace storyteller, narrators in Ming fiction regularly intoned ominous conventional wisdom on predators; their portrayals of women could be very sobering. This "storyteller," in the role of omniscient counselor, is a worried man. He knows a thing or two about women, none of it good, some of it cataclysmic.

In the first story of Feng Menglong's first collection, the narrator introduces his tale of love with words of caution. He advises: "This verse urges us not to diminish our essence and spirit with wine, lust, wealth and anger. . . . But of these four things, none does more damage than lust."[4] "Lust" (*se*) was the favorite word of this cautious moralist, for women were symbolic of *se*. "*Se*" means more, however, than sexuality and women; it also means delusion and spiritual contamination. The word *se* has, in fact, a canonical gravity to it, for it refers to the delusions of the five senses articulated by the teachings of Buddha. Women are not simply erotic; they are unclean, a form of evil, a terrible spiritual failing, a gate to hell.

Ironically, the prefaces of such tales often warned of what the story seemed to enjoy; "Never indulge in lust," went the usual advice, followed by a romantic story of sexual encounter. In fact, much of what the preface urged ran counter to the content of the attendant love story; Ming readers apparently enjoyed a little guilt with their romance. This tension between homily and narrative tells us something about the Ming paradox, however. The spirit of the age accommodated extremes: women were both malign and benign. This is why the storyteller came in handy. He was a folk figure, a cautious, urban everyman, armed with moral advice straight from the advice books, backed by centuries of watered-down Buddhism. He was the perfect foil for oracular gynephobia.

The ramifications of this damnation of the feminine were wide ranging, however. Any young woman was an agent provocateur, not only in the macrocosm of the body politic but also in an ordinary family. A female child could bring the cataclysm to her own home, to her own parents; she was just a mythic state toppler of narrow ambition. One household patriarch took special care to warn his family in his own book of Household Instructions. He was especially concerned with the arrival of a new bride into the house. She was young, fertile, erotic, and, by association, predatory; regulation was essential. "Most men lack resolve," admonished the patriarch, "and listen to what their women say. As a result," he warned, "blood relatives become estranged, and competitiveness, suspicion, and distance arise among them. Therefore, when a wife first comes into a family, it should be made clear to her that such things are prohibited."[5] A daughter-in-law was dangerous business in a house, and families had best take precautions (see Figure 5.2 for a particularly nasty example).

Feng Menglong, our Defoe of Ming mores, was fully versed in the tradition of the dangerous girl. Like other writers of the age, he knew of the disruption caused by the deviant daughter, and he often provided the awful details on just how such girls destroy. In one of his stories, "How Ji An Found an Eel at the River," Feng Menglong got quite explicit in detailing the horror of a young predator let loose on her family.[6]

Figure 5.2 "A Lovely Dream Is Hard to Achieve." A young bride despises her husband, and on the wedding night she wraps his braid around his neck and strangles him till he can neither talk nor breathe. At the same time she reaches down to his testicles and squeezes them like a "lion seizing a rabbit" (*Wu Youru huabao,* vol. 3, "Customs").

The plot of the tale is simple; it is the story of a girl's maturing. One day a man Ji An catches an eel from the river. The eel, however, is magical and pleads for his life. As Ji An carries the eel home for supper it cries from the basket, "If you let me go I'll give you untold riches, but if you kill me I'll make you rue the day." From this fairy-tale opening, things go sadly awry. The wife, in an unwary mood, kills the eel for supper. That night the couple, replete with the eel delicacy, make love and the mother conceives a child; the child is a daughter named Qingnu. Qingnu, of course, is not a nice person. Because of the unhappy fate of the eel, there is an unhappy curse on the child; she becomes, we discover, a twisted and dreadful offspring. Unlike Victorian heroines, however, who simply get themselves turned out of darkened doorways, this heroine drags her family into the abyss, as she becomes an unfilial, murderous adult.

In the first major episode of the story, we learn the sad details of Qingnu's first lapse. It occurs when Qingnu is a teenager, when Ji An is conveniently away. Qingnu is home taking care of the family shop along with her mother and their assistant Zhou San. When Ji An returns he notices something.

> Quite all of a sudden one morning Ji An said to his wife, "I want to have a word with you, but don't get angry with me."

"Go ahead, and say whatever it is," she replied.

"Over the last few days I've seen something about that Qingnu of ours. She does not act like a young girl."

"Well, she did not go out in either the day or the night, and she's done nothing else."

"No, not that. I've seen her exchanging looks with Zhou San."

That day the mother said nothing to her. But one day when Ji An was out she called Qingnu in. "My child, you are not to deceive me when I ask you about something."

"There's nothing going on," Qingnu replied. But her mother continued.

"For the last few days I've noticed something coarse about your person, and it is not at all suitable. Tell me the truth." Qingnu listened, but wouldn't reply. Instead she was all at a loss, changing color and blushing.

"There's got to be a reason for this!" her mother responded. Then she grabbed Qingnu and examined her body. She heaved a sigh and cried out bitterly, and in a burst of anger struck Qingnu. "Who ruined you?" she cried out.[7]

Love affairs and seductions were frequent subjects in Ming fiction, and Ming writers were skilled at describing the pull of sexual attraction, the approach-avoidance of obsessional lovers. This episode is not concerned with love, however; it is concerned with exposure. We are told nothing about the attraction between the two lovers; we are told only about her parents' suspicions and her mother's detective work. Qingnu is not a young woman infatuated with her lover Zhou San; she is an ill-tamed animal discovered in the home.

The introductory episode sets the tone for all the other sexual encounters that mark the girl's life, as this saga of the unclean continues. After the illicit affair with the shop assistant Zhou San, Qingnu is rapidly married off; the couple argue, however, and soon despise each other, and divorce follows. There is a second marriage; this time she becomes a concubine. Again, in her second marriage, there is more strife and, naturally, another seedy affair. Not content with the narrow circle of influence of a wife, Qingnu spreads her lethal influence into the town; as she matures as a woman, she matures as a predator, even becoming a serial murderess. To avoid exposure of her second affair, she and her lover kill her own stepson. The final resolution of this downward spiral is the ultimate act of social deviance; she destroys her own family; with the help of Zhou San, she returns home and kills her parents. At the conclusion of this tale of unhappily-ever-after, Qingnu and Zhou San are both executed for murder.

The implications of this reverse fairy tale are obvious. Maturity opens a terrible door for a culture; girls can become morally abject, atavistic adults, base and carnal and eel-like. True to the anxieties of the culture, as Qingnu grows up she devolves into a more primitive species, one dead of emotion like an eel. The emotional freeze in her character explains one stylistic feature of the story. The series of affairs that punctuate her life are told as a bland progression, a sad, flat tale. Her loves are neither passionate, nor charming, nor lusty, nor even ribald. This stylistic oddity is anything but accidental, however; for the lack of drama and erotic tension suggest that Feng Menglong was not interested in love or even lust, but in a type of feminine depravity—it is the depravity of the almost-human. Qingnu is the kind of woman who lacks human feeling, is deeply unromantic; she lacks desire, emotion, and conscience; she is the animal who cannot feel.

The locus of feeling for this story is clearly the family. Qingnu, however, is the opposite of the family; family allows filial affection, and Qingnu has no sense of it. She is a parasitic organism in the host environment, a grotesque among the normal. The eel's curse that informs Qingnu's life is thus more than a literary device, a conceit useful for explaining the

Color Plate 1 08.106. *Three Transcendants.* **15th century. Liu Jun. Chinese (Ming Dynasty), active 15th-century. Hanging scroll; ink and color on silk. Image: 133.3 × 83.25 cm; overall 243.0 × 105.5 cm. Museum of Fine Arts, Boston. Julia Bradford Huntington James Fund.**

Color Plate 2 *Figure Inebriated*, by Chen Hongshou (Collection of Mr. and Mrs. Wan-go
H.C. Weng, Lyme, New Hampshire).

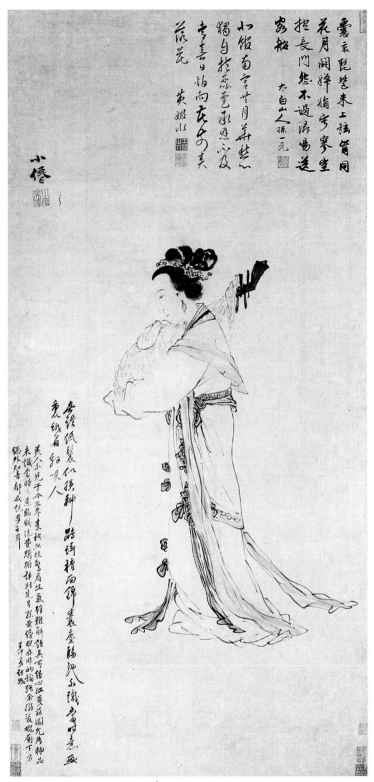

Color Plate 3 *Lady with a Lute*, by Wu Wei. Ink and color on paper, IMA60.36 (Indianapolis Museum of Art, gift of Mr. and Mrs. Eli Lilly, photograph © 1985 Indianapolis Museum of Art).

Color Plate 4 *A Portrait of the Geisha Gu Mei,* by Zhang Pudong, Qing Dynasty. Paper (Nanjing Museum).

Color Plate 5 *Gweilin, China. 1979. Retired worker* (© 1979 Eve Arnold. Magnum Photos, Inc. D96L-813/211).

Color Plate 6 *Inner Mongolia. China. 1979. Horse training for the militia* (© 1979 Eve Arnold.
Magnum Photos, Inc. D96L-813/217).

Color Plate 7 *The Female Generals of the Yang Clan Prepare for the Punitive Expedition against the West.* Contemporary New Year's print (author's collection).

Color Plate 8 *Eight Beauties Vie in Martial Arts.* Contemporary New Year's print (author's collection).

Color Plate 9 *Two Figures Studying Bamboo Painting*, anonymous, Chinese. Hanging scroll, ink and colors on silk; 145 cm × 104 cm (The Art Museum, Princeton University).

events; rather, it is a restatement of the myth of the predator. Qingnu has that predator's dullness, that eel-nature that shows first at puberty and forces her to reclaim her true identity; she is uncivilized, unfilial, sociopathic, and compulsively errant, and the story links them all. This is woman unmoved by gratitude or decency, woman as affective deviant.

Although such women do distress the civilized, yet one would hope that they at least remain mortal; imagine Qingnu as a demon. Unfortunately, however, women seemed particularly suited to shape shifting. In this branch of the predator's family tree, a beautiful woman tended toward the feral. That obvious line between the human and animal was, for her, unstable; as if by some fault of essential being, these border dwellers could not remain in the realm of the human, properly cultivated by the benign forces of civilization, the way men so reasonably did. Men remained firmly men, but women, a little too fluid in form, became other things. Nor was the tradition of the female shape shifter pure folklore. Ming intellectuals considered the problem of shape shifting as coolly as they considered the problem of any other phenomenon of nature. In essays and journals known as *suibi*, often cynical and always well-educated observers told of the female shape shifter, describing occurrences of foxes, snakes, cats, eels, and sometimes dragon shape shifters. There was a widespread belief in the literal existence of the female were-animal.

One of the more thorough examiners of the phenomenon was Lang Ying. Lang Ying collected his data as an ethnologist gathers data in the field. He collected anecdotes about the problem of shape shifters and made an ambitious collection of extant information on the habits and propensities of the Shandong fox-fairy:

> Shandong proliferates in foxes. . . . I had often heard that foxes could, by forming themselves according to their truest essence, transform into men or women in order to delude them. So, in the eighth year of the Jiajing Period, I went to Shandong to investigate these matters among the locals. They told me that by night the fox would sneak into the dwellings of the poor and disrupt the room and then go over to their beds where they slept. There they would suck in the breath that the people emit from the noses as they sleep. The victim then awakens as they feel their breath is stolen. . . .
>
> Also, the fox can shrink up its form, so that if there is a hole it can't get into, it just squeezes through it. [Besides these tricks] they can also transform themselves in order to commit licentious acts with men or women. Each fox forms a match according to its gender. . . . Also, they excel at amassing private wealth.[8]

Lang Ying here provides a dry discussion of the realities of fox fairies. As with most *suibi* writers of the Ming, he was a careful observer; elsewhere in his work he described the specific features of life in Hangzhou, the details of bronze mirrors, and practices of the Lantern Festival. To Lang Ying, the fox-fairy was simply one more phenomenon of Ming life.

Lang Ying was not alone in his detached recording of strange transformations. Xie Zhaozhe told of a female demon who was reported by a Buddhist monk as he traveled in the mountains. His story is perhaps more pathetic than frightening, but it is, in any case, evidence of a set of beliefs in demonic women that was common to authors of fiction as well as to authors of *suibi*. The anecdote begins with the flat statement that "a certain area of China was haunted by a demon":

> In Jinkong there was a demon who was actually able to scare people to death. Once, there was an itinerant monk who spent the night at a mountain temple with several other people. From far off

they heard the call of a goat. Later, it entered the room and approached the sleeping visitors, who in turn detected a foul odor from it. The monk then awoke and hit it with his sacred staff. The creature fell to the ground and the monk saw that it was a naked woman. They dispatched the thing to the local official. The family members of the woman hastened over and knelt before the official; they begged for her life, and so she was released into their hands. A few days later, the monk paid a call on the same local official and district. He asked his entourage about the woman and was told she was in fact a demon.[9]

Such female were-demons and were-animals were not folklore to Ming observers; and Ming authors of fiction were not exploiting the quaint and the colorful for their own purposes. The images of these women constituted a common stockpile of presumed fact that could, indeed, be explained. A woman's secret transformations, her love of discord, her desire for sexual encounter, her amorality, and even man's morbid fascination for her—all had theoretical foundations. If the Edwardian gentleman found each woman to be a separate enigma, the Ming gentleman thought each an explainable enigma. There was in place a phenomenology of the bizarre into which women fit. The erotic woman was anomalous in the same ways that unusual weather or animal prodigies might be. They weren't normal, but they were standard in their abnormalities. Intellectuals expended ponderous meditations on these subjects; there were great principles involved in the interpretation of the subnormal feminine, and the stories of eroticized women are rife with theory. Gender ideology, religion, physiology, and cosmology all helped explain her; science could be used to interpret her, religion to monitor her, and medicine to treat her. There were classification systems and subclassification systems; women would be understood.

The predatory woman was analyzed in the context of other strange events, within a phenomenology of the odd. Some events—such as strange births, prodigies of nature, and unusual weather—scholars labeled *yi biao*, manifestations of the unusual.[10] These events were seen as signs of heavenly favor or disfavor. Strange phenomena such as fox-fairies and long gestation periods were known as *shen qi*, deeply strange, extraordinary.[11] Nor were the observers too accepting; they could be cautious in ascribing unearthly influence, for they tested the accounts of these ghosts and were-animals. Some creatures were defined as truly magical, others found to be absurd. They attempted to distinguish among the genuinely mystical, the merely coincidental, or even the fraudulent. Some events were thought to be accidental (*ouran*), and other ostensibly magical practices were fakery. The label "deception of the masses" (*yu min*) was a common accusation leveled at such things as sword swallowing and shamanism. In one case, a report of a strange creature was found to be based on local hysteria. Lu Rong, one of the most cynical of Ming observers, sought to verify an account of a eighty-year-old granny-demon. Lu Rong had heard that "At the age of eighty, some sort of yaksha-demon loses her teeth, but then another set grows in. And, also, it was said that this woman would roam abroad at night and eat babies. People called her Old Maid Qiu. As a child, I'd been told about her."[12] Lu Rong, however, examined this account and found it to be based on hearsay and linguistic corruption. The Woman Qiu was a woman of a local village who "was by no means a demonic or wild creature."[13] But Lu's skepticism and his effort to distinguish between the demonic and the human sets in relief the assumptions that women could be demons.

The richest source on these feral women is fiction. There are vast amounts of lore about the erotic polymorph in both classical language stories and in vernacular fiction. These tales of shape shifting are typically love stories, but love stories with a gothic twist. The fox-fairy usually arrived to make love at night but decamped in the morning, leaving the obtuse male in a state of bewilderment. Many times these shape shifters were frightening, but often they were benign and even tragic. The husbands, of course, were consistently unsuspecting. Occasionally one of them might wonder why he never sees his wife without her clothes, or wonder why she needs a special tailor—to accommodate her fox tail—but generally they never suspected the true identity until too late.[14]

If women crossed the line into the realm of the animal, they also crossed the line from the living to the dead. The ghost lover, the wife who returns as a revenant, the seductress who turns out to be a demon—these were the common characters of love stories. A woman who appeared at night, clothed in white, standing mysteriously in a crowd, and who was sexually confident was very certainly a visitor from the world of the dead. Her charm, her beauty, her elegance had that whiff of the grave about her.

Once again there was theory; such women were phenomena to be explained. Ghosts were fact, naturally subject to analysis. In the Ming era, when religion credited the existence of the supernatural, ghosts were explainable. There were types of ghosts, theories on hauntings, types of manifestations, a spectrum of otherworldly phenomena to be interpreted. Indeed, ghosts had special status in traditional China. They were never far removed from the realm of the living, for, in the Ming, men and women inhabited an enchanted landscape, and this was not always bad news. The godly and the demoniac kept active watch over the affairs of man: ancestors, angry ghosts, city gods, and a pantheon of demons made their opinions known. Successes in business, illness, natural disasters, even advancement in office might all be due to the influence of the otherworld; the clouds of witnesses from the world beyond shimmered in the air, usually unseen but always capable of influence.

The fluid boundary between the worlds of the living and the dead was well attested. Indeed, Lang Ying, our researcher on fox-fairies, had many examples. One friend of his, a doctor, had told him of one ghostly encounter. The good doctor had been away practicing medicine in a distant town. Returning home, he met his old friend at the bridge that marked the entrance to the city. The two men passed a few moments catching up on the news of the town, and the doctor then went on his way. Later on, however, when the doctor repeated his conversation at the bridge, he learned the eerie news. "Why, he's been dead now for half a year," he was told. Lang Ying, like all his colleagues, had a theory for this strange encounter at the bridge. The event was bizarre but not unexplainable. "Ghosts mingle with mankind," he asserted, "but people don't recognize them as ghosts."[15]

This alliance with the supernatural was not necessarily frightening; if ghosts were everywhere, there was something common about them, and some could be helpful. Yuan Hongdao told of a story concerning his own brother, Yuan Zongdao. Zongdao was staying at an inn in Jingmen, when he dreamed of a spirit that said to him, "Get up quick!" The voice repeated the warning three times. Zongdao was awakened, but went back to sleep right away. The spirit appeared again and said to him, "Why don't you get up? I came here just to save you. Can't you see it?" And he rapped Zongdao's feet with a stick. Zongdao felt a jab of pain, so he grabbed his sheet as a cover and ran outside of the inn, just barely managing to escape the collapse of the entire building.[16] Ghosts existed in a type of fourth dimension; when conditions were right they appeared. Ghosts, however, had a special affinity with women. Men might be visited by ghosts, but women were likely to be ghosts and were especially prone to reappear after death. Lang Ying, who told the story of the surprised doctor, told of two female ghosts, "the case of Hong Yang who encountered a geisha who had died; as well as the case of an official who encountered his dead concubine."[17]

This female affiliation was thought a natural propensity, a basic alliance of like-bodied creatures. One scholar, Xie Zhaozhe, thought women were, by nature, more allied with the demonic and otherworldly. "Gentlemen devote themselves to fame and profit," he noted. "But women devote themselves to ghosts and gods. Their natures insure them thus. Nor can they escape themselves."[18] Xie thought this sexual polarity perfectly natural; reversing the roles was what was strange. "But if a woman avows a love of fame, then she is a sort of woman-man. And if a gentleman believes in ghosts and gods, then he may be said to lack the manly energies."[19]

Xie's explanation, however, left much unexplained. There was much more to this alliance of women with ghosts, a deeper explanation than simple tendencies. They were not simply drawn to the nether world, they were of the nether world. The reason was cosmology. Men, with all their manly energies, were of the earth, allied with the day, with the land of the living, and with the powers of the sun. Men were *yang*. Female energies, however, were *yin*, allied with the watery, the nocturnal, the fertile, and the quiescent. Women thereby contrasted with men. Ghosts, too, were *yin* in their cosmic energies; they, too, were watery and nocturnal. Scholars firmly articulated an alliance of the feminine with the ghostly, and authors of literature relied on this association. Indeed, tales of the supernatural were often set on moist spring nights, or by famous lakes and rivers. Classical stories of ghostly women were waterlogged; ghosts were watery, women were watery, and the two were alike in their basic element.

In one collection of stories, *Tales Told as the Lamp Burns Down,* the Ming author Qu You exploited the tradition of watery ghost-women. In one of his stories he provided ghost-theory as well, explaining how a man is contaminated by association with women. In this story of ghostly love, a young scholar foolishly began an affair with a mysterious beauty and naively fell in love with her despite the obvious signs of her excessive *yin* nature. Quickly, the man's "manly energies" became threatened, and a Daoist adept intervened. The priest had accurately read in the young man's aura an influence of demonic energies, or *yaoqi*. The Daoist painstakingly explained the dangers the man was in:

> Mankind is, in essence, pure *yang* at its most flourishing, whereas the demons are in essence the malign and contaminated elements of deepest *yin*. Now, if you, sir, abide together with a goblin of deepest *yin* and don't know it, and don't realize that you pass the night with a malign and contaminated being, your primal essence will be exhausted and the pernicious evil will control you. I am concerned that in these springtime years of your youth, you will become a sojourner in the nether world. How appalling![20]

Like evening shadows and moist nights, ghosts are the residue of the *yin* polarity. They are anathema to the full-blooded *yang* of the living, especially of living men; yet ghosts were a logical manifestation of the bipolarity of the cosmos. Qu You explains elsewhere that though ghosts are not intended to mix with humans, under certain watery, dark conditions they do manifest themselves:

> Thus are the paths of the living and the dead as far apart as the ends of the earth. . . . But even in this era of clarity and tranquillity, in this time of contentment, still might demons appear as delu-

sions and assume certain shapes. They may blend into the grasses and trees; or on nights when the sky is cloudy and moist, or just at dawn when the moon sets and Orion lies aslant, they make themselves heard, as, with a sighing in the beams, they gaze into your room unseen.[21]

The young scholar of the story, however, refused to heed the Daoist's warning and continued with his affair. Ultimately, he was drawn to the woman's coffin, where he died. Now he, too, was the essence of *yin*, and the narrator tells us at the end of the tale, "after this, when the day was deeply cloudy, or on nights when the moon was black, the people of the town all would see the ghosts of the scholar and the woman." The young man finally becomes a ghost, not by death, but by association.

If scholars analyzed these dangerous conditions, so did medical men, for men of science needed to interpret the feminine, to analyze the sources of female energy, and explain the *yin* problems that so naturally arose. The erotic, shape-shifting, or ghostly woman required thought, even cures. If she could be explained, then she could be treated. Not that physicians broke new ground in their analysis, for science exploited the same constructs that folklore and cosmology employed; scientific and religious typologies overlapped in that gray area of *yin*. Medical texts reinforced that sense that women were subject to malign influences. Wang Kentang was one of the most influential and prolific medical authors in the Ming; he was an excellent observer and a critical scientist, and his *Case Histories of Illustrious Physicians* is a carefully documented study. The observations on symptoms—detailed accounts of reported pain and dysfunction, his list of both failed and successful treatments, the tone of narration, and his citation of sources—all bespeak a meticulous, scientific mind. Yet even in the obvious and impressive rationalism of his observations, the metaphors of gender ideology held fast. Women are *yin* in their natures, and thus they are viewed and thus they are treated.

Overall, Wang Kentang devoted five chapters of his *Case Histories* to gynecology, wherein he articulated the theoretical basis for interpreting feminine physiology. The proper functioning of a woman's *yin* nature was based especially, according to Wang, on regulation of the *yin* or uterine blood, for women were governed by this "blood." *Yin* blood included both menstrual blood as well as the bloody products of birth. This type of "blood" was the source of illness and health in women; in a healthy or vigorous state it nurtured the embryo, in a state of depletion it caused illness that varied from amenorrhea to widespread systemic problems. Conversely, too much *yang* was equally dangerous. A *yang* heat could cause a variety of problems, such as fevers, numbness in the limbs, stomachache, eating disorders, seeing demons, dry mouth, and incoherent speech; all were caused by a "disastrous heat" or a "malign heat" entering the uterus or blood-dwelling.[22] Thus the products of the uterus defined the essential natures of women. Wang did not, of course, describe women as transformed snakes or eels, yet he characterized them as essentially *yin* in their natures, as tending to the pathological because of certain physiological traits.

In his chapters on gynecology, Wang described the pathology of the feminine. One of the illnesses he presented looks remarkably like the "illnesses" that occur in fiction: demonic possession. Women, because of their essential alliance with fertility, sexuality, and the *yin*, were subject to the demonic; their reliance on *yin* blood made them unstable receptacles for such influence. Pregnancy, in particular, was a time when the polluted and the demonic might intervene. He described in some detail two examples of demon-contact: the ghost embryo, and intercourse with demons. Wang explained the theoretical basis for the presence of demons: "But if there should be an arrhythmia in the natural state of a woman's essential physique, then the blood and *qi* are depleted and weak, and ghosts and the demonic can interfere in her proper Yin."[23] The symptoms of intercourse with demons were easily detected: irregular or threadlike pulse; refusal to see people; talking to oneself; sudden outburst of laughter or weeping. He prescribed for this condition medications to re-establish the balance in both the will and the body, and moxibustion to drive out the demon.[24]

Although "blood" governed women, it did not govern men. Man's basic essence had very little to do with the watery principles of *yin* properties. Men were perceived as being governed by semen; semen, however, was not linked to male fertility the way blood was linked to female fertility. Semen was perceived, by a magnificent leap of metaphor, as governing what in the Ming was considered an essentially masculine trait—rationality or thought. By medical definition, female physiology allied her with the phenomenon of reproduction—with the uterus and fertility—and male physiology tied him to the rational. Wang articulated the gender duality in his introduction to his section on gynecology.

> Now in men, semen is the governing principle, and in women it is blood. When in males the state of the semen flourishes, this is the dwelling of thought. But in females, where the supply of blood flourishes, this is where the embryo is sustained. And if there is some impediment to the flourishing of the blood then during their menstrual periods the state of the blood can be detected by the pulse emitted at the fingers and at points on the hands and feet.[25]

This sex-based allotment of the cerebral to the male may seem facile to some, but at least Doctor Wang had the problem under control; thankfully, laughter and weeping could be cured, although for the truly problematic patient, there was help from another source. Since women were subject to *yin* forces and the demonic was never distant, their hysterical laughter, sexual dreams, and other signs of *yin* complaints could be handled by religious intervention; anxious families with troubling women could summon either doctor or adept. Lu Rong, a Ming intellectual, tells of one Daoist adept who gained renown by treating a woman who had succumbed to her all-too-*yin*-like nature:

> Once, a woman of the district was affected by a strange illness. Each night, some creature would come and have intercourse with her. By day, she became gradually listless and exhausted, and no one had been able to cure this ailment. But the family heard of a Daoist adept who could exorcise demonic influence and they invited him in to visit her. The adept requested two youths to bathe; and he performed incantations and spewed water from his mouth and danced. As the dancing was about to end, he railed at them to get out. The two youths rushed out and cast themselves into the water. For quite a while they didn't come out and everyone stood by anxiously. After quite a time, the water suddenly boiled up, and the two youths together came out holding a great snake. On the head of the snake there were small horns. The creature was likely some sort of *jiao*-dragon. The youths fell prostrate to the ground and the woman began to feel revived. That night she began to sleep peacefully again, and the sickness did not return. The Daoist was well known for this afterwards, although later, when someone summoned him, he was not effective in his cure. Some people thought perhaps he had himself been impure in some way and had destroyed his powers. For the *jiao*-dragon is an evil creature . . . and those of spiritual arts who can move the spirits do so by attaining the utmost in moral purity, and thus spiritual creatures can be controlled by them.[26]

Snakes, eels, *jiao*-dragons—beware of anything slithery. Women were susceptible: too much water, too much slime, too much instability; as vessels ready for embryos, they are vessels as well for pathogens. The ordinary female has too much of raw nature about her, is too prone to the ghostly and the demonic. Women are not the only creatures subject to such corruption, however. Men are as well—but not without help. They require a virus, an agent for the *yin* sicknesses. This happy role is accorded to women. As a *yin* organism, a woman can infect a man; she can transform and contaminate with her love, becoming a transmitter for the demonic or diseased worlds, a catalytic agent for putrefaction. Love with her can, by medical and religious constructs, be fatal.

Fiction is filled with such infectious agents; one of the most infamous women in Chinese lore is just such a contaminating predator—Pan Jinlian, of the erotic novel *Jin Ping Mei*. Pan Jinlian is the archetypal femme fatale; her very name invokes her sexual identity, as it refers to the bound foot. But she is a femme fatale of the Ming variety, for her femininity relies on a web of references to the polluting predator. First and foremost she is the dominatrix; she is a state toppler, named for a medieval state toppler of the Qi Dynasty. Of course she is gorgeous; just a look "makes a man's soul fly to the heavens." And she is vital, a woman in constant action; she seeks, acquires, traps, and mates. She is tireless, omniscient, and omnipresent, a woman who never relents. When stymied in one affair, she seeks another. If she doesn't dominate sexually, she dominates with language; she excels at invective, and her daring is stunning. Like the grannies who so worried Shen Bang, Pan Jinlian can control, for Pan Jinlian is not afraid of naming anything. She is vulgar, direct, and fearless, and her accusations are potent. She can out-talk even her husband Ximen Qing, the master of the house. Who else would confront him returning from a liaison by ripping open his pants? She characterizes herself with remarkable accuracy: "Why, I'm a man, with no little kerchief upon my head; a ding-dong echo of proper old wife. For on my fist a man may stand, and on my arm a horse can walk. And I can walk over the face of any other."[27] In terms of her ferocious ability to dominate others, she is right.

Pan Jinlian, however, is more than the epitome of sexual dominance; she is the epitome of contaminating eroticism. Pan Jinlian kills whom she loves; all her mates die from sexual contact with her. One of the most infamous death scenes in Chinese literature occurs between her legs. In her final encounter with Ximen Qing, she murders him by stealing his manly energies through rape; his life ends in a gruesome spectacle of excessive intercourse. Pan Jinlian is voracious for intercourse and administers a sexual stimulant to the exhausted man; but even after Ximen Qing loses consciousness, she continues to apply the potion and continues to mount him; she rapes him continuously as he lies insensate. Ximen Qing's penis spews out semen, then air, his manly energies exhausted by her own inexhaustible *yin*. Finally, this predator, Pan Jinlian, this highly concentrated embodiment of *yin*, ends his life. Indeed, this murderous crouch is Jinlian's hallmark. Jinlian had killed her first husband in this position; the diminutive Wu Da was first poisoned and then suffocated by Jinlian as she crouched over him in a position of murderous sexual dominance (see Figure 5.3).

More than simply a grotesque aggressor and a murderess, Pan Jinlian is also a pathogen. She, like the ghosts that Qu You described and the diseased women Wang diagnosed, alters the men she finds. Through the medium of her sexuality, she spreads the disease of what she is. This unpleasant feature is discovered by the old man who takes her into his house as a servant. In the beginning of the novel he sexually exploits the thirteen-year-old Jinlian and then gets sick. The symptoms are classic; he presents all the hallmarks of exposure to *yin*. First he is afflicted by "pain in his loins, then runny eyes and a sniveling nose, then difficulty in urinating, then dizziness and stupor and wheezing and puffing, and then . . . suddenly one day,

Figure 5.3 Pan Jinlian poisoning her first husband, Wu Da (*Jin Ping Mei cihua, juan* 5).

the master of the house became disastrously afflicted by the coldness of *yin*. Alas and alack! He died!"[28] The disease carried by the female predator has an appropriate name: it's "the coldness of *yin*" that kills the master. Pan Jinlian, even as a child, is a carrier.

Intelligent men, informed of all these trouble spots, might be expected to avoid an obviously sexual women—might be expected to shun a woman whom the adept, the patriarch, and the neighbor have all warned against. But some men pursued the contaminant, driving headlong to their destruction. Intelligence was clearly not the problem; the issue was love. In this extended typology of the feminine, love compelled the male victim; it pulled him into its subculture of fear. Love was a type of enthrallment. To use the phrase of William Patrick Day, men became "lost in the circles of fear and desire."[29] An affair was not, in this lore, a revelation of love's awakening. It was a dark, morbid preoccupation, an *idée fixe*; love was like death—horror filled but fascinating. In this meta-metaphor, women had the dubious distinction of symbolizing the world of the erotic, the chaotic, the deviant. The female predator was a convenient catchall, a useful cipher; the Ming writer could use her to classify all the disturbing and discordant images that the erotic implied. With these metaphors, powerful erotic feelings were codified in the culture as weird. This, of course, may be the point of the entire construct. Women may represent the demonic not because of cosmology, but because cosmology takes the lead from psychology. Love is not demonlike because women are demonlike; rather, women are demonlike because a man's feelings bedevil him. Love is for him overwhelming and imprisoning, a product of dark obsessions he can't control; so he is left with the only form of control he can construct: metaphors of deviance.

As one granny was quick to point out, in fact, "that's just the way the man in the moon planned it." Overwhelming feelings should, in fact, surprise no one; the terror these women generated did not emanate from their shape shifting; it was based on the terrible truths they represented, for female demons had a nasty authenticity to them. Demonic women knew an ugly secret about men, no matter how well intentioned a man may have felt himself to be. These women knew how thin is the veneer of culture, and how often it is used to mask and control. Consequently, the lore of the predator shades into the lore of revelation. A predator can be the agent not just of danger, but also of ironic knowledge, offering to the reader the inescapable truth, punishing the deserving for smug delusions. Hypocrites seem her apt victims; they seek her out, only to end up in that place they richly deserve. She is like death, but it is a well-earned death. These women, in fact, have something of the inadvertent adept about them—shamanesses who detect the truth behind the hidden. Like exorcists, with their antennae up they see where "spirits shimmered among the live creatures,"[30] to use the phrase of Maxine Hong Kingston. This kind of predatory woman has the judges of hell in her lineage. Like ghosts they suggest a moral police force, but one whose morality is based on the the ironies of poetic justice. They see into the aura of men and notice what demons inform them; they detect, like the temple Daoist, whether a character has naked devils or golden soldiers of virtue in his retinue.

Many stories confirm this mythology that many women are predatory, but truthful, corrupting, but ironically revelatory. Even Pan Jinlian, the ur-predator, has a good deal of ironic knowledge in her character. Her final murder of Ximen Qing was poetic justice at its most colorful, as her character echoed the lore of terrible justice meted out to men. Her victim, Ximen Qing, had converted his domestic landscape into a dystopic gyneceum, his women becoming his whores. Pan Jinlian was simply his queen of wishes, giving him all that he demanded. Her name even suggests the demonic judge from hell in its echoes of the adept Pan, who was called to exorcise the demons of illness. Her name echoes as well the sense of judging, for the surname Pan is a Chinese pun on the verb "to judge."

Again Feng Menglong explored the lore; he told one tale of a presumptuous male, Daqing, who courted the abbess of a Buddhist nunnery. The young man abandoned his wife and family for a few days of easy sex. Infatuated with the beautiful woman, he had no qualms about the seduction. When the young scholar had completed his seduction and ensconced himself in the abbey, the abbess turned the tables and took the man captive; with the help of her pious assistants, she drained his manly energies with repeated sexual intercourse. He never returned home:

> So, Daqing resigned himself to his fate. Dressed up as a nun, he remained at the abbey to indulge himself in orgies, and the two nuns never left him alone. They were joined also by the two maids of the abbey; and sometimes they came together all in the same bed. . . . Now, even with only two blows of the ax, you can split apart one piece of dry wood; so how could one exhausted soldier stand up to such brazen enemies. The oil of the lamp was used up; the flame guttered and was dying. And finally it happened that the water in the water-clock drained all out and was gone.[31]

Daqing, like all heroes in cautionary tales, got what he wanted. But the women of the story did more than reveal the danger of his desires; they revealed the truth of them.

Those watery properties, so likely to elicit cures and exorcism, now seem, for these harsh predators, to suggest omnipotence. Hypocrites, no matter how stauch they stand as embodiments of *yang*, appear weak by contrast to the *yin* of these lethal judges. Their energy suggests, in fact, a watery force field, evokes the rushing waters of the adept Liu, or the rainstorms of the Shang shamaness. These avengers could drench the unwary and thereby change him, blending him in with their molecules. The predator is not just *yin* to her core; she is a process. In one of the most famous stories in Chinese myth, a shape shifting snake drains the vigor from a healthy young man with unconscious and effortless ease. The myth is called the story of Lady White; she is a snake woman, a woman of stunning beauty but deadly sexuality. The tellings and retellings of the tale have survived into the modern age, with films, cartoons, and even soap opera versions on television. One of the earliest versions, however, comes from a medieval collection of tales; this decidedly unsympathetic, classical tale reveals Lady White as a manifestation of *yin* element.

The story is set in the Tang Dynasty, during the second year of the reign period called Primal Harmony. It concerns a young man named Li Huang. "One day in the capital Li passed by a carriage with a large retinue of servants and stole a look inside to see who it was within. He was startled by what he saw: a woman of extraordinary beauty, clothed in white silk."[32] At this point, of course, the warning flags are up. The mystery and eroticism, the white clothes, the feminine trap, all meant one essential danger; the elements of the story were as well worn as any household adage, and the symbolism of it all crystal clear. A chance encounter was by definition an erotic encounter, and an erotic encounter meant the danger of *yin*. Manly energies were no match for it. Undeterred, however, the young man pursues her, and finds that she is called simply, but so very aptly, "Lady White." They meet and he is invited into the back apartments for a nice dinner:

> Six or seven served the meal, and when the two were done they summoned the wine and enjoyed some drinking. His stay turned into a visit of three days' time, and they enjoyed each other in

every way. Then on the fourth day . . . Li Huang took his leave and departed. But as he was mounting his horse to leave, his servant smelled something foul about his master. After Li returned, his family asked him where he'd been these several days. The scholar, however, could only summon his quilt and take to his bed, for he felt heavy of body and his head swam. His wife Lady Zheng sat beside him and told him what had happened in his absence. . . . But Li Huang only became increasingly frightened and said to his wife, "I will get up no more." After that he couldn't speak, and he felt his body dissolving beneath the quilt. When his wife pulled back the covers she saw that what had once been Master Li's body was now just a channel of water, and only his head remained.[33]

Too late for the husband, the horrified family learns that the mysterious woman is a great white snake; and they know that his misadventure has brought him the fate of many creatures of *yang*. His encounter is not described, however, as a form of adultery, a moral deviation, but as a serious lapse in hygiene. For in spending his three days with Lady White, he abandoned the space that defined him as vigorous and masculine, and crossed the boundary to the purely feminine. He spent three days in bed with a creature of the purest *yin*, a supine, watery, female creature, a being who was threefold damned. Thus his decline was a process of transformation: he is first a smell of putrefaction, then a man disoriented, and finally a flow of water. The woman, the creature of the *yin* polarity, changed his element.

It is a commonplace that sexuality unbinds personal constraints, and this can compromise the busy harmony of the collective; thus do cultures need to marginalize the erotic. This theme occurs in most cultures and obviously informs the myth of the female predator. As the erotic is made deviant, the rational and the controlled are configured as the norm, and the disruptive influences of love and sexual attraction are minimized. Within this construct of the predator we see the single-minded feminizing of the erotic. In the Ming, in politics, in the community, and in the family, the erotic and chaotic catalyst was female. Ming patriarchs of every stripe could call on the adages and wisdom of the ages to affirm this truth. Women were trouble, especially a fertile woman; like the predators and shape shifters of folklore and fiction, history and science, they had great disruptive powers. Emily Ahern's studies of contemporary China have discovered the same metaphors: for example, that a daughter-in-law, if fertile, is viewed as both necessary and contaminated, both powerful and polluted. The folklore of pregnancy especially expressed this divided perspective. A pregnancy was both bad luck and good luck; a pregnant woman was considered dangerous to brides and to children, and a mother, immediately postpartum, was considered contaminated; but the products of birth could be greatly prized. Obviously, the child was the treasure produced by the fertile wife, and even the placenta and the blood from menstruation and birth had magical properties.[34] Yet, as Mary Douglas has shown, the two polarities of power and pollution were two sides of the same coin;[35] for the power of female fertility inspired both fear and awe.

During the Ming, the most extraordinary expression of fear and awe was not, however, located in text but in practice; there was no more acute formulation of this sexual paradox than in the symbolism of the female foot. In the Ming, as in earlier periods, the arch of the foot was fractured in the practice known euphemistically as "foot binding." Laborers in the capital as well as farmers did not fracture the arches, but women whose function was predominantly that of wife, concubine, entertainer, or domestic employee did typically carry it out. As in most examples of mutilation, this marked the participant as a member of a caste and functioned as a complex cultural insignia, influenced by economic factors, the role of feminine culture, and religion. One important theme in the folklore of the foot, however, was the lore of the predator. The caste defined by the binding of the foot was one marked by the folk-lore of power and danger, one marked by terror of the erotic.

Central to the significance of the broken arch was the notion of deviance, for the distortion of the arch and the subsequent distorted gait suggested the subhuman; maiming the arch formed a clawlike foot and, with the foot no longer flat, women had a distorted, altered gait. If science considered woman's physiology as inconsistent with the normality of the masculine, then the irregularity of her walk also confirmed this. She was semihuman, not quite *homo erectus*. Nor was the fractured foot and the gait it produced the only significance of this ritual, for the binding itself was significant, suggesting the long process of the domestication of the feminine. This was not a sudden surgical fracture; it was a long process of containment and restriction. From approximately five years of age a girl's feet were bound tightly with six-foot-long bandages. Like the restrictions applied to midwives and the limitations through moral lecture applied to the daughters-in-law, the bandages gradually tightened as a woman achieved sexual maturity; and the binding created a physical equivalent of the myth of the female were-animal.

The fractured arch suggested deviance and also regulated sexuality. The bound foot was the chief erotic symbol in the Ming, yet as an emblem of sexuality, it was an evasive emblem, suggesting a euphemism for the sexual. Through this practice, the sexual was located at the bodily extremity, at the feet, a safe distance from actual sexual characteristics. Locating this abnormality exclusively on women further fixed the erotic exclusively on the female, making the quintessential symbol of the sexual a feminine trait. The fractured arches helped construct sexuality as both alien and feminine. A male foot was not erotic, nor were male scholars, nor male patriarchs, nor any other symbol of social order.

The wrapped, fractured, contained, feminine arch was thus the physical equivalent of the story of Lady White, of Bao Si, of Qingnu the dangerous girl, and of all other reconfigurations of the predatory woman. Both the ritual and the myth participated in the same mentalities and the same symbolic structures used to allay the cultural anxieties toward the erotic. Both reconfigured the feminine and the erotic as emblems of undomesticated, alien agents—cultural liabilities or risks—that had to be aggressively domesticated. Like were-beasts, the erotic female was both carnal and marginal, and her fractured arch reaffirmed her feral strangeness. Civilization, so dependent on family structure, lineage, and breeding, could well afford this particular symbol of the sexual. She was alien from the communal center, located in the dangerous margins, kept in abeyance, watched, and contained.

6

Recluses
and Malcontents

The greater part of what my neighbors call good I believe in my soul to be bad, and if I repent anything, it is very likely to be my good behavior. What demon possessed me that I behaved so well?

Henry David Thoreau, *Walden*[1]

The solitary recluse is the essential antihero, a self-declared alien in the clan and hierarchy. For the recluse, the security of the communal and the harmony of the domestic is deadening. The poet Baudelaire had a phrase for the recluse's compulsion: "*horreur du domicile*," a horror of the home.[2] In the West, Thoreau was chief among recluses, the archetypal refuser of comfort. For him, civilized life was deeply alienating; "*aes alienum*," he called it: life by "another's brass." By Thoreau's lights, man imprisoned himself within a "nutshell of civility,"[3] trapped himself among the "exuviae" of life. He saw man's natural state as solitude. Nor was Thoreau alone in his refusal of the communal. From John the Baptist to bohemian poets, recluses have populated the western imagination.

Of course, this distinguished association of lonely idealists is something of a men's club, at least in the West. The recluse in western lore is very likely to be a man; in the West, solitude is essentially a masculine trait.[4] Tough, lonely choices are for men. This sex-based definition of the recluse seems part of the natural order, for if men are the sex of solitude, women clearly are not. In western tradition, women are rarely alone; isolation seems too much for the weaker sex. Western feminine archetypes are bound firmly to the collective, have roots sunk deep into the village: the mother at the hearth, the wife at the loom, the bride by the bed. Women are the sex of the settled and of the domestic, the half of the species that *is* the communal and *is* the conjugal. Conversely, the solitary woman is an anomaly; in English the word "widow" is cognate with *vide*, to be empty. The implications are obvious: once a woman is no longer paired in conjugal stability, her life is a void, an emptiness, a life regarded as being without. It follows, then, through the analogic connections that circulate as logic, that a woman who has a life of solitude is relegated to, by definition, a pathology. Solitude is not a feminine trait—at least, not *naturally* a feminine trait.

Figure 6.1 *Portrait of the Ming Recluse Piao Xiang,* **by Chen Hongshou. Detail from** *Views of Sixteen Recluses,* **MA45, Leaf #15 (National Palace Museum, Taipei).**

There is, however, a significant lapse in this great sex-based division of type; it occurred in traditional China. In China the female recluse was as disdainful, rude, and aloof as any recluse; family cults notwithstanding, the female solitary enjoyed escape. Like Thoreau, she claimed her own pride of place, alien and remote though that place might have been. During the Ming, artists were the typical female solitaries, especially poets and sometimes painters; but other women took to the thatched hut as well. Historians, scholars. moralists, elder sisters, even filial women had studios where they alone would stay; and some women just declared themselves to be travelers. Whatever their roles, however, such women were not anomalous; they had a cultural legitimacy inscribed into the folklore of the feminine (see Figure 6.1).

Much of their legitimacy came from the authority of the adept. Solitude and mountain huts were contexts for sacred women; despite her secular life, the recluse could inherit—if not an aura of sanctity—at least a certain social tolerance. Solitary life for women, however, was not simply an isolated place for would-be adepts. It was an instinct, a deep craving, as compelling as the thirst for companionship, as powerful as the instinct for home. Thoreau called this instinct "elasticity," a need to travel freely and travel light. In Ming folklore the instinct had many names: "a love of mountains and streams," "free and easy wandering," or just plain "solitude." Whatever the term, however, women craved it as well as men. In the poets, wanderers, and shape shifters of the Ming, there was that same love of escape echoed by Thoreau. Women could be found—when they could be found at all—in hideaways as remote as a man's; they often refused life by "another's brass" and were just as likely to suffer from the "horror of the home" as men.

The female recluse of the Ming had thousands of incarnations, women who took to mountain retreats or solitary spaces to cultivate a life free of compromise. Rather than begin the
search for the archetype in the studios and thatched huts of specific women, I will start with
the recluse of myth, to seek the distillation of the type. There is one mythic solitary who was
a shape shifter, a woman who shifted from tiger to human to tiger. Her story first appeared
in medieval collections and continued in later revisions. In the Ming, Feng Menglong revived
the tale of the shape shifter–recluse in his *Compilation by the Historian of Love*.[5] The story
is a brief but poignant account of a creature pulled between two warring identities—one domestic, the other reclusive. He called her story "The Tiger Fairy."

The brief account of the woman opens with the journey of a young unmarried man named
Shentu Cheng. Master Shentu is traveling the mountains of Sichuan en route to take up a job
as a low-level officer of the Court. But his journey is a difficult one, for high in the mountains, in the middle of winter, he suddenly finds himself in a freezing and deadly snowstorm.
Fortunately, he comes upon a simple thatched hut, and even from the path he knows that inside is a "crackling fire and great warmth."[6] And sure enough, once inside, he is welcomed.
Within the hut are an old couple and their very bright, very literary, and very beautiful daughter. The old couple offer him warmed wine, and the four of them pass the time at literary
games by the fire as the storm rages outside. Of course, this moment of shelter from the
storm's savagery, in this simple setting of domestic comfort, proves to be prophetic. Master
Shentu falls in love, and in the few days it takes the storm to pass, he courts her. The parents
and the girl agree to his proposal of marriage, and she goes back to civilization as his bride.
Shentu Cheng then takes his new job, and the husband and wife settle in with ease. The bride
is a good wife, we are told. Because of her skills and strengths, they "make a fine home."
They "make friends with guests and wayfarers,"[7] so that "within only ten months Master
Shentu was well known." The bride herself is known to be kind. She is "generous to family
and clan" and cares for those in need. Eventually they have two children and have a life in
the village that is known to all as harmonious and useful. The mountain bride is domesticated, and happily so.

One day, however, Shentu Cheng finishes his job as a local officer, and it is now time to
return home. So Shentu, his wife, and their children all depart for the journey. Naturally they
travel the same route through those same ancient mountains where Shentu first discovered
his wife. They travel a while and are stopped one evening by the banks of a river. For no obvious reason, Shentu Cheng's wife has become morose. From the depths of her sadness, she
turns to her husband, and says in a manner that seems "suddenly to be deeply pained":[8]

> "I had written a poem for you, but preferred not to present it to you. But now, here, faced with
> this landscape, I cannot finally be silent." And so she chanted:

> > "Though the love between a man and a woman is strong,
> > Yet the desire for mountains and streams has its own depth.
> > I have often worried that my resolve would change:
> > That I'd turn my ungrateful back on our future years together."

> After she finished, she wept. She seemed to have some feeling of deep longing.[9]

Shentu Cheng hears his wife's poem, sees his wife's misery, and then responds: "Your
poem is certainly lovely," he deigns to say, "but these 'mountains and streams' are not
thoughts for the weaker sex."[10] Apparently, Shentu Cheng has forgotten his wife's origins

and missed the point. The landscape of the mountains is for any recluse—whether male or female—deeply attracting. Its wild rockscapes draw her as they drew Yuan Hongdao, Big Belly Li, and all other adepts and recluses. Master Shentu, however, is too much the solid citizen to see the signs. He responds obtusely and his wife continues to mourn. Finally, after twenty more days of mountain travel, of increased exposure to the mountain landscape, they arrive at the hut of the wife's parents.

> The hut itself was just as before; although now, it was empty; but Shentu and his wife decided they would stay there to stop over for the night. Because of the depths of his wife's thoughts and the depths of his wife's longings, she spent the whole day just sobbing and weeping. Then suddenly, at one corner of the wall, underneath an old pile of clothes, they came upon a tiger skin, all totally covered in dust and dirt. The wife caught sight of it and suddenly gave out a laugh of delight: "I had no idea this thing was still here!" Then she slipped the tiger skin over her back, and became, in an instant, a tiger. She roared, she growled, she snatched, she pounced; then she burst through the door and was gone. Shentu Cheng was gripped by terror; he took off at a run out the door.
>
> Then later, with his two children, he followed the path his wife had taken. But, finally, looking off to the mountains, he just cried. After several days it was clear that no one now knew where the tiger fairy had gone.[11]

The tiger fairy finally disappears the way adepts and mystics typically disappear. "No one knew where they went" is the phrase that typically concludes these biographies. The little folk tale does more, however, than depict a strange disappearance; it casts escape as an instinctual drive, a drive that rivals the instinct for society and home. The two instincts are signaled by the two places the woman inhabits: the village and the mountains. Nor are her two compulsions ranked; the tiger fairy is both good wife and good tiger. Her domestic instinct is clearly valid; she is happy at first with her husband, with her children, and within her community; indeed, she chants a line of poetry avowing her love: "the love between a man and a woman is strong." But for the tiger fairy this love of home proves to be the weaker instinct. Gradually, even unwillingly, as the woman moves deeper into the mountains, her need for the mountains reawakens. First, her nostalgia is expressed in the poem she feels compelled to chant, next she lets out the laughter of freedom at the sight of the tiger hide, and finally she flees back into the mountains in her rediscovered tiger shape as, unwillingly or not, she sheds that "nutshell of civility." Her final escape resolves the conflict felt by the creature; for though she lives for a time among men, with a husband, children, and village life to show for it, yet no amount of time served in conjugal happiness completely erases "the love of mountains and streams." Ultimately, the domestication of the tiger fairy doesn't take.

Is it possible, however, that the solitary woman was a creature only of myth, or that solitude in women was a luxury available only to the initiate? It might seem that only adept status legitimized solitude, and that without it a woman was confined to the domestic altars. But women of the Ming did imitate the hermit; they did cultivate solitude with the same enthusiasm as did men, although as with male recluses, reclusive life could have companions. Many female recluses were part-time escapists, as gentry recluses also had families, or recluse-artists invited friends and mates.

Eremitism for women often meant latitude. "I closed the gate, and relied on suiting myself," declared one recluse-poet.[12] Naturally, schedules were the first to go. "By the little railing I arise from sleep as the sun approaches noon," said another woman.[13] Ease was not the hallmark of the eremitic life, however. As these women abandoned the codes of domestic life and shut out the demands of others, they established their own brand of discipline and rigor. The women in solitary seclusion were tinged, in fact, with a type of fanaticism. Poets such as Yuan Hongdao adopted the eremitic life with a sense of rebellion, play, and eccentricity; female recluses—whether poets, scholars, or hikers—could have a harsher style. The reclusive female was severe, more the ascetic than was the male iconoclast. In his "Sixteen Portraits of Recluses," Chen Hongshou painted the recluse Piao Xian as a bookish, somber woman (see Figure 6.1).

One of the most famous female recluses of the Ming was the poet Lu Qingzi, who authored several collections of poetry. In her most famous collection, the *Gallery of the Clouds Reclining*, she described her mountain retreat at Cold Mountain where she, along with her husband, "cultivated ascetic seclusion."[14] It is no surprise she picked Cold Mountain. It had been famous since the seventh century as a monastic escape from the contamination of the world. Lu wrote a number of poems there about her reclusive life: "Dwelling in the Mountains," "In the Village," "The Grass Hut." In one of her reclusive poems, "On Dwelling in Idleness," she defined the solitary escape. The solitude she described, however, was anything but "empty"; it was not robbed of life or stripped of value or vitality, and it had nothing of the widow's loneliness in it. Rather this space was intimate, calm, and rich in sensation. The poem opens with the typical hallmarks of the recluse: the shut gate and the path overgrown with weeds.

On Dwelling in Idleness

> I close my gate. I rely on suiting myself.
> In the little alley creepers and grass are grown deep.
> The color of the willow makes the spring birds call.
> The play of light on the waves grows tranquil in the evening shadow.
> The fallen petals blanket the covered ground.
> The high clouds grow still over the nearby grove.
> If you ask about the purpose of this dark (*you*) house;
> There is but the plain zither at the end of the bed.[15]

There is much of the conventional in this poem; Lu describes the typical retreat from the vulgarity of the world—the isolated house, the refusal of company, and the poet at the zither. But in Lu's retreat there is more than a sense of isolation from the herd. For although there is in the poem a clear progression from the excluded exterior to private interior, from untrodden path and shut gate to the bedroom inside, yet there is not simply a sense of the diminishing of contact and sensation. Rather the reverse is true: the details of this inward progress emphasize an expansion of sensations. In this private, interior world the poem reveals a richly complete world where there is a feeling of sensuality, not denial; the images of the small landscape—the play of the changing light and the muffled sounds on the ground—create a lush middle section of the poem. Even her perceptions are enhanced; she detects now the subtle and gradual changes within the gate. There is then an intense, meditative stillness that comes over the setting of the poem. Lu Qingzi employs one especially telling word to describe her place of escape. The term for "dark"—*you*—was commonly applied to the recluse's style, especially that of the female recluse; women who took to seclusion, as well as their retreats, their poetry, and their behavior were depicted as "dark." But what did this word mean? Certainly it meant to be secluded or to be withdrawn, but it had additional connotations as well. It meant finely nuanced, subtle, secret, mysterious, and uncanny. Far from a sense of emptiness in these spaces, there was a sense of strangeness or even echoes of sanctity; ordinary space had been mystified.

Despite the "dark" aspects of these retreats, however, eremitism in these women has sounded to some like a timid, overly refined withdrawal from life: sedate, passive, "quietist"; the retreat of these women has looked like an insipid contentment. Indeed, the folklore of the recluse, especially of the female recluse, has suffered from Disneyfication in which the intensity of the recluse has been taken out. The solitude of these women, however, was anything but sedate, the small spaces anything but bland; rather, solitary space was the setting for the withdrawal of the artist, the scholar, the reader, or the musician. "Serene" is, in fact, the last word to apply to her. Solitude in these female escapees is rather a calling and a compulsion, a necessity closely allied with the need for creative work (see Figure 6.2).

The Ming poet Wu Qi was one of these inward poets—withdrawn, mysterious; her verses were called dreamlike and subtle. In Wu Qi's life there are no traces of the passive—rather, an obsessional drive. Her biographers have been quick to point out her passion for work, noting that, even as a child, she displayed an intense craving for a solitary and creative life. The first to note her need for the scholar's life were her parents. "As a child Wu Qi was precociously clever; at five she could complete a poem after once having seen it. Her parents saw that she was brilliant, far beyond the abilities of others, and so arranged for her to have a teacher. As a young girl she composed poetry, and as a young woman she wrote prose pieces. She labored at writing day and night without rest. Though her parents saw her excessive zeal, they could do nothing to stop her."[16] Her drive to write led her finally to decisively and permanently repudiate the conventional life of a domesticated woman. Finally, "this young scholar set aside her hairpins and ornament, and sought then her sheet of paper, as if she'd found an ancient jade." Like the tiger fairy who finds the old tiger skin in the corner of the hut, the poet retrieves her own emblem of solitude—"her sheet of paper"—as the rediscovered emblem of a basic instinct. Ultimately, Wu Qi completely abandoned the "exuviae" of civilization; widowed after twenty years of marriage, Wu Qi joined a group of other women writers and broke off association with men, and with one of her friends she set off on a tour of the sites around the Qiantang River in the area of Hangzhou.[17]

This note of asceticism runs through many of the portraits of female recluses. They were often rigorously self-disciplined, assuming a monasticism in their lives that rivaled the strictness of taking orders. Many of these recluses, in fact, acquired disciples or lived in monastic retreats. The poet Shen Yixiu was one such reclusive poet, a devout Buddhist who believed that her verses should serve to "awaken the world." Her own cousin became her disciple, taking the name of the Person of the Single Way. The two of them wrote and meditated in their study called the Study of the Valley's Echo. The disciple described their daily ritual: "Each day 'my sister' chanted the Sanskrit texts, which formed our regular lessons. She would sit with eyes intent, reading Buddhist scripture."[18] This religious intensity did not shock her family; rather, they considered her both brilliant and devout. The solitary woman was sheltered and legitimized by religion.

Not surprisingly, these poets needed mountains; travel clearly attracted them, and many made pilgrimages to savage, isolated sites. Mountains conveyed permanence and transcendence; they disrupted the hold of the mundane, liberating the recluse from the ordinary and the unmystified space, offering a sense of the divine. One well-known writer, the poetess

Figure 6.2   Lady Guan of the Wei period, known for her achievements as a poet and painter, especially for her paintings of bamboo. All the women in her family were talented artists. Famous also as a scholar of Buddhist texts and as a devout woman. Shown with the typical accoutrements of the hermitage life: ink, brushes, books and flower arrangement (*Wu Youru huabao,* vol. 1, "One Hundred Beauties Past and Present").

Qing Lanzhen, was famous for her mountain travel. Her friend, the writer Zhu Jingyan, said her poetry was suffused with the feel of the mountains.[19] She was not a devout Buddhist like Shen, nor a studious prodigy like Wu Qi, but like the adepts, she "took to the hiker's stick" (see Figure 6.3). In one of her poems, she described a journey she made:

Going Mountain Climbing with My Sister

Linked companions as a pair; here and everywhere we take in the magnificent sites.
Now mixed, now distinct, the ancient trees and clouds.
There are places where the trimmed bamboo has never been cut.
No mountain lacks the green pine's growth.[20]

Another poet, Wang Hui, of the Qing era, also needed to travel; she described her journey from the bounds of her town into the foliage of the mountains.

On the Shanyin Road

When I exit the city
from the watchtower gate

I lose completely
all sense of spatial limits,
passing ten miles through
the cool shade of the hills.
Water and land rise to view
by turns and sink away;
my course lengthens out
open and endless.
Hills and mountaintops draw apart,
each contour like no other;
bamboo and trees interlace
making dense forest.
Who would know
under this impenetrable growth
a stream is gliding through?
On the stone bridge
the road is obvious,
then I round a bend
and confuse east and west.
No one else in sight
here in the mist
hushed, alone
mountain flowers so red.[21]

Figure 6.3 **"Climbing Great Peaks"** (*Wu Youru huabao*, vol. 1, "Remarkable Women from All Over").

These mountain landscapes were more than places of solitude; they were the site for the recluse's work. Lu Qingzi, the poet above who described the life behind the "shut gate," described a mountain studio. Lu's poem "On Dwelling in the Mountains" opens with an expansive spectacle. Then from the wild views the poet shifts her gaze to the intimate landscape of her study and her books; both the studio and the mountain are the setting for the recluse's work (see Color Plate 9).

On Dwelling in the Mountains (II)

The color of the trees: a thousand-layered green.
The depth of the ravine: a flow of ten thousand cliffs.
As the birds call, the shadows in the flowers grow warm.
In the autumn the maple leaves fall by the stone gate.
As the mallet strikes, the Sanskrit text is heard;
I climb the stairs to my studio gallery.
Attentive to karma I search through my Buddhist library.
But isn't this just a search for the Daoist Cinnabar Hill?[22]

But being alone was not just a setting for work or escape; it was also, for the women who described it, a type of sensation or cast of mind. Solitude interested the female recluses as a type of feeling or a quality of intelligence. Solitude had for them all the hallmarks of any sentiment; it had features of nuance and tone, and levels of intensity, and could be subject to the explorations all poets level at forms of affect. Just as lyric poets write about love, as novelists write about alienation, and as dramatists explore the nature of revenge, these reclusive women interpreted the qualities of being alone. Their poetry explored how, in isolation, perceptions are shaped and clarified, and how the self achieves a type of definition.

In a state of solitude, the recluse finds a certain quality of mind that is both settled and sharply focused. Thoreau's word for this state was "deliberate." For Ming recluses there was the same sense of reduction and acuteness. Solitude sensations suggest the mind of the nighttime predator: relaxed, ready, and focused. Night imagery is often allied with the poems describing the hermit's life; "Sitting at Night," "Reading at Night," "The Courtyard at Night," "Writing at Night" are common titles for poems by reclusive women. There is nothing surprising in this, for night simplifies and eliminates. What is surprising is the ease with which these reclusive women adapted to this world. They appeared to inhabit the private spaces that night affords with facility, like an animal settling into its lair, at home in the dark. In one such poem, "Just Sitting," the poet Woman Yin described a world of night. The landscape has all the marks of the solitary escape: night, privacy, and the quieted space. In this quieted space the poet can develop an animal-like sharpness in her perceptions.

Just Sitting

Night deepens, the fall moon grows cold.
A slight mist drops down from the leaves.
The four walls chill now just a bit.
The clear night: it's the time I listen to the zither.[23]

In this brief quatrain there is, ironically, a kind of ascetic sensuality. In the contained space, within the four simple walls, the world is completely perceived. The poet notes the dim light of the moon, the slight edge of discomfort from the increased feeling of cold, the subliminal perception of the falling dew, and finally the expectation of the sound of the zither. At the same time, the sensations are nuanced. Like the nocturnal animal, the poet seems acutely attuned to the small events. From the opening phrase—"Night deepens . . ."—the poem presents a carefully absorbed process. No ordinary diurnal creature, this observer is aware of the variety of changes that take place in the dark. Her isolation in the quieted space has not deadened her perceptions, but has sharpened them, clarified her instincts for observing fine detail, and prepared her ear for listening to the zither. Hence, despite the restricted nature of these hermitage spaces, perceptions expand; the powers of intuition are heightened and tactile sensations grow sharp. The contained gardens, sites at night, the courtyards at dusk, the simple rooms with one lantern, and a gauze curtain ruffled in the wind are not negative spaces, stripped of interest. They are small landscapes that are deeply inviting. "Solitude" is in some sense the wrong word. For the recluse is not naming an absence of people—a void—nor an emptied space nor a state of aloneness. She is describing instead a richness of calmed space. Whereas feminine solitude in the West often suggests abandonment, in the Ming it suggests an acquisition of vividly sensed space.

The poet Zhu Jingyan was one woman who loved seclusion and who wrote about it often. She was a member of a gentry family, a woman raised within the conventions of the harsh code of filial obligation. Yet she assumed the dark spaces and took as her pen name "Stillness Retreat." In one poem, "Written in the Midst of Illness," she defined the sensations. In this poem Zhu intensifies the feeling of the solitary night by adding the imagery of sickness, using the image to redouble the other effects of the night and contained space. Illness adds a primitive, atavistic feel, enhances the sense of the world pared down to her own immediate space, and augments a sense of the precise perception of the specific moment. The poem suggests a return to the essentials of self definition, the feeling of "a tribal person alone"[24] to use the phrase of Maxine Hong Kingston.

Written in the Midst of Illness

> I have plucked away the stem of the cold lantern; my dreaming is unfinished.
> I'm wrapped in my covers. I have sat here now, in grave solemnity, on till midnight.
> The Barbarian reed pipe blows; I can't tell from where.
> The plum petals now all fallen; moonlight floods the the village.[25]

The title sets the inward nature of the setting: more than do the space of her bedroom and the setting of midnight, this woman's illness narrows the perspective of the poet. Her body is the filter of her observations, creating a physical perimeter that cuts her off from others as clearly as does the night or the shut gate. In this night scene, however, she is anything but confined or passive; rather she appears to be at attention. Enveloped in her covers, the poet sits up in bed as midnight approaches. Her austere dignity—her "grave solemnity"—suggests a soldier's calm, gives us a feeling that, now that the trivial has fallen away, she has, with appropriate decorum, prepared for something. Orderly, she has cleaned up the signs of her waking hours when the lantern was lit; now she accepts the dark as she trims down the used wick. This landscape is clearly the recluse's apt space; there is a kind of cool self-containment and expectant readiness about the woman that echo other depictions of the recluse's meditative solitudes.

At the same time, the narrator is not defined just by the four walls of her bedroom. In her perfect stillness, she seems to be listening into other spaces beyond the room and beyond the rational world. The first other-realm the poet invokes is the world of the subconscious; the image of dreams not finished suggests a recent immersion in the subconscious world, and suggests as well the world of imagination or fantasy, of that half of the mind allied with the night. That this world is "unfinished" implies a continuity between the waking and dream states. The eerie pipe suggests a second exotic world, the world of the borderlands, a place of open horizons. The image of moonlight then summarizes both the above themes of the subconscious and the exotic, echoes the sense of nocturnal, not-rational perception. Unlike the sun, which suggests illumination by rational thought, the moon suggests nighttime or subconscious perceptions. The still, moonlit landscape further intimates an alien space. In this poem it brightens the village, but a village lit bright at night is an antivillage, a village that— for a time—no longer belongs to the diurnal and the gregarious. This narrow space of her bedroom has thus become a kind of exotic space.

Ultimately, these recluse-poets trace their ancestry back to the adepts. Many reclusive artists took pen names that evoked the tradition of feminine mysticism. The writer Wu Qi had two names: Buddha Brow, and the Zhi Transcendent; the poet Wu Xiao called herself the Icy Transcendent. Others took names such as Quiet Retreat, the Daoist of the Azure Sky, and the Daoist of the Grass Cloak. In their poetry they described adept themes, especially sacred journeys and magical flight. The Daoist of the Azure Sky described the arrival of autumn in the mountains in her poem "New Autumn": "The color of the moon fills the screen and increases my joy. . . . Softly I set my spirit to wander out beyond creation."[26] Beyond the obvious evocations of adept themes and names are the implications of the recluse's characterization of space. When Madame Yin sits sensing the walls of her room now chilling "a bit," and when Zhu Jingyan sits erect like a warrior, tuned to the sounds of exotic space, there is a suggestion of a kind of inner alchemy. We seem to be watching a secularized adept who has turned her back on the conscious and common, opened the immediate world with her sharpened perceptions, and—with an uncanny sense of the subliminal—become a mystic of the minutely sensed, inner world. Thus has she transformed ordinary space into mystified expanded space. The real adept, of course, has control of the exotic spaces described in scripture, the wild places that Tan Yang Zi visited while her father kept guard. These recluse-poets only take control of the confined space—the intimate landscapes of the mountain hut or the study; but through their perceptions—their interpretation of the sensation of solitude—they are both stationary and traveling.

The instinct for seclusion, however, was not limited to recluses, mystics, and solitary poets; sometimes women of the village also despised the village. For these women—wives, daughters, concubines, or matriarchs, lodged in domestic stability—mountain travel was impossible; they were too limited by circumstance to escape. Still, even in these women, there were powerful traces of the tiger fairy. There is a sense of women who have compromised out of dire necessity, yet who are ready to exit. For them, their apparent domestication is, on closer look, something of a failed experiment. Their solutions were severely limited, however—the "horror of the home," the "longing for mountains and streams," could not be expressed through escape. Rather, these recluses' longing was limited to small domestic rebellions: to refusals, to complaints, to protests, and to fury.

For these domestic renegades, what palled most was compromise. Like the filial woman and the religious adept, they abhorred the servile nature of domestic life, the need to bend to another. Thoreau agreed; they "labor under a mistake," he said, and live "a fool's life." "How many a poor immortal soul have I met well-nigh crushed and smothered under its load, creeping down the road of life."[27] Ming recluses were equally disdainful of the need to do another's labors. The word they disliked the most was *shi*, "to serve"; to serve a man or a first wife was smothering, and they despised obedience. Such women were still confined to the village, however, so they became in their constraint domestic renegades confined to home.

A regional historian of the Ming told the story—famous for generations, he maintained—of one such domestic renegade. This young girl—who came to be called Elder Maiden Xia—had the fierceness of the warrior-adepts. Like the young warrior who easily took up her sword by the bedside, she also despised compromise, but her fierceness was confined to the setting of her family, and her protest limited to domestic refusal. For her story was not the story of a mystic but rather that of a malcontent. This is the story of the bookish and resolute Elder Maiden Xia. Her story begins with the conventional history of her family.

The Elder Maiden Xia was from Peizhou. Her father, Xia Zixiao had passed the official examination in the Wanli period. For generations throughout the dynasty his family had grown famous in the region for the distinctions they gained in government service. Thus if anyone thought of a good marriage, they would necessarily think of the women of the Xia family.

Xia Zixiao had three daughters. When the Elder Maiden Xia grew to be fifteen years old, it was time to find her a husband, The local matrons repeatedly sought out the girl and their father was in agreement. But Elder Maiden avowed that she hated the way women were subservient to men. "What limits are there to a man's passions?" she argued, "And when a woman's demeanor is always adapting, and she values only the man's opinion, then her sense of the Unchanging Way will also adapt. It is a misfortune indeed that I was born a female, for a female must serve a man, and I do not wish to." And so she set aside creams and cosmetics, and then used linen for cloth, and removed all ornament. Of course, her parents were horrified. They demanded she explain herself and urged her to change, but her will was fixed, and there was nothing to be done about it. The family just wept and grieved.

The years passed by and she grew older, and people began to call her the Elder Maiden. Now the Maiden loved to study; and she and her brothers would debate and analyze the lofty arguments of the ancient and modern authors. In these debates the brothers were usually defeated.

By nature the Elder Maiden was severe and august; often she would use her own knowledge of the rites to chasten not only those below her but even those above her. Hence everyone in her family was in awe of her.[28]

Elder Maiden Xia was clearly a difficult woman. Her obdurate nature made her refuse the obvious path of marriage. Of course, her family objects to her decision. The mother and especially the father—with his distinguished lineage of ancestors in government service—resolutely advocate the domestic, but as our story acknowledges, they were helpless to change her. The instinct for refusal was too strong. Her refusal, however, was not without tradition; for the Elder Maiden's step-by-step transition is not just an abandonment of the domestic, but rather an imitation of the ascetic. When she "set aside creams and cosmetics," she reflected the recluse; when she studied the classics and argued their fine points, she suggested the religious teacher; when she refused to serve a husband who would compromise her sense of the "Unchanging Way," she imitated the nun. Elder Maiden Xia did indeed refuse the communal, but she did not refuse the feminine, for although she refused the role of wife, she embraced the role of adept. She became a sort of religious teacher of her own family, a displaced recluse, and the family itself was converted, transformed from patriarchal village to monastic hall. Her brothers and even her family elders became her students, as she instructed, debated, and chastened them on points of morality and ritual.

Accommodations were not always possible, however. Elder Maiden Xia's refusal to serve a man forced compromise on her family. Her brothers were apparently willing to be instructed by this proud woman of the "Unchanging Way." But not all families submitted. For women in these families, there were few options except rage. For them the angry complaint held the only trace of the adept's fierceness. Feng Menglong, who preserved the story of the Tiger Fairy in his *Compilation by the Historian of Love*, also told the story of a furious domestic malcontent. This brief narration tells of a miserable and fiercely defiant concubine, and her fury echoes that of other such women trapped in a loathsome conjugal arrangement. What is especially interesting about this account, however, is that it is a first-person account: the fury of this malcontent is told by the woman herself. Feng Menglong maintains in his anecdote that he found this fragment of a woman's life on the walls of a posthouse in the town of Xinjia:

> I was born and grew up in Kuaiji. At an early age I began to study calligraphy and history. As soon as I reached adulthood, I was made a concubine to a man from Yan. . . . Oh, that I, with the contemplative temperament of an anchoress, should be forced to serve an insensitive military man. . . . But for a person imprisoned in a cage, what difference can death make. I am not afraid of anything except being buried in some desolate, barren field, with not a trace, not even a few words remaining—and therefore I [have] restrained myself from giving in to death immediately, waiting rather until everyone else was sound asleep, when I stealthily came from the backyard. Now, grinding the black ink slab moistened with my tears, I have written these poems upon the wall, in the hope that someone sympathetic might read them and lament my untimely birth. Then, even though I may have passed away, there will still be something of me left behind.
>
> Rose garment already half dust-covered,
> Accompanying me, a single dying lamp.
> Just as, after the red rain of pear blossoms,
> The stripped trees, pitiable, show nothing of spring.
>
> Roaming all day then, midst tigress and leopard,
> Harboring feelings now, still, deeply regretful;
> Creator—created, not purposeless—I,
> Leaving behind to the talented, story-beginnings.[29]

The story of this woman had wide circulation; it was a folk tale told in several versions, an exemplar of the type. Whether she ever existed we don't know, but she was emblematic of the enraged concubine, with her manifesto of a domestic malcontent. Like most malcontents, there were the overtones of the adept; her "temperament of an anchoress," her contempt for her life with "a military man," and even her ability to compose poetry all seem drawn from the same pool of myth. She does, indeed, suggest the recluse, but a thwarted recluse with no means of escape. She can only be a mutant of the archetype, her journey to exotic space arrested. What does remain to her is a distilled rage, her "indignation," and her deep regret for a lost life. She remains in the village, but despises it; she writes poetry, but composes only in secret; she invokes the tradition of the anchoress, but only as her "temperament." The Woman at the Posthouse, an anonymous concubine, stands as a silenced exemplar of this tradition.

Some domestic malcontents, however, did more than compose poetry in silence; they became noisy, complaining, vindictive, and vitriolic. These malcontents were the so-called furious women, a well-known category of the feminine, described at length by intellectuals and satirized by playwrights. They appeared as stock figures in everything from joke books to family admonitions. They were an established social class, a subspecies of the domesticated woman, or of the warrior, or of both. The name for them, *du fu*, is often translated as "jealous woman," and indeed, their jealousy of other women was very much part of their lore. As the stories of these women make clear, however, sexual jealousy was not so much the issue as was dominance. Although they could certainly be seen as the purest manifestations of feminine envy, still many of them displayed more rage and contempt than jealousy. They were furious at civilization, at weakness, at compromise; these traits were not linked to envy of other women, but rather seem to spring from some deep sense of superiority. The *du fu* was an implacable enemy, often vicious, typically arrogant, and habitually terrifying, especially to men. She was a true dominatrix. In the context of Ming patriarchy there would seem no place for the fiercely contemptuous woman; Ming culture was patterned on strict filial norms that explicitly named men as superior in status to women. But she did exist. The deeply disdainful, harshly superior, wickedly vitriolic, brilliantly argumentative woman was well known and well feared. Dorothy Ko points out the lineage of these women; dating from the medieval period, they were thought to be a phenomenon of clan pride. A vitriolic woman was loathe to yield her clan status to her husband's dominance.[30] One brief anecdote gives a fine sense of the intensity of these women, gives a sense of these *du fu* as a feminine gargoyle. These women of vitriol were filled with a corrosive disdain, so immune that no creature—human or supernatural—dared to challenge them. The entire neighborhood knew their capabilities, nicknaming them the "Five Tigers."

> In the Jiang family, there were five sisters who were truly furious women (*du fu*). The five of them all loathed their neighbors, and so they were known in the area as the Five Tigers. Now there was in the town a house that was known to be haunted, and no one dared to live in it.
>
> The Five Tigers heard about it; and they laughed: "How could there be any such thing?!" So one night they entered the house, each one of them carrying a knife; they sat themselves down in the central hall and remained until dawn. During the night, the Five Tigers heard not one ghost nor one goblin. So now you see that these women were feared even by the ghosts. How much more should they be feared by us men!![31]

The Five Tigers were lethal; neighbors and patriarchs all were relegated to meek silence, and all were happy to give this category of women a wide berth.

If neighbors were wary of these women, husbands were terrorized, for the most infamous of these women of vitriol were the furious wives. They were, according to one sober observer, a domestic death sentence: "A lifetime with such a woman is one of mankind's greatest misfortunes."[32] They were inescapable and controlled the household economy, the household property, and the servants. "At least," said our harried scholar, "you could run from the cruelty of parents, or tyrants, or even violent friends," but the frightened husband had to "meet with his tyrant every time he comes home."[33] The problem was that these women loved the heat of verbal battle, and they were good at it; they "mulled over anger and chewed on insults."[34] Debate and insult were grist for their mill. They conspired together as well; they were known for their feminine alliances: "When vitriolic women support each other it is like some evil visited on you for some terrible karma of the past."[35] Nor was the furious woman confined to the home. She could also be found in Court; for even worse than the vitriolic wife was the vitriolic ruler, the royal woman who terrorized. Empresses and royal mothers or consorts could fit this terrible stereotype; royal authority combined with a vitriolic woman's rage could transform a woman into a national disaster.

The source of their power was their intensity; they could inundate the hapless spouse. One of these oft-sighted *du fu* was an infamous harridan; she raged at her husband and punished his behavior like a demonic nanny. Whenever he returned late from work, she would flog him and yank his beard until his face was covered with blood. All the man's friends felt sorry for him. Finally, however, the wife died; his personal demon was removed, his home was now his own. His friends all rejoiced at his liberation but were surprised when the husband became deeply depressed and, shortly afterwards, went into a sad decline and himself died.[36] (see Figure 6.4 for three tiger-sisters of the Qing.)

This phenomenon was not a cultural oddity. Indeed, the fear of vitriolic women was sufficiently well known to be classified. There were terms for it. "Gynephobia," in the literal sense of "fear of the feminine," was well described; and although the husband with the bloodied beard may not have received comfort from the labels his wife was known for, at least the labels meant he was not alone. There were two common expressions for the fear of women. One was *ju nei*, a formal expression that means, literally, "terror of the back apartments"; it is a rather elegant expression for an atavistic response. The second one was *wei fu*, which means literally "fear of the wife." Of course, there were explanations; intellectuals mused over the causes of such fear.

Figure 6.4 "'Flower Tiger' Waxes Wroth." There were three married women so vitriolic that they were known as the Three Tigers: Yellow Tiger, White Tiger, and Flower Tiger. All three of the women had daughters who were just as fierce as their mothers. When Mr. Li married the daughter of the youngest sister, he tried to "regulate his wife and bring her into submission." The young bride, however, went back home and complained to her mother. The mother, Flower Tiger, then gathered her sisters to go to Li's house, and the three of them smacked him about to teach him a lesson (*Wu Youru huabao*, vol. 2, "Anecdotes of Past and Present").

One scholar thought that the vitriolic woman was a particular problem of the Ming era: "During the Song dynasty, because of the teachings of Zhu Xi, there were few vitriolic women. Now in our era, however, as his teachings have declined, vitriolic women proliferate."[37]

Sober debate aside, however, the scared husband and furious wife made great material; if Ming readers worried about it, they also thought it funny. Joke books, plays, and short fiction contained scores of humiliated husbands and domineering wives. In *A Treasury of Jokes*, Feng Menglong told of a minor rebellion staged by a clique of timorous husbands, a rebellion destined to fail.

> There was a group of husbands who all lived in fear of their wives. One day they all gathered together to come up with a plan to free themselves from their constant state of fear, and reestablish thereby their proper spousal authority. But someone, who thought to give them all a bit of a scare, reported to them: "Each one of your wives has heard all about this meeting! They're on their way to give you each a beating!!"
>
> When they heard this, they raced off in a mass and scattered, leaving one man alone who just sat tight; and so it seemed as if only one man remained unafraid. But on closer examination, what actually happened, was that the man was frozen to his seat, scared to death.[38]

Such warring factions were common stereotypes in the Ming, ready-made for the humiliating anecdote. Of course, the joke was consistently the same. The man of the house commanded reverence; the little woman of the house annihilated him. Still the jokes proliferated; no matter how many times the husband said "yes, dear" as the wife engulfed him in fury, it was always funny. One husband grumbled at his wife's conduct, as men of dignity are wont to do; but this timorous husband grumbled at his own pathetic errand: he was sent by his spouse to borrow thumb pinchers from a neighbor so his wife could squeeze his fingers with them. Then there was the "furious woman," consumed with rage, determined to give her husband a beating. The poor man ran off to the bedroom and hid away from her blows. "Come out!" she commanded. "No!!" he replied. "When a bold man says no," he continued staunchly from under the bed, "he means no!"[39] In all these jokes there was something of gallows humor; the furious woman was an assault on the hierarchy of male over female, but she was too distressing to be purely comical.

The furious woman could not have done it alone, however. She was an echo of deeper disruptions, a surface quake that derived from a source, for at the heart of this troubling gargoyle were the recluses, adepts, and mythic creatures who felt themselves entitled to fury. In her viciousness, the furious woman echoed the warrior Maid Eleven, who reached for a broadsword when her brother-in-law threatened; or she suggested Elder Maiden Xia, the "severe and august" daughter who refused to serve. There were even hints of the filial woman, with her "heart of iron and stone." Despite the customary view of her as sexually jealous, this *du fu* was far more complex. In the Ming there was a grudging admiration for her; her astounding capacity for rage was epic in its grandeur. One man observed that such women were awe inspiring for their "stern authority."[40] Even in the short account of the Five Tigers there was a certain respect, a touch of neighborhood pride: right next door there were women who could scare away ghosts. Like a famous site—a great lake or strange stone—these women were something to be remarked on to visitors, larger than life, fascinating to watch, at least when safe at a distance. Not surprisingly, tigers were the typical familiars of such women—their alter egos, their epithets, or their alternate shape. Both were nocturnal and solitary, at home in the antihome of alien landscapes, and very difficult to domesticate.

7
Conclusion

A joke circulating in the late Ming involved a conversation between two women:

A girl, not yet married, went to her sister-in-law in a private moment and asked her, "Is 'that business' a little enjoyable?"

"What," replied the sister-in-law, "could be enjoyable about 'that business'? The truth is, the affairs between man and wife are fixed and ordained by the *Great Rites of the Duke of the Ancient Kingdom of Zhou*."

Some time later, after the girl had herself been married, she came back to her family for a visit. As soon as she saw her sister-in-law, she went right over to her to say:

"You are such a liar!"[1]

Jf wit is the voice of the unconscious, then the sexuality of this girl was the unconscious undercurrent of Ming domestic life. In response to the girl's shy question—a question posed in the anxious euphemism of the uninitiated—the sister-in-law provided the official version of sexual relations. Citing the authority of the *Rites of Zhou*, the ancient canon of the Confucian school, she redrew private life absent the erotic, eliminating all that the erotic implies: a sense of play, of wickedness, of individuality, and of arrogance; hers was the public text that codified primness. What public speech omits, however, a joke names, and with the declaration of "You are such a liar!" the girl rebutted the evasive half-truth of the libido police. Naturally, the rebuke erupted in comic form, as comedy is the typical avenue for the uncensored; and briefly, at least in this private interchange, the good Duke was overturned. Of course, there have been many overturnings—so many that it is reasonable to say that this joke is not an ellipsis of standard decorum but a revelation of standard alternatives. These alternatives are the eels and white snakes, the flying warriors and grannies, the shape shifters and state topplers. Like a crude lineage or tentative shadow family, they are the authority for the girl's punch line. Her blunt response invokes all of them; she mimics the tiger sisters' attack on the son-in-law and the tiger fairy's flight, confounding that rigid equation of home with woman with the *Rites of Zhou*.

This book's exploration of this guild of archetypes has seen the forthright, the prominent, and even the baroque versions—the extremes and grotesques. That is partly the nature of archetypes; they delineate in large sizes. These women, however—the predators, the mystics, the grannies, the mates in excellence—were not rigidly of type. Rather, it should be noted that women would assume them briefly; they sometimes mimicked the type as it suited them, becoming the soldier or the scholar, the granny or the virago, and then returning to the mundane. That shopper of Beijing assumed myth in a blink; from meek traveler by the market gate to a sudden, ready warrior, she recalibrated her umbrella to give the fool a poke.

The woman Liu Shuying was one of these late Ming role shifters. Without any consideration for the categories argued by academics, she assumed a different mask to meet the changing disasters of the end of the Dynasty. Liu was the daughter of an aristocratic family in the southern province of Jiangxi. When she was only seven, her father was killed by the corrupt eunuch-official Wei Zhongxian, and the widow of the general, Woman Xiao, had to raise the child alone. Liu's mother did not instruct her solely in the ways of family piety, however, but educated her from her husband's books; she taught Liu Shuying swordsmanship, military strategy, and Chan Buddhism. In 1644, when the dynasty fell, Liu—not surprisingly—responded like a soldier. She reviled the Manchu and, using her family wealth and property, recruited an army of a thousand, trained her recruits, and held out in the South for two years. As a warrior, Liu was also a gallant; weak men disgusted her. When the Ming general Zhang Xianbi was hesitating between Ming and Manchu, she flew into a rage and struck at him with her sword. The general cowered behind a pillar, and his guard drew their arms. "Such cowards!" she accused. "I am a mere woman, and yet you take up arms!"[2] With the final collapse of all pockets of resistance, however, Liu was left with failure, although she still had one more archetype to invoke. Like the tiger fairy and its many solitary descendants, Liu retired from the common lives of common men and women to a small hut; she called her place "the Lotus Boat." There she lived with her aged mother, and the two passed their lives together reading sutras.[3]

Liu was soldier, gallant, recluse, and daughter, according to the needs of the time. The archetypes were not larger-than-life, overarching deities with rigid modes of being, nor were they strict masks once worn, never removed; they were costume changes.

Not that this was a paradox. The lore gives a sense not of neat categories, but of a turmoil of energies. The feminine was in essence protean, not so much alternating among these several personae as being all of them. The physics of the feminine—the principle of *yin*—gives ultimate shape to this tumble of roles. *Yin* notions inform the list of feminine characteristics—water, fertility, love, power, and danger—and serve to both unify the list and sustain it in the culture. Women thus slip in and out of the relevant categories, from doctor to consort to tiger to matchmaker. Even the most heavily codified woman of the Ming, the chaste widow, seems to show some *yin* elasticity. In defiance of the sharp delineation of her as Confucian exemplar,[4] she suggests in some incarnations other feminine archetypes. As drought-relieving cult figure, she suggests the burned shamanesses, dragon brides, snake women, and rain deities.

There is one myth that expresses best the protean nature of the feminine: Lady White, the infamous snake-wife-warrior, is the best testimony to the tendency to shape shift within the *yin*. In popular versions retold over the millennia, she is a doctor ministering to the poor, a slimy snake emerging in a spring rain, an aggressive lover pursuing the innocent, a soaring warrior, a thief, and a reverential wife; she is, in fact, all the women of this book. But she is not trading archetypes; rather, she is revealing one while she masks another. Her most important archetype, however, is her puny one, for she is most purely herself when she is reduced in form, when she is most human. In those moments, at least in the brilliant version by Feng Menglong, she is only a mortal woman and very charming.[5] Her appeal is not in the ferocious extremes, but in the reduction. She may pursue her lover like a demon, steal clothes, steal money, rage like a beast at priests and adepts, reveal her ugly, gigantic animal form, and command the waters, but the high changes of the grotesque are less potent than her charm as a woman weakened by love. When she is finally captured, she gives a look that all recall from the story: "As they all looked on, she assumed her original form of a white snake, three feet long. But even then she raised her eyes to look up and gaze at Xu Xuan."[6] This sweet look she gives seems more the essential character of White Snake than her other masks. Indeed, the power of this story seems to lie not in the ways Lady White confounds the world of men, but in the way she is seduced by the privilege of being all too human. Perhaps this is why, with all these extraordinary permutations, she is most eloquent avowing her weak self, that self least bound to nature, most needful of society, that fragile human animal that needs the protection of clothes. When accused by a priest of being a shape shifter—which, of course, she most certainly is—she says, "How, sir, can I be the malign demon you say I am? Does not my jacket have a seam? Don't I cast a shadow beneath the sun?"[7]

If Lady White moves readily from myth to mortal, her human imitators move easily from mortal to myth. There seems to be, in fact, a special proximity of the mythic with the ordinary. These archetypes, in their close latency, are constant below the rational surface. Of course, the folklore of the dangerous is not so ready on the lips as the *Rites of Zhou*; but still, such immediacy, such proximity to the feminine tells us about the common readiness of the roles. These archetypes were available, part of the mentalities of the time, written or told in an easy vocabulary, not so much private speech as informal speech. This collection of women has been sustained in a web of traditions that is flimsy, a web largely constructed in non-canonical, nonhegemonic texts, some half-erased by the processes of cultural censorship. Yet, like earlier versions of an evolving book, these myths are both ancient and persistent; and, whether faintly readable or not, whether preserved as canon or not, they comprise the beginning of the document.

Notes

Preface

1. Howard Nemerov, *Figures of Thought* (Boston: Godine, 1978), p. 69.
2. Henry Adams, "The Dynamo and the Virgin," in *The Education of Henry Adams, an Autobiography* (New York: Time Books, 1964), p. 172.
3. A. L. Rowse, *A Cornishman at Oxford* (London: Jonathan Cape, 1962), pp. 151–52.

Chapter One. Background: The Great Ming

1. Johan Nieuhof, et al., *An Embassy from the East India Company of the United Provinces, to the Grand Tartar Cham . . .* (1669), p. 135.
2. Wai-kam Ho, "The Late Ming Literati: Their Social and Cultural Ambiance," in *The Chinese Scholar's Studio: Artistic Life in the Late Ming Period. An Exhibition from the Shanghai Museum*, ed. Chu-Tsing Li and James C.Y. Watt (London: Thames and Hudson, 1987), p. 27.
3. *Ming shi, juan* 301 (Beijing: Zhonghua shuju, 1974), p. 7709.
4. Ray Huang, *1587, A Year of No Significance* (New Haven and London: Yale University Press, 1981), p. 5.
5. For discussions of miraculous aspects of the filial woman, see Mark Elvin, "Female Virtue and the State in China," *Past and Present* 104 (August 1984): 111–52.
6. Ibid., pp. 116–18. Also see Jonathan Chaves, "Moral Action in the Poetry of Wu Chia-chi (1618–84)," *Harvard Journal of Asiatic Studies* 46 (1986): 409; Katherine Carlitz, "Shrines, Governing-Class Identity, and the Cult of Widow Fidelity in Mid-Ming Jiangnan," *Journal of Asian Studies* 56, no. 3 (August 1997): 612–40.
7. T'ien Ju-K'ang, *Male Anxiety and Female Chastity. A Comparative Study of Chinese Ethical Values in Ming-Ch'ing Times* (Leiden: E. J. Brill, 1988), p. 10.
8. Frederic Wakeman, Jr., *The Great Enterprise: The Manchu Reconstruction of Imperial Order in Seventeenth-Century China*, 2 vols. (Berkeley: University of California Press, 1985), p. 654.
9. Elvin, "Female Virtue," p. 118. And in Feng Menglong, "Shen zhi lue," *juan* 2, in *Jia shen ji shi* [1644], ed. Feng Menglong, (Xuanlan tang congshu, Nanjing: Nanjing Central Library, 1941), pp. 4a–5b.
10. Hung Ming-shui, "Yuan Hung-tao and the Late Ming Literary and Intellectual Movement" (Ph.D. diss., University of Wisconsin, 1975), p. 112.
11. James Peter Geiss, "Peking under the Ming (1368–1644)" (Ph.D. diss., Princeton University, 1979), pp. 47–48.
12. Ibid., p. 172.
13. Albert Ch'an, *The Glory and Fall of the Ming Dynasty* (Norman: University of Oklahoma Press, 1982), p. 274.

14. Ibid., p. 18.

15. Geiss, "Peking under the Ming," pp. 76–77.

16. Victoria B. Cass, "Female Healers in the Ming and the Lodge of Ritual and Ceremony," *Journal of the American Oriental Society*, *Festschrift dedicated to Edward H. Schafer* 106 (March 1986): 234–36. For a variety of feminine occupations for women in Beijing, see Li Jiarui, *Beiping fengsu lei zheng* (Shanghai: Commercial Press, 1931) pp. 151–53; for treatment of Palace women pre-Ming, see Priscilla Ching Chung, *Palace Women of the Northern Sung 960–1126* (Leiden: E. J. Brill, 1981).

17. Wakeman, *The Great Enterprise*, pp. 92–97, pp. 665–66.

18. Jonathan Spence, *The Memory Palace of Matteo Ricci* (New York: Viking, 1983), p. 227.

19. Albert Ch'an, "Late Ming Society and the Jesuit Missionaries," in *East Meets West, The Jesuits in China, 1582–1773*, ed. Charles E. Ronan and Bonnie B.C. Oh (Chicago: Loyola University Press, 1988), p. 168.

20. Geiss, "Peking under the Ming," p. 105.

21. Xie Zhaozhe, *Wu za zu* (Taibei: Xinhua shuju, 1971), *juan* 8, p. 16b.

22. Chun-shu Chang and Shelley Hsüeh-lun Chang, *Crisis and Transformation in Seventeenth-Century China: Society, Culture and Modernity in Li Yü's World* (Ann Arbor: University of Michigan Press, 1992), p. 159.

23. Yu Huai, *Banqiao zaji*, in *Zhao dai cong shu*, ed. Zhang Chao (Shanghai: Shanghai guji chubanshe, 1990), p. 3149.

24. Craig Clunas, *Superfluous Things: Material Culture and Social Status in Early Modern China* (Urbana: University of Illinois Press, 1991), p. 146.

25. Qian Qianyi, *Lie chao shiji xiao zhuan* (Shanghai: Zhunghua, 1959), p. 765, describing Ma Shouzhen; Yu Huai, *Banqiao zaji*, p. 3150.

26. John Meskill, *Gentlemanly Interests and Wealth on the Yangtze Delta* (Ann Arbor, Mich.: Association for Asian Studies, no. 49, 1994), pp. 141–55.

27. Chang and Chang, *Crisis and Transformation*, p. 153.

28. Ibid., p. 2.

29. Jonathan Chaves, ed. and trans., *The Columbia Book of Later Chinese Poetry: Yüan, Ming and Ch'ing Dynasties (1279–1911)* (New York: Columbia University Press, 1986), p. 93.

30. A Ying, *Xiao shuo xian tan* (Shanghai: Gudian wenxue, 1958), p. 12.

31. Xie Zhaozhe, *Wu za zu*, *juan* 2, p. 3b.

32. Ibid., p. 90.

33. K. T. Wu, "Ming Printing and Printers," *Harvard Journal of Asiatic Studies* 7, no. 3 (1942–43): 221–26.

34. Dorothy Ko, *Teachers of the Inner Chambers: Women and Culture in Seventeenth-Century China* (Stanford, Calif.: Stanford University Press, 1994), p. 62. See also Joanna Handlin, "Lü K'un's New Audience: The Influence of Women's Literature on Sixteenth-Century Thought," in *Women in Chinese Society*, ed. Margery Wolf and Roxanne Witke (Stanford, Calif.: Stanford University Press, 1975), pp. 13–38.

35. Tan Yunxian, *Nü yi zayan* "preface," in *Lidai funü zhuzo kao*, ed. Hu Wenkai (Shanghai: Shanghai guji chubanshe, 1957), pp. 201–02.

36. Wakeman, *The Great Enterprise*, p. 139. Also see Joanna Handlin, *Action in Late Ming Thought: The Reorientation of Lü K'un and Other Scholar-Officials* (Berkeley: University of California Press, 1983); Patrick Hanan, *The Chinese Vernacular Story* (Cambridge: Harvard University Press, 1981).

37. Spence, *The Memory Palace*, pp. 96–97.

38. Patrick Hanan, "The Text of the *Chin P'ing Mei*," *Asia Major*, n. s. 9 (1962): 47.

39. Charles O. Hucker, *The Censorial System of Ming China* (Stanford, Calif.: Stanford University Press, 1966), pp. 197–224.

40. Wakeman, *The Great Enterprise*, pp. 92–108; André Levy, "Exentrisme et excentricité," and "L'Apologie du roman," in *Le Conte Chinois en langue vulgaire du XVII siècle* (Paris: Ecole Française d'Extrême-Orient, 1980), pp. 265–74 and 282–94. Also see Li Chi, *The Travel Diaries of Hsü Hsia-k'o* (Hong Kong: Hong Kong University Press, 1974), pp. 26–27, for a discussion of foreign influences on southern intellectuals.

41. Feng Menglong, *Qing shi lei lue*, "Preface," in *Guben xiao shuo jicheng*, ed. Zhou Lin et al. (Shanghai: Shanghai guji chubanshe, 1990), pp. 4b-5a.

42. Richard Wang, "The Cult of Qing: Romanticism in the Late Ming Period and the Novel *Jiao Hong Ji*," *Ming Studies* 33 (August 1994): 15–17.

43. For a few of the many discussions of *qing* and its role in late Ming art and society, see Hanan, *The Invention of Li Yu*; C. T. Hsia, "Time and the Human Condition in the Plays of T'ang Hsien-tsu," in *Self and Society in Ming Thought*, ed. William Theodore de Bary (New York: Columbia University Press, 1970), pp. 253–54; Li Hua-yuan Mowry, trans., *Chinese Love Stories from the "Ch'ing Shih"* (Hamden, Conn.: Archon, 1983); Robert Hegel, *The Novel in Seventeenth Century China* (New York: Columbia University Press, 1981); Ko, *Teachers of the Inner Chambers*, pp. 68–112; Wang, "The Cult of Qing"; Kang-i Sun Chang, *The Late Ming Poet Ch'en Tzu-lung: Crises of Love and Loyalism* (New Haven and London: Yale University Press, 1991), pp. 9–18; Chou Chih-p'ing, *Yüan Hung-tao and the Kung-an School* (New York: Columbia University Press, 1988).

44. Hung Ming-shui, "Yuan Hung-tao and the Late Ming Literary Movement," p. 49–51.

45. A. Levy, "L'Apologie du roman," pp. 282–94; John Ching-yu Wang, *Chin Sheng-t'an* (New York: Twayne, 1972).

46. Wang, *Chin Sheng-t'an*, p. 20.

47. Ibid.

48. Feng Menglong, *Qing shi lei lue*, *juan* 4, p. 36.

49. Judith Zeitlin, "Shared Dreams: The Story of the Three Wives Commentary on the Peony Pavilion," *Harvard Journal of Asiatic Studies* 54, no. 1 (1994): 127–30; see also Ko, *Teachers of the Inner Chambers*, pp. 68–78.

50. Wakeman, *The Great Enterprise*, pp. 148–49; Ko, *Teachers of the Inner Chambers*, pp. 266–78.

51. Some couples vowed fidelity by imitating wedding ceremonies, marking their promises with formal vows; there developed an expectation among the elites and geishas that a geisha of quality would marry up and marry out and find not just a husband but a husband of consequence. The official Qian Qianyi married the geisha Liu Shi, and Dong Xiaowan married the literatus Mao Xiang.

52. Yuan Hongdao, "Zui Souzhan," in *Yuan Zhonglang quanji* (Shanghai: Dafan shuju, 1935); Jonathan Chaves, trans., *Pilgrim of the Cloud: Poems and Essays from Ming China* (New York and Tokyo: Weatherhill, 1978), pp. 110–12.

53. Anna Seidel, "A Taoist Immortal of the Ming Dynasty: Chang San-feng," in *Self and Society in Ming Thought*, ed. William Theodore de Bary (New York: Columbia University Press, 1970), pp. 483–531.

54. James Cahill, *The Compelling Image, Nature and Style in Seventeenth-Century Chinese Painting* (Cambridge: Harvard University Press, 1982) p. 108.

55. James C.Y. Watt, "The Literati Environment," in *The Chinese Scholar's Studio: Artistic Life in the Late Ming Period*, ed. Chu-Tsing Li and James C.Y. Watt (New York: Thames and Hudson, 1987), p. 5.

56. A. Levy, " Excentrisme et excentricité," p. 269.

57. Geiss, "Peking under the Ming," p. 31.

58. Chang and Chang, *Crisis and Transformation*, pp. 155–58.

59. Meskill, *Gentlemanly Interests*, pp. 100–05.

60. Clunas, *Superfluous Things*, p. 181.

61. Ibid., p. 156.

62. A. Levy, "Excentrisme et excentricité," p. 270.

63. Hanan, *The Invention of Li Yu*, p. 44.

64. Watt, "The Literati Environment," p. 6.

65. Pei-yi Wu, *The Confucian's Progress: Autobiographical Writings in Traditional China* (Princeton: Princeton University Press, 1990), p. 260.

66. Watt, "The Literati Environment," p. 6.

67. Ibid.

68. Rolf A. Stein, *The World in Miniature: Container Gardens and Dwellings in Far Eastern Religious Thought*, trans. Phyllis Brooks (Stanford, Calif.: Stanford University Press, 1990), p. 114.

69. Clunas, *Superfluous Things*, passim; also see his *Fruitful Sites: Garden Culture in Ming Dynasty China* (Durham, N.C.: Duke University Press, 1996).

70. Clunas, *Superfluous Things*, pp. 34–36.

71. Stein, *The World in Miniature*, p. 29.

72. Ibid., p. 5, citing De Groot.

73. Stein, *The World in Miniature*, p. 29.

74. Ibid., p. 36.

Chapter Two. Geishas

1. Marsha Weidner, Ellen Johnston Laing, Irving Yucheng Lo, Christina Chu, and James Robinson, *Views from Jade Terrace: Chinese Women Artists, 1300–1912* (Indianapolis: Indianapolis Museum of Art; New York: Rizzoli, 1988), p. 85.

2. Yu Huai, *Ban qiao zaji*, in *Zhaodai congshu*, ed. Zhang Chao (Shanghai: Shanghai guji chubanshe, 1990), p. 3149; also in Howard Levy, *A Feast of Mist and Flowers: The Gay Quarters of Nanjing at the End of the Ming* (Yokohama: no pub., 1966), p. 52. Also see Paul S. Ropp, "Ambiguous Images of Courtesan Culture in Late Imperial China," in *Writing Women in Late Imperial China*, ed. Ellen Widmer and Kang-i Sun Chang (Stanford, Calif.: Stanford University Press, 1997), pp. 31–41.

3. Yu Huai, *Ban qiao zaji*, p. 3147.

4. Ibid., p. 3153.

5. Qian Qianyi, *Lie chao shiji xiao zhuan* (Shanghai: Zhonghua, 1959), p. 764.

6. H. Levy, *Feast of Mist and Flowers*, p. 18, citing *Chibei outan*, *juan* 12, p. 166. Another Ming writer, Zou Shu, tells of one young girl of fourteen who worked as a maid and reported to her new owners that she had been captured by bandits and sold in the marketplace. From Zhou Sun, *Shi mei ci ji*, in *Zhaodai cong shu*, ed. Zhang Chao (Shanghai: Shanghai guji chubanshe, 1991), p. 3227. Hangzhou itself was famous for its marketing of women; see Dorothy Ko, *Teachers of the Inner Chambers: Women and Culture in Seventeenth Century China* (Stanford, Calif.: Stanford University Press, 1994), p. 261.

7. Zhao Shijie, comp., *Lidai nüzi wenji* (Beijing: Saoye shan fang, 1928), *juan* 3, p. 36.

8. Qian Qianyi, *Lie chao shiji xiao zhuan*, p. 760.

9. Ko, *Teachers of the Inner Chambers*, p. 286.

10. Ibid., p. 286.

11. E. H. Schafer, "Pleasure Boats of the Tang," in "Schafer Sinological Papers"; Marsha Wagner, *The Lotus Boat: The Origins of Chinese Tz'u Poetry in T'ang Popular Culture* (New York: Columbia University Press, 1984); also see Dorothy Ko, "The Written Word and the Bound Foot: A History of the Courtesan's Aura," in *Writing Women in Late Imperial China*, ed. Ellen Widmer and Kang-i Sun Chang (Stanford, Calif.: Stanford University Press, 1997), pp. 74–100; also Zhang Zhongjiang, *Jinü yu wenxue* (Taibei: Kangnai sheng, 1971).

12. Wang Shunu, *Zhongguo changji shi* (Shanghai: Shanghai guji chubanshe, 1988), p. 234.

13. Ibid.

14. H. Levy, *Feast of Mist and Flowers*, pp. 19–20, quoting Cao Dazhang, *Qinhuai shi nü biao*.

15. H. Levy, *Feast of Mist and Flowers*, p. 19, citing the *Ming shilu*.

16. Yu Huai, *Ban qiao zaji*, p. 3151.

17. Ibid., p. 3149.

18. Zou Shu, *Shi mei ci ji*, *Zhaodai congshu*, ed. Zhang Chao (Shanghai: Guji chubanshe, 1990), p. 3227.

19. Yu Huai, *Ban qiao zaji*, p. 3148.

20. H. Levy, *Feast of Mist and Flowers*, p. 5; Richard Barnhart, *Painters of the Great Ming: The Imperial Court and the Zhe School* (Dallas: Dallas Museum of Art, 1973), p. 229. For a consideration of Western perceptions of the feminine, see Rey Chow, *Woman and Chinese Modernity: The Politics of Reading between East and West* (Minneapolis: University of Minnesota Press, 1991).

21. There is considerable literature on this shift; for a good overview, see John Meskill, "The New Temper," in *Gentlemanly Interests and Wealth on the Yangtze Delta* (Ann Arbor: Association for Asian Studies, 1994), pp. 157–74. See also C. T. Hsia, "Time and the Human Condition in the Plays of T'ang

Hsien-tsu," in *Self and Society in Ming Thought*, ed. William Theodore de Bary (New York: Columbia University Press, 1970), pp. 252–53.

22. Hung Ming-shui, "Yuan Hung-tao and the Late Ming Literary and Intellectual Movement" (Ph.D. diss., University of Wisconsin, 1974), p. 99.

23. Patrick Hanan, *The Invention of Li Yu* (Cambridge: Harvard University Press, 1981), p. 69.

24. Meskill, *Gentlemanly Interests*, p. 164; also see Nelson Wu, "Tung Ch'i-ch'ang (1555–1636): Apathy in Government and Fervor in Art," in *Confucian Personalities*, ed. Arthur Wright and Denis Twitchett (Stanford, Calif.: Stanford University Press, 1962), pp. 260–93. For a discussion of the "anomie" of the late Ming, see Chang and Chang, *Crisis and Transformation*, pp. 152–54.

25. Meskill, *Gentlemanly Interests*, p. 32. For discussions of the southern economy, see also Fu Yiling, *Mingdai Jiangnan shimin jingji shitan* (Shanghai: Shanghai renmin chubanshe, 1957), pp. 24–56, 78–100. For discussion of extravagance, see Craig Clunas, *Superfluous Things: Material Culture and Social Status in Early Modern China* (Urbana: University of Illinois Press, 1991). The government passed sumptuary laws to stymie the outlays of cash that were a function of the new luxurious living; laws prevented locals from using gold for their utensils, gold lacquer for screens, and silver and jade for vessels (Clunas, *Superfluous Things,* p. 149). One local magistrate forbade the construction of huge festival lanterns, made often with silks and embroidery, consuming hours of labor, all with the intention of being set ablaze in a holiday bonfire (p. 146). See also Ho P'ing-ti, "The Salt Merchants of Yang-chou: A Study of Commercial Capitalism in Eighteenth Century China," *Harvard Journal of Asiatic Studies* 17, no. 1–2 (1954): 130–68.

26. H. Levy, *Feast of Mist and Flowers*, p. 17, citing Yoshikawa Kojiro. Also see Willard Peterson, *Bitter Gourd: Fang I-chih and the Impetus for Intellectual Change* (New Haven and London: Yale University Press, 1979).

27. Andre Levy, "Excentrisme et excentricité," in *Le Conte chinois en la langue vulgaire du XVII siècle* (Paris: L'Ecole Française d'Extrême en Orient, 1980), p. 269.

28. Ibid., p. 269.

29. Richard Wang, "The Cult of Qing: Romanticism in the Late Ming Period and in the Novel *Jiao Hong Ji*," *Ming Studies* 33 (August 1994): 23.

30. Feng Menglong, *Qing shi lei lue*, juan 4, p. 3b.

31. Ibid.

32. Ibid.

33. Michael Holquist, "How to play Utopia. Some brief notes on the distinctiveness of utopian fiction," in *Game, Play, Literature, Yale French Studies*, no. 41(1968): 112.

34. Ibid.

35. Ibid.

36. Feng Menglong, *Qing shi lei lue*, juan 4, pp. 3b–4a. Feng is here exploiting a paranomastic gloss from the Han.

37. Yu Huai, *Ban qiao zaji*, p. 3148.

38. Ibid.

39. Mao P'i-chiang (Mao Xiang), *The Reminiscences of Tung Hsiao-wan*, trans. Pan Tze-yen (Shanghai: Commercial Press, 1931), p. 31.

40. Mao Xiang, *Yingmu an yiyu*, in *Zhaodai cong shu*, ed. Zhang Chao (Shanghai: Shanghai guji chubanshe, 1990), p. 3234.

41. Ibid.

42. Feng Menglong, *Qing shi lei lue*, juan 4, pp. 3b–4a.

43. Peterson, *Bitter Gourd*, pp. 133–45.

44. Yu Huai, *Ban qiao zaji*, p. 3150.

45. Mao P'i-chiang, *Reminiscences of Tung Hsiao-wan*, p. 49.

46. James Cahill, "The Three Zhangs, Yangzhou Beauties, and the Manchu Court," *Orientations* (October 1996): 60. Also see Wu Hung, "Beyond Stereotypes: The Twelve Beauties in Qing Court Art and *The Dream of the Red Chamber*," in *Writing Women in Late Imperial China*, ed. Ellen Widmer and Kang-i Sun Chang (Stanford, Calif.: Stanford University Press, 1997).

47. Yu Huai, *Ban qiao zaji*, p. 3149.

48. Allan H. Barr, "The Wanli Context of the Du Shiniang Story," *Harvard Journal of Asiatic Studies* 57, no. 1 (June 1997), pp. 107–41. Professor Barr discusses several texts treating the geisha, espe-

cially Song Maocheng's *Jiuyueji* and Pan Zhiheng's *Geng shi*, as well as the several texts detailing the story of the geisha Bai Huan (see pp. 123–24). Irving Yucheng Lo, in "Daughters of the Muses in China," in *Views from Jade Terrace: Chinese Women Artists, 1300–1912*, ed. Marsha Weidner et al., refers to a compendia of works on the geisha, p. 39, n.46.

49. Mao Xiang, p. 3235.

50. Rolf Alfred Stein, *The World in Miniature: Container Gardens and Dwellings in Far Eastern Religious Thought*, trans. Phyllis Brooks (Stanford, Calif.: Stanford University Press, 1990), p. 91.

51. Cass, "Celebrations at the Gate of Death," pp. 28–43.

52. Yu Huai, *Ban qiao zaji*, p. 3150.

53. Ibid.

54. Chen Yinke, *Liu Rushi biezhuan* (Shanghai: Shanghai guji chubanshe, 1980), vol. 2, p. 469.

55. Yu Huai, *Ban qiao zaji*, p. 3149.

56. Kang-i Sun Chang, *The Late Ming Poet Ch'en Tzu-lung: Crises of Love and Loyalism* (New Haven: Yale University Press, 1991), p. 22.

57. Lo, "Daughters of the Muses," p. 43.

58. Yu Huai, *Ban qiao zaji*, p. 3149.

59. Weidner et al., *Views from Jade Terrace*, "Catalogue," "Xue Susu," p. 84, n. 2.

60. Lo, "Daughters of the Muses," p. 43.

61. Mao Xiang, *Xing mei an yuyi*, p. 3233.

62. Weidner et al., *Views from Jade Terrace*, "Catalogue," "Dong Bai," p. 99.

63. Wai-yee Li, "The Late Ming Courtesan: Invention of a Cultural Ideal," in *Writing Women in Late Imperial China*, p. 70.

64. Chen Yinke, *Liu Rushi bie zhuan*, p. 468.

65. Qian Qianyi, *Lie chao shiji zhuan* (Shanghai: Zhonghua, 1959). p. 746; Yu Huai, *Yingmei an yuyi*, p. 3149.

66. Yu Huai, *Yingmei an yuyi*, p. 3152.

67. Li Jiarui, *Beiping fengsu lei zheng* (Shanghai: Commercial Press, 1931), p. 396.

68. Li, "The Late Ming Courtesan," p. 61.

69. Ibid., pp. 61–63.

70. Yu Huai, *Ban qiao zaji*, p. 3152.

71. Feng Menglong, *Qing shi lei lue*, juan 4, p. 1a.

72. Ibid.

73. Mao Xiang, *Ying mei an yuyi*, p. 3233.

74. Barr, "The Wanli Context," pp. 135–36.

75. Li, "The Late Ming Courtesan," pp. 59–61.

76. Qian Qianyi, *Lie chao zhiji xiaozhuan*, pp. 763–64.

77. Li, "The Late Ming Courtesan," pp. 62–64. Ko, *Teachers of the Inner Chambers*, p. 281. Qian Qianyi describes a geisha who married a knight errant (*Liechao shiji xiao zhuan*, p. 759).

78. Tseng Yü-ho, "Hüeh Wu and Her Orchids in the Collection of the Honolulu Academy of Arts," *Arts Asiatiques* 2, no. 3 (1955): 205–7.

79. Ibid., pp. 197–98.

80. Yu Jianhua, *Zhong guo meishujia renming cidian* (Shanghai: Renmin meishu chubanshe, 1981), cited in Weidner et al., *Views from Jade Terrace*, "Catalogue," "Xue Susu," p. 82.

81. Qian Qianyi, *Lie chao shiji xiao zhuan*, p. 770.

82. Barr, "The Wanli Context," p. 122.

83. Qian Qianyi, *Lie chao shiji xiao zhuan*, p. 770.

84. Ibid.

85. See especially Ko, *Teachers of the Inner Chambers*, pp. 59–65.

86. James Cahill, "The Painting of Liu Yin," in *Flowering in the Shadows: Women in the History of Chinese and Japanese Painting*, ed. Marsha Weidner (Honolulu: University of Hawaii Press, 1990). pp. 103–22. Also see Kang-i Sun Chang, "Ming and Qing Anthologies of Women's Poetry and Their Selection Strategies," in *Writing Women in Late Imperial China*, pp. 154–55.

87. Chen Yinke, *Lin Rushi bie zhuan*, pp. 343–44.

88. Ibid., p. 344.

89. Ibid., p. 69.

90. Ibid., p. 35.

91. Chen Zilong helped publish her first collection of poetry, and Wang helped publish her "Notes and Poems." *Zhou zheng yuan gao* (Suzhou, 1986) p. 3.

92. Weidner, et al., *Views from Jade Terrace*, "Catalogue," "Liu Shi (Yin)," pp. 99–100.

93. Also see Chang, *The Late-Ming Poet Ch'en Tzu-lung*, pp. 19–40; Ko, *Teachers of the Inner Chambers*, pp. 274–78.

94. Chen Yinke discusses the travel of women, especially geishas, *Liu Rushi bie zhuan*, p. 470.

95. Ibid., p. 458.

96. Ibid., p. 462.

97. Ibid., p. 445.

98. Ibid., p. 471.

99. Ko, *Teachers of the Inner Chambers*, p. 284.

100. Chen Yinke, *Liu Rushi bie zhuan*, p. 471.

101. Ibid., pp. 60–61.

102. Ibid., pp. 81–82.

103. Ibid., p. 434.

104. Chen Yinke, *Liu Rushi bie zhuan*, pp. 433–40.

105. Ibid., pp. 434.

106. Ibid., p. 437.

107. Ibid., p. 438.

108. Yu Huai, *Ban qiao zaji*, p. 3149.

Chapter Three. Grannies

1. Maxine Hong Kingston, *The Woman Warrior: Memoirs of a Girlhood Among Ghosts* (New York: Knopf, 1977), p. 67.

2. *Jin Ping Mei, juan* 12, p. 18b.

3. Shen Bang, *Wanshu zaji* (Taibei: Guting shushi, 1960).

4. Xie Zhaozhe, *Wu za zu*, (Taibei: Xinhua, 1971), p. 31b.

5. E. H. Schafer, "Ritual Exposure in Ancient China," *Harvard Journal of Asiatic Studies* (1951): 130–84. For discussions of gender, ideology, and especially of the notions of power and danger, see Charlotte Furth, "Concepts of Pregnancy, Childbirth, and Infancy in Ch'ing Dynasty China," *Journal of Asian Studies* 46 (February 1987): 7–35; Emily Ahern, "The Power and Pollution of Chinese Women," in *Studies in Chinese Society*, ed. Arthur Wolf (Stanford, Calif.: Stanford University Press, 1978), pp. 269–90. Also see Mary C. Douglas, *Purity and Danger: An Analysis of Concepts of Pollution and Taboo* (New York: Praeger, 1966); and Karen Paige and Jeffrey Paige, *The Politics of Reproductive Ritual* (Berkeley: University of California Press, 1981); for the theme of the gossip see Marina Warner, *From the Beast to the Blond*, (New York: Farrar, 1984).

6. Schafer, "Ritual Exposure," pp. 160–64.

7. E. H. Schafer, *The Divine Woman: Dragon Ladies and Rain Maidens in T'ang Literature* (Berkeley: University of California Press, 1973), pp. 12–19.

8. Schafer, "Ritual Exposure," p. 137.

9. Michael Loewe, *Chinese Ideas of Life and Death: Faith, Myth and Reason in the Han Period (202 B.C.–A.D. 220)* (London: George Allen and Unwin, 1982), p. 106.

10. Schafer, "Ritual Exposure," p. 150.

11. Xie Zhaozhe, *Wu za zu, juan* 6, p. 31b.

12. Huang Liuhong, *A Complete Book Concerning Happiness and Benevolence: A Manual for Local Magistrates in Seventeenth Century China*, trans. Djang Chu (Tucson: University of Arizona Press, 1984), p. 609.

13. *Da Ming huidian*, ed. Shen Shixing (Taibei: Dongnan shu baoshe, 1963), "libu," *juan* 71, section 29, pp. 1a–5a.

14. Victoria B. Cass, "Female Healers in the Ming and the Lodge of Ritual and Ceremony," *Journal of the American Oriental Society* 106 (March 1986): 240. For treatments of female healers, see Angela Leung, "Autour de la naissance; la mère et l'enfant en Chine aux XVI et XVII siècles," *Cahiers Internationaux du Sociologie* (1984): 51–69.

15. Xie Zhaozhe, *Wu za zu, juan* 5, pp. 10a–b.

16. Shen Bang, *Wanshu zaji*, pp. 74–76.

17. Ibid., p. 74.

18. Ibid., p. 76.

19. Ibid., p. 75.

20. Ibid.

21. Ibid.

22. Ibid.

23. Ibid., p. 74.

24. Another powerful wet-nurse of the Palace kept her own son with her in the Palace. Woman Lu was wet-nurse to Emperor Shi Zong. Her son, Lu Bing (1510–1560), rescued the young prince, Shi Zong (1522–1566), from the Palace during a fire. Lu Bing eventually served as Commissioner in Chief of the Embroidered Uniform Guard. *Ming Shi* (Beijing: Zhonghua, 1974), p. 307; also mentioned in Jiao Hong, *Xian zheng lu* (Shanghai: Shanghai shudian, 1986), *juan* 109, pp. 11a–14a.

25. Yao Guangxiao, ed., *Ming Shi lu* (Beijing: Academia Sinica, 1940), "Xi zong," *juan* 10, p. 2b. For additional sources on Wet-nurse Ke, see Ulrich Hans-Richel Mammitzsh, "Wei Chung-hsien (1568–1628): A Reappraisal of the Eunuch and the Factional at the Late Ming Court" (Ph.D. diss., University of Hawaii, 1968); Wang Chunyu and Du Wanyan, *Ming chao huanguan* (Beijing: Ci Jincheng chubanshe, 1989); Liu Royu, *Zho zhong zhi, juan* 14 (*Congshu jicheng*) (Shanghai: Commercial Press, 1937); Gu Yingtai, *Ming shi jishi benmo, juan* 71 (*Siku quan shu*) (Taibei: Taiwan shangwu yinshuguan, 1983); Frederic Wakeman, Jr., *The Great Enterprise: The Manchu Reconstruction of Imperial Order in Seventeenth-Century China*. 2 vols. (Berkeley: University of California Press, 1985), pp. 89–90, 356n.

26. Charles Hucker, *The Censorial System of Ming China* (Stanford, Calif.: Stanford University Press, 1966), p. 210.

27. Ibid.

28. Shen Bang, *Wanshu zaji*, p. 76.

29. Loewe, *Chinese Ideas of Life and Death*, p. 110.

30. Shen Bang, *Wanshu zaji*, p. 74.

31. Ibid.

32. Shen Defu, *Wanli ye hu bian* (Beijing: Zhonghua, 1959), pp. 1576–1577.

33. Shen Bang, *Wanshu zaji*, p. 74.

34. *Jin Ping Mei ci hua* (Hong Kong: Taipingshuju, 1982), *juan* 2, p. 7a.

35. Ibid.

36. Feng Menglong, "Jiang Xingge chong hui zhen zhu shan," *Gu jin xiao shuo* (Beijing: Renmin wenxue, 1958), *juan* 1, pp. 18–19.

37. Feng Menglong, *Shan ge* (Beijing: Guan de dong, 1962), *juan* 5, p. 40.

38. Ibid., *juan* 7, p. 56.

39. *Jin Ping Mei, juan* 2, pp. 7b–8a.

40. Ibid., p. 81.

41. Robert M. Torrance, *The Comic Hero* (Cambridge: Harvard University Press, 1978), pp. 12–17.

42. Ibid., p. 150.

43. Feng Menglong, "Maiyou lang du zhan hua kui," *Xing shi heng yan* (Hong Kong: Zhonghua, 1983), *juan* 3, p. 39.

44. *Jin Ping mei, juan* 2, p. 9a.

45. Ibid.

46. Feng Menglong, "Maiyou lang du zhan hua kui," p. 38.

47. *Jin Ping Mei, juan* 2, p. 9b.

48. Jean Mulligan, trans., *The Lute, Kao Ming's P'i-p'a chi* (New York: Columbia University Press, 1980), p. 45.

49. Ibid.

50. Northrop Frye, *Anatomy of Criticism: Four Essays* (Princeton: Princeton University Press, 1957), p. 173.

51. Ibid.

52. Maria Kotzimanidou, "A Study of the Go-Between in Arabic and Spanish Literature," University of California, Berkeley, Comparative Literature Seminar, manuscript, p. 13. See also G. Ruggiero, *The Evolution of the Go-Between in Spanish Literature Through the Sixteenth Century* (Berkeley: University of California Press, 1966).

53. Bang Yuanying, *Wen chang zalu*, Si bu bei yao edition (Shanghai: Commercial Press, 1936), p. 20.

Chapter Four. Warriors and Mystics

1. Suzanne Cahill, *Transendence and Divine Passion: The Queen Mother of the West in Medieval China* (Stanford, Calif.: Stanford University Press, 1993), p. 50.

2. *Feng Shen yanyi* (Shanghai: Commercial Press, 1937), *juan* 53, p. 505.

3. Ling Mengchu *Chu ke pai'an jingqi* (Xining: Quehai renmin chubanshe, 1984), *juan* 4.

4. Brigitte Berthier, *La Dame du-bord-de-l'eau* (Nanterre: Société d'Ethnologie, 1988), pp. 31–32.

5. Ann Waltner, "T'an-yang-tzu and Wang Shih-chen: Visionary and Bureaucrat in the Late Ming," *Late Imperial China* 8, no. 1 (June 1987): 113. For discussion of visionaries, Daniel L. Overmeyer, *Folk Buddhist Religion: Dissenting Sects in Late Traditional China* (Cambridge: Harvard University Press, 1976); Susan Naquin, "The Transmission of White Lotus Sectarianism in Late Imperial China," in *Popular Culture in Late Imperial China*, ed. David Johnson, Andrew J. Nathan, and Evelyn S. Rawski (Berkeley: University of California Press, 1985), pp. 255–91; Beata Grant, "Female Holder of the Lineage: Lingji Chan Master Zhi yuan Xianggang (1579–1654)," *Late Imperial China* 17, no. 2 (December 1996): 51–76; Yu Songqing, *Nankai: xue bao* 5 (1982), pp. 31–32.

6. Waltner, "T'an-yang-tzu and Wang Shih-chen," p. 116.

7. Xie Zhaozhe, *Wu za zu* (Taibei: Xinhua shuju, 1971), *juan* 8, p. 43b.

8. Wang Jianzhang (1708–1778), *Liedai xianshi* (Changshu baofangke, 1881), *juan* 8, p. 53b.

9. Ibid.

10. Ibid.

11. Hung Ming-shui, "Yuan Hung-tao and the Late Ming Literary and Intellectual Movement" (Ph.D. diss., University of Wisconsin, 1974), p. 209.

12. Albert Ch'an, *The Glory and Fall of the Ming Dynasty* (Norman: University of Oklahoma Press, 1982), pp. 272–73.

13. Shen Bang, *Wanshu zaji* (Taibei: Guting shushi, 1960), p. 203.

14. Ibid., p. 195.

15. Shen Defu, *Wanli ye hu bian* (Beijing: Zhong hua, 1959), p. 1858; and in Wang Jianzhang, *Liedai xianshi*, *juan* 8, pp. 51a–b.

16. Liu Tong, *Di Jing jingwu lue* (Shanghai: Gudian wenxue, 1957), pp. 89–90; Shen Bang, *Wanshu zaji*, pp. 164, 171, 182.

17. Shen Bang, *Wanshu zaji*, p. 182.

18. Ibid.

19. Liu Tong, *Di Jing jingwu lue*, p. 90.

20. Xie Zhaozhe, *Wu za zu*, *juan* 11, p. 25a.

21. "Hui Zhen Ni," in *Gujin tushu jicheng*, ed. Chen Menglei and Jiang Tingxi (Taibei: Wen xing shudian, 1964), "Shen yi dian," *juan* 205, "Nuns," 2, p. 2106.

22. Sun Shi, *Gujin tushu jicheng*, "Shen yi dian," *juan* 258, "Transcendents," p. 2588.

23. James Geiss, "Peking under the Ming (1368–1644)" (Ph.D. diss., Princeton University, 1979), p. 194.

24. Albert Ch'an, *The Glory and Fall of the Ming Dynasty*, p. 272.

25. Ibid., p. 80.

26. Ibid., p. 272.

27. Waltner, "T'an-yang-tzu and Wang Shih-chen," p. 109.

28. Xie Zhaozhe, *Wu za zu, juan* 8, p. 43a.

29. *Ming shi*, ed. Zhang Tingyu (Beijing: Zhonghua shuju, 1974), *juan* 154, p. 17b; *juan* 175, p. 1a.

30. Hong Mai, *Yi jian zhi* (Taibei: Ming wen shuju, 1982), pp. 1544–45.

31. Ibid., p. 1545.

32. Ibid.

33. Ibid.

34. "Liu fu ren," *Hu guang tong zhi*, Siku quan shu, vol. 533, p. 2572.

35. Ibid., p. 17b.

36. Ibid., p. 18a.

37. Ibid.

38. Ibid.

39. Ibid., p. 18b.

40. Ibid.

41. Shen Bang, *Wanshu zaji*, p. 207.

42. Ibid., p. 206.

43. Ibid., p. 214.

44. See Suzanne Cahill, *Transcendence and Divine Passion: The Queen Mother of the West in Medieval China* (Stanford, Calif.: Stanford University Press, 1993), pp. 32–43; E. H. Schafer, *Pacing the Void: T'ang Approaches to the Stars* (Berkeley: University of California Press, 1977); Isabel Robinet, *Meditation taoïste* (Paris: Dervy Livres, 1977); Kristofer M. Schipper, "The Taoist Body," *History of Religions* 17, nos. 3 and 4 (1978); Catherine Despeaux, "L'Ordination des femmes Taoïstes sous les T'ang," *Études chinoises* 5, nos. 1–2 (1986): 57–100.

45. Schafer, *Pacing the Void*, p. 241. Also discussed in Isabel Robinet, "Randonnés extatiques des taoïstes dans les astres," *Monumenta Serica* 32 (1976): 159–62. Also see her *Meditation taoïste*.

46. Ibid.

47. Waltner, "T'an-yang-tzu and Wang Shih-chen," p. 115.

48. Ibid., p. 15.

49. Ibid.

50. Hou Ching-lang, "The Chinese Belief in Baleful Stars," in *Facets of Taoism*, ed. Holmes Welch and Anna Seidel (New Haven and London: Yale University Press, 1979), pp. 193–228; on p. 201, Hou treats a handbook used by sorcerers and mediums. See also the discussion of spirit-medium texts published in Taiwan in 1981 and 1984, based on seances at temples in Taizhong, in Gary Seaman, *The Journey to the North: An Ethnographical Analysis and Annotated Translation of the Chinese Folk Novel "Pei-yu-chi"* (Berkeley: University of California Press, 1984), pp. 12–23; Seaman cites Anthony Yu's discussion of the two texts in Yu's *Journey to the West*, vol. 1 (Chicago: University of Chicago Press, 1977), pp. 13–14. See also Jack Potter, "Cantonese Shamanism," in *Religion and Ritual in Chinese Society*, ed. Arthur P. Wolf (Stanford, Calif.: Stanford University Press, 1974), pp. 210–12 and David Hawkes, "The Quest of the Goddess," in *Studies in Chinese Literary Genres*, ed. Cyril Birch (Berkeley: University of California Press, 1974), pp. 42–68.

51. *Shan hai jing xiao zhu*, ed. Yuan Ke (Chengdu: Bashu shushe, 1993), *juan* 1, pp. 4–5.

52. For treatment of the journey in a variety of folklores, see Lois Fusek, "The Kao T'ang Fu," *Monumenta Serica* 30 (1972–73): 392–425. There is an extensive literature on sacred mountains and mountain travel; see, for example, Terry F. Kleeman, "Mountain Deities in China: The Domestication of the Mountain God and the Subjugation of the Margins," *Journal of the American Oriental Society* 114, no. 2 (April–June 1994): 226–38; and Michel Soymie, *Le Lo-Feou Chan, étude de geographie religieuse* (Paris: École Française d'Extrême-Orient, 1956).

53. Rolf A. Stein, *The World in Miniature: Container Gardens and Dwellings in Far Eastern Religious Thought*, trans. Phyllis Brooks (Stanford, Calif.: Stanford University Press, 1990), pp. 106–11.

54. Ling Mengchu, *Chuke pai an jing qi, juan* 4, "Cheng Yuanyu dian lu dai changqian; Shiyi Niang yun fengcong tanxia." See also Shen Defu, *Wanli ye hu bian, juan* 28, pp. 1858–1860, for treatment of women warriors.

55. Ling Mengchu, *Chuke pai an jing qi*, p. 75.

56. Ibid., p. 72.

57. Ibid., p. 74.

58. Ibid.

59. Ibid.

60. Ibid., pp. 74–75.

61. James J.Y. Liu, *The Chinese Knight Errant* (Chicago: University of Chicago Press, 1967); C. T. Hsia, "The Military Romance," in *Studies in Chinese Literary Genres*, ed. Cyril Birch (Berkeley: University of California, 1974), pp. 339–90.

62. Wu Youru, *Wu Youru huabao* (Shanghai: Shanghai guji shudian, 1983), citing the *Ming shi*, *ji* 2a, p. 25b.

63. Peng Pai, *Zhongguo lidai nüjie* (Taizhong: Xueren wenhua, 1980), pp. 8–14, 257–316.

64. Lü Xiong, *Nüxian waishi* (Shanghai: Shanghai guji chubanshe, 1991).

65. André Levy, "Le serpent blanc en Chine et au Japon, excursions à travers les variations d'un thème," in *Études sur le conte et le roman chinois* (Paris: École Française d'Extrême-Orient, 1971), pp. 101–06.

66. Roxanne Witke, "The Transformation of Attitudes Towards Women During the May Fourth Era of Modern China" (Ph.D. diss., University of California, Berkeley, 1970), pp. 54–57.

67. Wu Youru, *Wu Youru huabao*, *ji* 9b, p. 2b.

68. Ibid., *ji* 11b, p. 15a.

Chapter Five. Predators

1. Gore Vidal, "Sex and the Law," in *Reflections from a Sinking Ship* (Boston: Little, Brown, 1969), p. 109.

2. *Jin Ping Mei cihua* (Hong Kong: Taiping Shuju, 1982), *juan* 1, pp. 2a–3b.

3. Tadao Sakai, "Confucianism and Popular Educational Works," in *Self and Society in Ming Thought*, ed. William Theodore de Bary (New York: Columbia University Press, 1970), pp. 352–60. See also Cynthia Brokaw, *The Ledgers of Merit and Demerit: Social Change and Moral Order in Late Imperial China* (Princeton: Princeton University Press, 1991).

4. Feng Menglong, "Jiang Xingge chonghui zhen zhu shan," in *Gu jin xiaoshuo* (Beijing: Renmin wenxue, 1958), *juan* 1, p. 1.

5. "Family Instructions," trans. Clara Yu, in *Chinese Civilization and Society: A Sourcebook*, ed. Patricia Buckley Ebrey (New York and London: Free Press, 1981), p. 164.

6. Feng Menglong, "Ji Yafan jin man chanhuo," in *Jing shi tongyan* (Hong Kong: Zhonghua shuju, 1963), *juan* 20, pp. 261–72.

7. Ibid., p. 263.

8. Lang Ying, *Qi xiu lei gao* (Beijing: Zhonghua, 1961), *juan* 48, pp. 705–06. Also see Wang Mao, *Ye ke congshu* (Shanghai: Shanghai guji chubanshe, 1939), *juan* 6, p. 6a.

9. Xie Zhaozhe (Taibei: Xunhua shuju, 1971), *juan* 5, pp. 15b–16a.

10. Ibid., pp. 17b–18a.

11. Ibid.

12. Lu Rong, *Shu yuan za ji* (Cong shu jicheng. Shanghai: Commercial Press, 1937), *juan* 7, pp. 11a–b.

13. Ibid.

14. For discussion of fox-fairy stories, see Judith Zeitlin, *Historian of the Strange: Pu Songling and the Chinese Classical Tale* (Stanford, Calif.: Stanford University Press, 1993); Allan Barr, "The Disarming Intruders: Alien Women in *Liaozhai zhiyi*," paper presented at the Association for Asian Studies Annual Meeting, panel on Gender Dynamics in Seventeenth Century Fiction and Drama, Boston, 1987. Also see Allan Barr, "A Comparative Study of Early and Late Tales in *Liaozhai zhiyi*," *Harvard Journal of Asiatic Studies* 45, no. 1 (June 1985): 157–202.

15. Lang Ying, *Qi xiu lei gao, juan* 49, pp. 717–18.

16. Hung Ming-shui, "Yuan Hung-tao and the Late Ming Literary and Intellectual Movement" (Ph.D. diss., University of Wisconsin, 1974), pp. 34–35.

17. Lang Ying, *Qi xiu lei gao*, pp. 718.

18. Xie Zhaozhe, *Wu zu zu* (Taibei: Xinhua shuju, 1971), *juan* 8, p. 1a.

19. Ibid.

20. Qu You, "Mudan deng ji," in *Qian deng xin hua* (Shanghai: Shanghai gudian wenxue, 1957), p. 52.

21. Ibid.

22. Wang Kentang, *Zheng zhi zhun sheng* (Taibei: Hai hong bao chai, 1974), *juan* 11, pp. 16b–18a. For discussion of the configuration of the feminine in medical texts, see Charlotte Furth, "Blood, Body, and Gender: Medical Images of the Female Condition in China, 1600–1850," *Chinese Science* 7 (1986): 43–66.

23. Wang Kentang, *Zheng zhi zhun sheng, juan* 1, p. 12a.

24. Ibid.

25. Ibid., pp. 1a–b.

26. Lu Rong, *Shu yuan zaji, juan* 7, p. 11a–b.

27. *Jin Ping Mei, juan* 1, pp. 2b–3a. Also see for discussion Victoria B. Cass, "Celebrations at the Gate of Death: Symbol and Structure in *Jin Ping Mei*" (Ph.D. diss., University of California, Berkeley, 1979), pp. 130–43.

28. Ibid., p. 10b.

29. William Patrick Day, *In the Circles of Fear and Desire, A Study of Gothic Fantasy* (Chicago: University of Chicago Press, 1985), pp. 1–11.

30. Kingston, *The Woman Warrior*, p. 14.

31. Feng Menglong, "He Daqing yi hen yuanyang tiao," in *Xing shi heng yan*, p. 299.

32. Tan Zhengbi, *San Yan Liang Pai ziliao* (Shanghai: Shanghai guji chubanshe, 1980), p. 338. Also discussed in André Levy, "Le Serpent Blanc en Chine et au Japon," in *Études sur le conte et le roman chinois* (Paris: École Française d'Extrême-Orient, 1971), pp. 97–113.

33. Tan Zhengbi, *San Yan Liang Pai ziliao*, p. 338.

34. Emily Ahern, "The Power and Pollution of Chinese Women," in *Studies in Chinese Society*, ed. Arthur Wolf (Stanford, Calif.: Stanford University Press, 1978), pp. 269–90.

35. Mary C. Douglas, *Purity and Danger: An Analysis of Concepts of Pollution and Taboos* (New York: Praeger, 1966), pp. 4–14.

Chapter Six. Recluses and Malcontents

1. Henry David Thoreau, *Walden* (New York: Thomas Y. Crowell, 1961), p. 11.

2. Charles Baudelaire, "Mon coeur mis à nu," in *Journeaux intimes*, vol. 21 (Paris: Librairie Jose Corti, 1949), verse 36, p. 74; also in Bruce Chatwin, *The Songlines* (New York: Viking, 1987).

3. Thoreau, *Walden*, p. 6.

4. Teresa de Lauretis, "Desire in Narrative," in *Alice Doesn't: Feminism, Semiotics, Cinema* (Bloomington: University of Indiana Press, 1984), pp. 103–57.

5. Feng Menglong, *Qing shi lei lue, juan* 21, pp. 29a–31b. Li Hua-yuan Mowry has translated this story in *Chinese Love Stories from the "Ch'ing-shih"* (Hamden, Conn.: Archon, 1983), pp. 136–39.

6. Ibid., p. 29a.

7. Ibid., p. 30a.

8. Ibid., p. 30b.

9. Ibid.

10. Ibid.

11. Ibid., p. 31b.

12. *Lidai nüzi shiji*, ed. Zhao Shijie and Zhu Xi (Taibei: Kuangwen, 1972), *juan* 7, p. 9b.

13. *Lidai funü zhuzuo kao*, ed. Hu Wenkai (Shanghai: Shanghai guji chubanshe, 1985), p. 204.

14. Hu Wenkai, *Lidai funü zhuzuo kao*, pp. 169–70.

15. Zhao Shijie and Zhu Xi, *Lidai nüzi shiji*, *juan* 7, p. 9b.

16. Hu Wenkai, *Lidai funü zhuzuo kao*, p. 105.

17. Ibid., p. 104.

18. Ibid., p. 113.

19. Ibid., pp. 177–78.

20. Zhao Shijie and Zhu Xi, *Lidai nüzi shiji*, *juan* 4, p. 11a.

21. Maureen Robertson, "Voicing the Feminine: Constructions of the Gendered Subject in Lyric Poetry by Women of Medieval and Late Imperial China," *Late Imperial China* 13, no. 1 (June 1992): 88.

22. Zhao Shijie and Zhu Xi, *Lidai nüzi shiji*, *juan* 7, p. 9b.

23. Ibid., *juan* 4, p. 9b.

24. Kingston, *The Woman Warrior*, p. 17.

25. Zhao Shijie and Zhu Xi, *Lidai nüzi shiji*, *juan* 6, p. 8a.

26. Ibid., *juan* 8, p. 14a.

27. Thoreau, *Walden*, p. 4.

28. *Chongqing fu zhi*, cited in *Gujin tushu jicheng*, "Jia yuan dian," *ci* 421, *juan* 344, "Ming Lun," p. 3406.

29. Li Hua-yuan Mowry, trans., "The Woman at the Posthouse," in *Love Stories from "Ch'ing-shih"* (Hamden, Conn.: Archon, 1983), pp. 107–8.

30. Dorothy Ko, *Teachers of the Inner Chambers: Women and Culture in Seventeenth Century China* (Stanford, Calif.: Stanford University Press, 1994), pp. 106–10.

31. Xie Zhaozhe, *Wu za zu*, *juan* 8, p. 14a.

32. Ibid., p. 8a.

33. Yenna Wu, *The Chinese Virago: A Literary Theme* (Cambridge and London: Harvard University Press, Council on East Asian Studies, 1995), p. 119.

34. Xie Zhaozhe, *Wu za zu*, *juan* 8, p. 8a.

35. Ibid.

36. Wu, *The Chinese Virago*, p. 119.

37. Xie Zhaozhe, *Wu za zu*, *juan* 8, p. 13a.

38. Feng Menglong, *Xiaofu*, cited in Lu Yunzhong, *Zhongguo lidai xiaohua yi bai pian* (Hong Kong: Commercial Press, 1985), p. 88.

39. Lu Yunzhong, *Zhongguo lidai xiaohua*, pp. 72, 76.

40. Xie Zhaozhe, *Wu za zu*, *juan* 8, pp. 9a–b.

Chapter Seven. Conclusion

1. Feng Menglong, *Xiao fu*, *juan* 9, p. 1b.

2. Wang Qimo, *Quan Ming zhong yi biezhuan* (Suzhou: Guanglu guji chubanshe, 1991), *juan* 30, p. 4b.

3. Ibid., p. 5a.

4. See, for example, Glen Dudbridge, *The Legend of Miao Shan* (London: Ithaca Press, 1978).

5. Feng Menglong, "Bai Niang Zi yong zhen Leifeng Ta," *Jing shi tongyan* (Hong Kong: Zhonghua shuju, 1983), *juan* 28.

6. Ibid., p. 431.

7. Ibid., p. 447.

Bibliography of English Sources

Adams, Henry. *The Education of Henry Adams, an Autobiography*. New York: Time Books, 1964.

Ahern, Emily. "The Power and Pollution of Chinese Women." In *Studies in Chinese Society*, edited by Arthur Wolf, 269–90. Stanford, Calif.: Stanford University Press, 1978.

Armstrong, Nancy. *Desire and Domestic Fiction: A Political History of the Novel*. New York: Oxford University Press, 1987.

Bakhtin, M. M., and Michael Holquist. *The Dialogic Imagination: Four Essays*. Austin: University of Texas Press, 1981.

Barnhart, Richard. *Painters of the Great Ming: The Imperial Court and the Zhe School*. Dallas: Dallas Museum of Art, 1993.

Barr, Allan H. "A Comparative Study of Early and Late Tales in *Liaozhai zhiyi*." *Harvard Journal of Asiatic Studies* 45, no. 1 (June 1985): 157–202.

———. "The Disarming Intruders: Alien Women in *Liaozhai zhiyi*." Paper presented at the Association for Asian Studies Annual Meeting, panel on Gender Dynamics in Seventeenth Century Fiction and Drama, Boston, 1987.

———."The Wanli Context of the Du Shiniang Story." *Harvard Journal of Asiatic Studies* 57, no. 1 (June 1997): 107–41.

Baudelaire, Charles. *Journeaux intimes*. Paris: Librairie Jose Corti, 1949.

Berthier, Brigitte. *La Dame-du-bord-de-l'eau*. Nanterre: Société d'ethnologie, 1988.

Boodberg, Peter A. *Selected Works of Peter A. Boodberg*. Edited by Alvin P. Cohen. Berkeley: University of California Press, 1979.

Brokaw, Cynthia. *The Ledgers of Merit and Demerit: Social Change and Moral Order in Late Imperial China*. Princeton: Princeton University Press, 1991.

Bynum, Caroline Walker. *Holy Feast and Holy Fast: The Religious Significance of Food to Medieval Women*. Berkeley: University of California Press, 1987.

Cahill, James. *The Compelling Image: Nature and Style in Seventeenth-Century Chinese Painting*. Cambridge: Harvard University Press, 1982.

———. "The Painting of Liu Yin." In *Flowering in the Shadows: Women in the History of Chinese and Japanese Painting*, edited by Marsha Weidner, 103–22. Honolulu: University of Hawaii Press, 1990.

———. "The Three Zhangs, Yangzhou Beauties, and the Manchu Court." *Orientations* (October 1996): 59–68.

Cahill, Suzanne. "Performers and Female Taoist Adepts: Hsi Wang Mu as the Patron Saint of Women in Medieval China." *Journal of the Oriental American Society* 106 (1986): 155–68.

———. *Transcendence and Divine Passion: The Queen Mother of the West in Medieval China*. Stanford, Calif.: Stanford University Press, 1993.

Carlitz, Katherine. "Shrines, Governing-Class Identity, and the Cult of Widow Fidelity in Mid-Ming Jiangnan." *Journal of Asian Studies* 56, no. 3 (August 1997): 612–40.

———. "The Social Uses of Female Virtues in Late Ming Editions of *Lienü Zhuan.*" *Late Imperial China* 12, no. 2 (Dec. 1991): 117–52.

Cass, Victoria B. "Celebrations at the Gate of Death: Symbol and Structure in *Jin Ping mei.*" Ph.D. diss., University of California, Berkeley, 1979.

———. "Female Healers in the Ming and the Lodge of Ritual and Ceremony." *Journal of the American Oriental Society, Festschrift dedicated to Edward H. Schafer* 106 (March 1986): 233–40.

———. "Revels of Gaudy Night." *Chinese Literature: Essays, Articles and Reviews* 4, no. 2 (July 1982): 213–31.

Ch'an, Albert. *The Glory and Fall of the Ming Dynasty.* Norman: University of Oklahoma Press, 1982.

———. "Late Ming Society and the Jesuit Missionaries." In *East Meets West: The Jesuits in China, 1582–1773,* edited by Charles E. Ronan and Bonnie B.C. Oh, 153–72. Chicago: Loyola University Press, 1988.

Chang, Chunshu. "Kung Shang-jen and his *Tao-hua shan.*" In *China: Linguistics and Literary Criticism,* edited by Graciela de la Lama, 231–35. Mexico City: El Colegio de Mexico, 1982.

———. "The World of P'u Sung-ling's Liao-chai chih-i: Literature and the Intellegentsia during the Ming-Ch'ing Dynastic Transition." *Journal of the Institute of Chinese Studies of the Chinese University of Hong Kong* 6, no. 2 (1973): 401–23.

Chang, Chun-shu, and Shelley Hsüeh-lun Chang. *Crisis and Transformation in Seventeenth-Century China: Society, Culture and Modernity in Li Yü's World.* Ann Arbor: University of Michigan Press, 1992.

Chang, Kang-i Sun. "Ming and Qing Anthologies of Women's Poetry and Their Selection Strategies." In *Writing Women in Late Imperial China,* edited by Ellen Widmer and Kang-i Sun Chang, 147–70. Stanford, Calif.: Stanford University Press, 1997.

———. *The Late Ming Poet Ch'en Tzu-lung: Crises of Love and Loyalism.* New Haven and London: Yale University Press, 1991.

Chatwin, Bruce. *The Songlines.* New York: Viking, 1987.

Chaves, Jonathan. "Moral Action in the Poetry of Wu Chia-chi (1618–84)." *Harvard Journal of Asiatic Studies* 46 (1986): 387–469.

———, ed. and trans. *The Columbia Book of Later Chinese Poetry: Yüan, Ming and Ch'ing Dynasties (1279–1911).* New York: Columbia University Press, 1986.

Chou, Chih-p'ing. *Yüan Hung-tao and the Kung-an School.* New York: Columbia University Press, 1988.

Chung, Priscilla Ching. *Palace Women in the Northern Sung 960–1126.* Leiden: E. J. Brill, 1981.

Cleary, Thomas, trans. and ed. *Immortal Sisters: Secrets of Taoist Women.* Boston and Shaftsbury, Dorset: Shambhala, 1989.

Clunas, Craig. *Fruitful Sights: Garden Culture in Ming Dynasty China.* Durham, N.C.: Duke University Press, 1996.

———. *Superfluous Things: Material Culture and Social Status in Early Modern China.* Urbana: University of Illinois Press, 1991.

Cohn, Don J., trans. and ed. *Vignettes from the Chinese Lithographs from Shanghai in the Late Nineteenth Century.* Hong Kong: Chinese University of Hong Kong (a *Renditions* paperback), 1987.

Day, William Patrick. *In the Circles of Fear and Desire: A Study of Gothic Fantasy.* Chicago: University of Chicago Press, 1985.

de Bary, William Theodore, ed. *Self and Society in Ming Thought.* New York: Columbia University Press, 1970.

De Lauretis, Teresa. "Desire in Narrative." In *Alice Doesn't: Feminism, Semiotics, Cinema,* 103–57. Bloomington: University of Indiana Press, 1984.

Despeux, Catherine. "L'ordination des femmes Taoïstes sous les T'ang." *Études chinoises* 5, nos. 1–2 (1986): 53–100.

Douglas, Mary C. *Purity and Danger: An Analysis of Concepts of Pollution and Taboos.* New York: Praeger, 1966.

Dudbridge, Glen. *The Legend of Miao Shan.* London: Ithaca Press, 1978.

Ebrey, Patricia Buckley, ed. *Chinese Civilization and Society: A Sourcebook*. New York and London: Free Press, 1981.

Elvin, Mark. "Female Virtue and the State in China." *Past and Present* 104 (August 1984): 111–52.

Franke, Wolfgang. "Historical Writing During the Ming." In *Cambridge History of China*. Vol. 7, *The Ming Dynasty, 1368–1644*, pt. 1, 726–82. Cambridge: Cambridge University Press, 1988.

Frye, Northrop. *Anatomy of Criticism: Four Essays*. Princeton: Princeton University Press, 1957.

— — —. *The Secular Scripture: A Study of the Structure of Romance*. Cambridge: Harvard University Press, 1976.

Furth, Charlotte. "Androgynous Males and Deficient Females: Biology and Gender Boundaries in Sixteenth and Seventeenth-Century China." *Late Imperial China* 46, no. 1 (1987): 7–36.

— — —. "Blood, Body, and Gender: Medical Images of the Female Condition in China, 1600–1850." *Chinese Science* 7 (1986): 43–66.

— — —. "Concepts of Pregnancy, Childbirth, and Infancy in Ch'ing Dynasty China." *Journal of Asian Studies* 46, no. 1 (AAS Symposium Volume) (February 1987): 7–35.

Fusek, Lois. "The Kao T'ang Fu." *Monumenta Serica* 30 (1972–73): 392–425.

Geiss, James Peter. "The Chia-ching Reign, 1522–1566." In *The Cambridge History of China*. Vol. 7, *The Ming Dynasty, 1368–1644*, edited by Frederick Mote and Denis Twitchett, 440–510. Cambridge, England, and New York: Cambridge University Press, 1977.

— — —. "Peking under the Ming (1368–1644)." Ph.D. diss., Princeton University, 1979.

Goodrich, L. Carrington, and Fang Chaoying, eds. *Dictionary of Ming Biography, 1368–1644*. 2 vols. New York: Columbia University Press, 1976.

Grant, Beata. "Female Holder of the Lineage: Lingji Chan Master Zhiyuan Xianggang (1597–1654)." *Late Imperial China* 17, no. 2 (December 1996): 51–76.

Guisso, Richard W., and Stanley Johanessen, eds. "Women in China, Current Directions in Historical Scholarship." *Historical Reflections* 8, no. 3 (Symposium Volume) (Fall 1981).

Hanan, Patrick. *The Chinese Vernacular Short Story*. Cambridge: Harvard University Press, 1981.

— — —. *The Invention of Li Yu*. Cambridge: Harvard University Press, 1988.

— — —. "The Text of the *Chin P'ing Mei*." *Asia Major* n. s. 9 (1962): 1–57.

Handlin, Joanna. *Action in Late Ming Thought: The Reorientation of Lü K'un and Other Scholar-Officials*. Berkeley: University of California Press, 1983.

— — —. "Gardens in Ch'i Piao-chia's Social World, Wealth and Values in Late-Ming Kiangnan." *Journal of Asian Studies* 51, no. 1 (February 1992): 55–81.

— — —. "Lü K'un's New Audience: The Influence of Women's Literature on Sixteenth Century Thought." In *Women in Chinese Society*, edited by Margery Wolf and Roxanne Witke, 13–38. Stanford, Calif.: Stanford University Press, 1975.

Hawkes, David. "The Quest of the Goddess." In *Studies in Chinese Literary Genres*, edited by Cyril Birch, 42–68. Berkeley: University of California Press, 1974.

Hegel, Robert E. *The Novel in Seventeenth-Century China*. New York: Columbia University Press, 1981.

Ho, P'ing-ti. *The Ladder of Success in Imperial China: Aspects of Social Mobility, 1368–1911*. New York: Columbia University Press, 1962.

— — —. "The Salt Merchants of Yang-chou: A Study of Commercial Capitalism in Eighteenth-Century China." *Harvard Journal of Asiatic Studies* 17, nos. 1–2 (1954): 130–68.

Ho, Wai-kam. "The Late Ming Literati: Their Social and Cultural Ambiance." In *The Chinese Scholar's Studio: Artistic Life in the Late Ming Period. An Exhibition from the Shanghai Museum*, edited by Chu-Tsung Li and James C.Y. Watt, 23–36. London: Thames and Hudson, 1987.

— — —, ed. *The Century of Tung Ch'i Ch'ang, 1555–1636*. Kansas City, Mo.: Nelson Atkins Museum of Art, 1992.

Holquist, Michael. "How to play Utopia, Some brief notes on the distinctiveness of utopian fiction." *Game, Play, Literature, Yale French Studies*, no. 41 (1968): 106–23.

Hou, Ching-lang. "The Chinese Belief in Baleful Stars." In *Facets of Taoism*, edited by Holmes Welch and Anna Seidel, 193–228. New Haven and London: Yale University Press, 1979.

Hsia, C. T. "The Military Romance." In *Studies in Chinese Literary Genres*, edited by Cyril Birch, 336–90. Berkeley: University of California Press, 1974.

———. "The Scholar Novelist and Chinese Culture: A Reappraisal of Ching-hua yüan." In *Chinese Narrative*, edited by Andrew Plaks, 266–305. Princeton: Princeton University Press, 1977.

———. "Time and the Human Condition in the Plays of T'ang Hsien-tsu." In *Self and Society in Ming Thought*, edited by William Theodore de Bary, 249–90. New York: Columbia University Press, 1970.

Huang, Liuhong. *A Complete Book Concerning Happiness and Benevolence. A Manual for Local Magistrates in Seventeenth Century China*. Translated by Djang Chu. Tucson: University of Arizona Press, 1984.

Huang, Ray. *1587, A Year of No Significance*. New Haven and London: Yale University Press, 1981.

Hucker, Charles O. *The Censorial System of Ming China*. Stanford, Calif.: Stanford University Press, 1966.

———. "Su-chou and the Agents of Wei Chung-hsien, 1626." In *Two Studies on Ming History*, edited by Charles Hucker, 41–83. Ann Arbor: University of Michigan Center for Chinese Studies, 1971.

Hummel, Arthur, ed. *Eminent Chinese of the Ch'ing Period*. 2 vols. Washington, D.C.: U.S. Government Printing Office, 1943–44.

Hung, Ming-shui. "Yuan Hung-tao and the Late Ming Literary and Intellectual Movement." Ph.D. diss., University of Wisconsin, 1975.

Johnson, David, Andrew Nathan, and Evelyn Rawski, eds. *Popular Culture in Late Imperial China*. Berkeley: University of California Press, 1985.

Kingston, Maxine Hong. *The Woman Warrior: Memoirs of a Girlhood Among Ghosts*. New York: Knopf, 1977.

Kleeman, Terry. "Mountain Deities in China: The Domestication of the Mountain God and the Subjugation of the Margins." *Journal of the American Oriental Society* 114, no. 2 (April–June 1994): 226–38.

Knoepflmacher, Ulrich. *Laughter and Despair, Readings in Ten Novels of the Victorian Era*. Berkeley: University of California Press, 1971.

Ko, Dorothy. "The Complicity of Women in the Qing Good Woman Cult." In *Family Process and Political Process in Modern Chinese History*, Pt. 1. 2 vols. Taibei: Academia Sinica, Institute of Modern History, 1992.

———. "Pursuing Talent: Education and Women's Culture in Seventeenth and Eighteenth Century China." *Late Imperial China* 13, no. 1 (June 1992): 9–39.

———. *Teachers of the Inner Chambers: Women and Culture in Seventeenth-Century China*. Stanford, Calif.: Stanford University Press, 1994.

———. "The Written Word and the Bound Foot: A History of the Courtesan's Aura." In *Writing Women in Late Imperial China*, edited by Kang-i Sun Chang and Ellen Widmer, 74–100. Stanford, Calif.: Stanford University Press, 1997.

Kotzimanidou, Maria. "A Study of the Go-Between in Arabic and Spanish Literature." University of California, Berkeley, Comparative Literature Seminar, manuscript.

Lau, Joseph, and Y. W. Ma. *Traditional Chinese Stories: Themes and Variations*. New York: Columbia University Press, 1978.

Leung, Angela. "Autour de la naissance: la mère et l'enfant en Chine aux XVI et XVII siècles." *Cahiers Internationaux du Sociologie* (1984): 51–69.

Levenson, Joseph R. "The Amateur Ideal in Ming and Early Ch'ing Society: Evidence from Painting." In *Chinese Thought and Institutions*, edited by John K. Fairbank, 320–41. Chicago: University of Chicago Press, 1957.

Levy, André. "L'Apologie du roman." In *Le Conte Chinois en langue vulgaire du XVII siècle*, 282–94. Paris: École Française d'Extrême-Orient, 1980.

———. "Exentrisme et excentricité." In *Le Conte Chinois en langue vulgaire du XVII siècle*, 265–74. Paris: École Française d'Extrême-Orient, 1980.

———. "Le Serpent Blanc en Chine et au Japon: Excursions à travers les variations d'un thème." In *Études sur le conte et le roman chinois*, 97–113. Paris: École Française d'Extrême-Orient, 1971.

Levy, Howard. *A Feast of Mist and Flowers: The Gay Quarters of Nanjing at the End of the Ming*. Yokohama, no pub., 1966.

Li, Chi. *The Travel Diaries of Hsü Hsia-k'o*. Hong Kong: Hong Kong University Press, 1974.

Li, Wai-yee. "The Late Ming Courtesan: Invention of a Cultural Ideal." In *Writing Women in Late Imperial China*, edited by Kang-i Sun Chang and Ellen Widmer, 46–73. Stanford, Calif.: Stanford University Press, 1997.

Liu, James J.Y. *The Chinese Knight Errant*. Chicago: University of Chicago Press, 1967.

Liu, Ts'un-yan. *Buddhist and Taoist Influences on the Chinese Novel I: Feng-shen yen-i*. Wiesbaden, W. Germ.: Harrassowitz, 1962.

Lo, Irving Yucheng. "Daughters of the Muses of China." In *Views from Jade Terrace: Chinese Women Artists, 1300–1912*, edited by Marsha Weidner, Ellen Johnston Lang, Irving Lo, Christina Chu, and James Robinson. 41–63. Indianapolis: Indianapolis Museum of Art; New York: Rizzoli, 1988.

Loewe, Michael. *Chinese Ideas of Life and Death: Faith, Myth and Reason in the Han Period (202 B.C.–A.D. 220)*. London: George Allen and Unwin, 1982.

Mair, Victor. "Language and Ideology in the Written Popularizations of the *Sacred Edict*." In *Popular Culture in Late Imperial China*, edited by David Johnson, Andrew J. Nathan, and Evelyn S. Rawski, 325–59. Berkeley: University of California Press, 1985.

Mammitzsh, Ulrich Hans-Richel. "Wei Chung-hsien (1568–1628): A Reappraisal of the Eunuch and the Factional at the Late Ming Court." Ph.D. diss., University of Hawaii, 1968.

Mann, Susan. "*Fuxue* (Women's Learning) by Zhang Xuecheng (1738–1801), China's First History of Women's Culture." *Late Imperial China* 13, no. 1 (June 1992): 40–56.

———. "Widows in Kinship, Class, and Community Structures of Qing Dynasty China." *Journal of Asian Studies* 46, no. 1 (February 1987): 37–56.

Mao P'i-chiang (Mao Xiang). *The Reminiscences of Tung Hsiao-wan*. Translated by Pan Tze-yen. Shanghai: Commercial Press, 1931.

Maspero, Henri. "Legendes mythologiques dans le *Chou King*." *Journal asiatique* 102 (1924): 1–100.

McLaren, Ann E. *The Chinese Femme Fatale: Stories from the Ming Period*. University of Sydney, East Asian Series no. 8, 1994.

McMahon, Keith. "A Case for Confucian Sexuality: The Eighteenth-Century Novel, *Yesou Puyan*." *Late Imperial China* 9, no. 2 (December 1988): 32–55.

———. *Misers, Shrews, and Polygamists: Sexuality and Male-Female Relations in Eighteenth-Century Fiction*. Durham, N.C.: Duke University Press, 1995.

Meskill, John. *Gentlemanly Interests and Wealth on the Yangtze Delta*. Ann Arbor, Mich.: Association for Asian Studies, no. 49, 1994.

Mote, Frederick. "A Millennium of Chinese Urban History: Form, Time, and Space Concepts in Soochow." *Rice University Studies* 59 (fall 1973): 35–65.

———. *The Poet Kao Ch'i*. Princeton: Princeton University Press, 1962.

Mowry, Hua-yuan Li, trans. *Chinese Love Stories from the "Ch'ing-shih."* Hamden, Conn: Archon, 1983.

Mulligan, Jean, trans. *The Lute, Kao Ming's P'i-p'a chi*. New York: Columbia University Press, 1980.

Naquin, Susan. "The Transmission of White Lotus Sectarianism in Late Imperial China." In *Popular Culture in Late Imperial China*, edited by David Johnson, Andrew J. Nathan, and Evelyn S. Rawski, 255–91. Berkeley: University of California Press, 1985.

Nemerov, Howard. *Figures of Thought*. Boston: Godine, 1978.

Ng, Vivian W. "Ideology and Sexuality: Rape Laws in Qing China." *Journal of Asian Studies* 46, no. 1 (February 1987): 57–70.

Nieuhof, Johan, et al. *An embassy from the East-India Company of the United Provinces, to the Grand Tartar Cham, Emperour of China, delivered by their Excell[en]cies, Peter de Goyer and Jacob de Keyzer, at his imperial city of Peking: wherein the cities . . . ports, rivers, &c. in their passages from Canton to Peking are ingeniously described*. 1669. Reproduction of original in Huntington Library, Los Angeles, Calif. Ann Arbor, Mich.: University Microfilms, 1972.

O'Flaherty, Wendy D. *Women, Androgynes, and Other Mythical Beasts*. Chicago: University of Chicago Press, 1980.

Ono, Kazuko. *Chinese Women in a Century of Revolution, 1850–1950*. Translated by Kathryn Bernhardt, edited by Joshua A. Fogel. Stanford, Calif.: Stanford University Press, 1989.

Overmeyer, Daniel. "Alternatives: Popular Religious Sects in Chinese Society." *Modern China* 7, no. 2 (April 1981): 153–90.

— — —. *Folk Buddhist Religion: Dissenting Sects in Late Traditional China*. Cambridge: Harvard University Press, 1976.

— — —. "Women in Chinese Religions: Submission, Struggle, Transcendence." In *From Benares to Beijing: Essays on Buddhism and Religion in Honour of Professor Jan Yun-hua*, edited by Koichi Shinohara and Gregory Schoper, 91–120. Oakville, Ontario: Mosaic Press, 1991.

Pagels, Elaine H. *The Gnostic Gospels*. New York: Vintage, 1981.

Paige, Karen, and Jeffrey Paige. *The Politics of Reproductive Ritual*. Berkeley: University of California Press, 1981.

Paul, Diana Y., and Frances Wilson. *Women in Buddhism: Images of the Feminine in Mahayana Tradition*. 2d ed. Berkeley: University of California Press, 1985.

Peterson, Willard. *Bitter Gourd: Fang I-chih and the Impetus for Intellectual Change*. New Haven and London: Yale University Press, 1979.

Poggioli, Renato. *The Theory of the Avant Garde*. Cambridge: Belknap Press of Harvard University Press, 1968.

Potter, Jack. "Cantonese Shamanism." In *Religion and Ritual in Chinese Society*, edited by Arthur P. Wolf, 207–31. Stanford, Calif.: Stanford University Press, 1974.

Robertson, Maureen. "Voicing the Feminine: Constructions of the Gendered Subject in Lyric Poetry by Women of Medieval and Late Imperial China." *Late Imperial China* 13, no. 1 (June 1992): 63–110.

Robinet, Isabel. *Meditation taoïste*. Paris: Dervy Livres, 1977.

— — —. "Randonnés extatiques des taoïstes dans les âstres." *Monumenta Serica* 32 (1976): 159–273.

Ropp, Paul S. "Ambiguous Images of Courtesan Culture in Late Imperial China." In *Writing Women in Late Imperial China*, edited by Ellen Widmer and Kang-i Sun Chang, 31–41. Stanford, Calif.: Stanford University Press, 1997.

— — —. "Love, Literacy, and Laments: Themes of Women Writers in Late Imperial China." *Women's History Review* 2, no. 1 (1993): 107–41.

— — —. "The Seeds of Change: Reflections on the Condition of Women in the Early and Mid Ch'ing." *Signs: Journal of Women in Culture and Society* 2, no. 1 (Autumn 1976): 5–23.

Rowse, A. L. *A Cornishman at Oxford*. London: Jonathan Cape, 1962.

Ruggiero, G. *The Evolution of the Go-Between in Spanish Literature Through the Sixteenth Century*. Berkeley: University of California Press, 1966.

Ruhlmann, Robert. "Traditional Heroes in Chinese Popular Fiction." In *Confucianism and Chinese Society*, edited by Arthur F. Wright, 122–57. New York: Atheneum, 1964.

Sakai, Tadao. "Confucianism and Popular Educational Works." In *Self and Society in Ming Thought*, edited by William Theodore de Bary, 331–66. New York: Columbia University Press, 1970.

Schafer, E. H. "The Capeline Cantos, Verses on the Divine Loves of Taoist Priestesses." *Asiatische Studien* 32, no. 1 (1978): 5–65.

— — —. *The Divine Woman: Dragon Ladies and Rain Maidens in T'ang Literature*. Berkeley: University of California Press, 1973.

— — —. *Pacing the Void: T'ang Approaches to the Stars*. Berkeley: University of California Press, 1977.

— — —. "Pleasure Boats of the Tang." In "Schafer Sinological Papers." Manuscript.

— — —. "Ritual Exposure in Ancient China." *Harvard Journal of Asiatic Studies* (1951): 130–84.

— — —. "Three Divine Women of South China." *Chinese Literature: Essays, Articles, Reviews* 1 (January 1979): 31–42.

Seaman, Gary. *The Journey to the North: An Ethnographical Analysis and Annotated Translation of the Chinese Folk Novel "Pei-yu-chi."* Berkeley: University of California Press, 1987.

Schipper, Kristofer M. "The Taoist Body." *History of Religions* 17, nos. 3 and 4 (1978): 355–86.

— — —. *The Taoist Body*. Translated by Karen C. Duval. Berkeley: University of California Press, 1993.

Seidel, Anna. "Buying One's Way to Heaven: The Celestial Treasury in Chinese Religions." *History of Religions* 17 (1978): 419–31.

———. "A Taoist Immortal of the Ming Dynasty: Chang San-feng." In *Self and Society in Ming Thought*, edited by William Theodore de Bary, 483–531. New York: Columbia University Press, 1970.

Seigel, Cecilia Sagawa. *Yoshiwara: The Glittering World of the Japanese Courtesan*. Honolulu: University of Hawaii Press, 1993.

Soymie, Michel. *Le Lo-Feou Chan, étude de géographie religieuse*. Paris: École Française d'Extrême Orient, 1956.

Spence, Jonathan. *The Death of Woman Wang*. New York: Penguin Press, 1978.

———. *The Memory Palace of Matteo Ricci*. New York: Viking, 1983.

Spence, Jonathan, and John Wills, Jr., eds. *From Ming to Ch'ing: Conquest, Region and Continuity in Seventeenth-Century China*. New Haven: Yale University Press, 1979.

Spitzer, Leo. *Linguistics and Literary History*. Princeton: Princeton University Press, 1974.

Stein, Rolf A. *The World in Miniature: Container Gardens and Dwellings in Far Eastern Religious Thought*. Translated by Phyllis Brooks. Stanford, Calif.: Stanford University Press, 1990.

Strickmann, Michel. "The Mao Shan Revelations: Taoism and the Aristocracy." *T'oung Pao* 63 (1977): 1–64.

———. "On the Alchemy of T'ao Hung-ching." In *Facets of Taoism*, edited by Holmes Welch and Anna Seidel, 123–93. New Haven: Yale University Press, 1979.

Struve, Lynn. *Voices from the Ming-Qing Cataclysm, China in Tiger's Jaws*. New Haven and London: Yale University Press, 1993.

Sung, Marina H. "The Chinese *Lieh-nü* Tradition." *Current Directions in Historical Scholarship in China: Historical Reflections* 8 (Summer 1981): 363–74.

Tanaka, Issei. "The Social and Historical Context of Ming-Ch'ing Local Drama." In *Popular Culture in Late Imperial China*, edited by David Johnson, Andrew J. Nathan, and Evelyn S. Rawski, 143–60. Berkeley: University of California Press, 1985.

Thoreau, Henry David. *Walden*. New York: Thomas Y. Crowell, 1961.

T'ien, Ju-K'ang. *Male Anxiety and Female Chastity: A Comparative Study of Chinese Ethical Values in Ming-Ch'ing Times*. Leiden: E. J. Brill, 1988.

Torrance, Robert M. *The Comic Hero*. Cambridge: Harvard University Press, 1978.

Trigault, Nicolas, ed. *China in the Sixteenth Century: The Journals of Matthew Ricci, 1583–1610*. Translated by Louis J. Gallagher. Foreword by Richard J. Cushing. New York: Random House, 1953.

Tseng, Yu-ho. "Hsüeh Wu and Her Orchids in the Collection of the Honolulu Academy of the Arts." *Arts Asiatiques* 2, no. 3 (1955): 197–208.

Vidal, Gore. *Reflections upon a Sinking Ship*. Boston: Little, Brown, 1969.

Wagner, Marsha. *The Lotus Boat: The Origins of Chinese Tz'u Poetry in T'ang Popular Culture*. New York: Columbia University Press, 1984.

Wakeman, Frederic, Jr. *The Great Enterprise: The Manchu Reconstruction of Imperial Order in Seventeenth-Century China*. 2 vols. Berkeley: University of California Press, 1985.

———. "Romantic Stories and Martyrs in 17th-Century China." *Journal of Asian Studies* 63 (August 1984): 631–61.

Waltner, Ann. "T'an-yan-tzu and Wang Shih-chen: Visionary and Bureaucrat in the Late Ming." *Late Imperial China* 8, no. 1 (June 1987): 105–33.

Wang, John Ching-yu. *Chin Sheng-t'an*. New York: Twayne Publishers, 1972.

Wang, Richard. "The Cult of Qing: Romanticism in the Late Ming Period and in the Novel *Jiao Hong Ji*." *Ming Studies* 33 (August 1994): 12–55.

Warner, Marina. *Alone of All Her Sex: The Myth and the Cult of the Virgin Mary*. London: Picador, 1976.

———. *From the Beast to the Blonde: On Fairy Tales and Their Tellers*. New York: Farrar, Straus and Giroux, 1994.

Watt, Ian. *The Rise of the Novel*. World Authors Series. Berkeley: University of California Press, 1972.

Watt, James C.Y. "The Literati Environment." In *The Chinese Scholar's Studio: Artistic Life in the Late Ming Period*, edited by Chu-Tsing Li and James C.Y. Watt, 1–13. New York: Thames and Hudson, 1987.

Weidner, Marsha, Ellen Johnston Laing, Irving Yucheng Lo, Christina Chu, and James Robinson. *Flowering in the Shadows: Women in the History of Chinese and Japanese Painting*. Honolulu: University of Hawaii Press, 1990.

————. *Views from Jade Terrace: Chinese Women Artists, 1300–1912*. Indianapolis: Indianapolis Museum of Art; New York: Rizzoli, 1988.

Widmer, Ellen. "The Epistolary World of Female Talent in Seventeenth Century China." *Late Imperial China* 10, no. 2 (December 1989): 1–43.

————. "Fox Fairy Tales in the *Tai Ping guangji*." Manuscript, Harvard University, no date.

————. "Xiaoqing's Literary Legacy and the Place of the Woman Writer in Late Imperial China." *Late Imperial China* 13, no. 1 (June 1992): 111–55.

Witke, Roxanne. "The Transformation of Attitudes Towards Women During the May Fourth Era of Modern China." Ph.D. diss., University of California, Berkeley, 1970.

Wolf, Margery. *The House of Lim: A Study of a Chinese Farm Family*. New York: Appleton-Century-Crofts, 1968.

Wolf, Margery, and Roxanne Witke, eds. *Women in Chinese Society*. Stanford, Calif.: Stanford University Press, 1975.

Wu, Hung. "Beyond Stereotypes: The Twelve Beauties in Qing Court Art and *The Dream of the Red Chamber*." In *Writing Women in Late Imperial China*, edited by Ellen Widmer and Kang-i Sun Chang. Stanford, Calif.: Stanford University Press, 1997.

Wu, K. T. "Ming Printing and Printers." *Harvard Journal of Asiatic Studies* 7, no. 3 (1942–43): 203–60.

Wu, Nelson. "Tung Ch'i-ch'ang (1555–1636): Apathy in Government and Fervor in Art." In *Confucian Personalities*, edited by Arthur Wright and Denis Twitchett, 260–93. Stanford, Calif.: Stanford University Press, 1962.

Wu, Pei-yi. *The Confucian's Progress: Autobiographical Writings in Traditional China*. Princeton: Princeton University Press, 1990.

Wu, Yenna. *The Chinese Virago: A Literary Theme*. Cambridge and London: Harvard University Press, Council on East Asian Studies, 1995.

————. *The Lioness Roars: Shrew Stories from Late Imperial China*. Cornell East Asian Series 81. Ithaca: Cornell University East Asia Program, 1995.

Yeh, Catherine. "Reinventing Ritual: Late Qink Handbooks for Proper Customer Behavior in Shanghai Courtesan Houses." *Late Imperial China* 19, no. 2 (December 1998): 1–63.

Yu, Ying-shih. "Toward an Interpretation of the Intellectual Transition in Seventeenth Century China." *Journal of the American Oriental Society* 100, no. 2 (April–June 1980): 115–25.

Yuan Hongdao. *Pilgrim of the Clouds: Poems and Essays from Ming China*. Translated by Jonathan Chaves. New York and Tokyo: Weatherhill, 1978.

Zeitlin, Judith. *Historian of the Strange: Pu Songling and the Chinese Classical Tale*. Stanford, Calif.: Stanford University Press, 1993.

————. "The Petrified Heart: Obsession in Chinese Literature, Art and Medicine." *Late Imperial China* 12, no. 1 (June 1991): 1–26.

————. "Shared Dreams: The Story of the Three Wives Commentary on the Peony Pavilion." *Harvard Journal of Asiatic Studies* 54, no. 1 (1994): 127–79.

Bibliography of Chinese and Japanese Sources

A Ying 阿英. *Xiaoshuo xian tan* 小說閒談 [Discussing Fiction]. Shanghai: Gudian wenxue, 1958.

Chang Bide 昌彼得, compiler. *Mingdai banhuaxuan chuji* 明代版畫選初輯 [Selected Wood Block Prints from the Ming Dynasty, First Edition]. 2 vols. Taibei: Guoli zhongyang tushuguan, 1969.

Chen Dongyuan 陳東原. *Zhongguo funü shenghuo shi* 中國婦女生活史 [A History of the Lives of Chinese Women]. Shanghai: Shangwu yinshuguan, 1928. Reprint. Taibei: Shangwu, 1981.

Chen Menglei 陳夢雷, Jiang Tingxi 蔣廷錫, and others, eds. *Gujin tushu jicheng* 古今圖書集成 [Imperial Collectanea of Texts Old and New]. 10,040 *juan* in 800 volumes, 1725. Reprint. Taibei: Wenxing shudian, 1977.

Chen Yinke 陳寅恪. *Liu Rushi biezhuan* 柳如是別傳 [Unofficial Biography of Liu Rushi]. 3 vols. Shanghai: Shanghai guji chubanshe, 1980.

Chen Yuanjing 陳元靚. *Sui shi guangji* 歲時廣記 [Miscellany on the Calendar]. Shanghai: Commercial Press, 1939.

Da Ming huidian. 大明會典 [Ming Imperial Documents]. Compiled by Shen Shixing 申時行. Edited by Xu Pu 徐溥. Taibei: Dongnan shubaoshe, 1963.

Dianshizhai huabao 點石齊畫報 [Pictorial of the Engraved Stone Studio]. Edited and published by Shanghai guji shudian, 1983.

Ding Bing 丁丙, comp. *Wulin zhanggu congbian* 武林掌故叢編 [Collectanea of Legends from Hangzhou]. 26 vols. Qiantang: Dingshi Jiahuitang, 1883. Reprint. Taibei: Jinghua shuju, 1967.

Dong Guo Xiansheng 東郭先生. *Ji jia feng yue* 妓家風月 [The Geisha and the High Romantic]. Shanxi: Beiyue wenyi chubanshe, 1990.

———. *Xianhua Jinpingmei* 閒話金瓶梅 [Random Talks on the *Jin Ping Mei*]. Taibei: Shishi chubanshe, 1978.

Du ji 妒記 [Accounts of Female Jealousy]. Attributed to Yu Tongzhi 虞通之. Reprint. Lu Xun 魯迅, comp., *Gu xiaoshuo gouchen* 古小說鉤沈 [Selected Ancient Tales], in *Lu Xun quanji* 魯迅全集 [Collected Works of Lu Xun] vol. 8. *Lu Xun quanji* chubanshe, 1948.

Feng Menglong 馮夢龍. *Gu jin xiao shuo* 古今小說 [Stories Old and New]. Beijing: Renmin wenxue, 1958.

———, comp. *Guazhir* 掛枝兒 [A Collection of the Guazhir Songs]. Edited by Guan Dedong 關德棟, 2 vols. Beijing: Zhonghua shuju, 1962.

———. *Jia shen jishi* 甲申記事 [A History of 1644]. In *Feng Menglong quanji.* Edited by Wei Tongxian, vol.13. Nanjing: Nanjing Central Library, 1941.

———. *Jing shi tongyan* 警世通言 [Perceptive Words to Startle the World]. Hong Kong: Zhonghua shuju, 1983.

———. *Qing shi lei lue* 情史類略 [The Compilation by the Historian of Love]. In *Guben xiaoshuo jicheng*, fascicle 634-635. Shanghai: Shanghai guji chuban she, 1990.

———. *Shan ge* 山歌 [Mountain Songs]. Beijing: Guan de dong, 1962.

———. *Xiaofu* 笑府 [A Treasury of Jokes]. *Feng Menglong quanji.* Edited by Wei Tongxian, vol.41. Shanghai: Shanghai guji chubanshe. 1990.

———. *Xing shi heng yan* 醒世恒言 [Constant Words to Awaken the World]. Hong Kong: Zhonghua shuju, 1983.

Feng sheng yen yi 封神演義 [The Investiture of the Gods]. Shanghai: Commercial Press, 1937.

Fu Yiling 傅衣凌. *Mingdai jiangnan shimin jingji shitan* 明代江南市民經濟試探 [An Inquiry into the Economy of the Jiangnan District in the Ming Dynasty]. Shanghai: Shanghai renmin chubanshe, 1957.

Gong Zhebing 宮哲兵. *Funü wenzi he yaozu qianjia tong* 婦女文字和瑤族千家峒 [Women Writers from Yao Territories]. Beijing, 1986.

Hangzhou lishi congbian bianji weiyuanhui 杭州歷史叢編編輯委員會, ed. *Yuan-Ming-Qing mingsheng Hangzhou* 元明清名城杭州 [Hangzhou, a Renowned City in the Yuan, Ming and Qing Dynasties]. Zhejiang: Zhejiang renmin chubanshe, 1990.

He Lezhi 何樂之, ed. *Mingkan mingshantu banhuaji* 明刊名山圖版畫集 [Collected Pictures of Famous Mountains from the Ming]. Shanghai: Renmin meishu chubanshe, 1958.

Hong Mai 洪邁. *Yi jian zhi* 夷堅志 [What Master Yi Jian Recorded]. Taibei: Ming wen shuju, 1982.

Huguang tongzhi. 湖廣通志. Edited by Mai Zhu 邁柱. Siku quanshu. Vol. 533-540.

Hu Wanchuan 胡萬川. *Huaben yu caizijiaren xiaoshuo zhi yanjiu* 話本與才子佳人小說之研究 [Huaben Texts and the Stories of Gifted Scholars and Women of Excellence]. Taibei: Daan chubanshe, 1994.

Hu Wenkai 胡文楷, ed. *Lidai funü zhuzuo kao* 歷代婦女著作考 [An Examination of Women's Writing Through the Dynasties]. Shanghai: Shanghai guji chubanshe, 1985.

Huang Zongxi 黃宗羲. *Ming ru xue an* 明儒學案 [Confucian Learning in the Ming Dyansty]. Si bu bei yao, vol.394-397. Taibei: Zhonghua shuju, 1984.

Jiao Hong 焦竑. *Xian zheng lu* 獻徵錄 [Court-presented Biographies]. Shanghai: Shanghai shudian, 1986.

Jin Ping Mei cihua 金瓶梅詞話 [The Flower in the Golden Vase]. Lanling Xiaoxiaosheng 蘭陵笑笑生 [pseud]. Facsimile reprint of the Ming Wanli edition. Hong Kong: Taiping shuju, 1982.

Kong Lingjing 孔另境. *Zhongguo xiaoshuo shiliao* 中國小說史料 [Historical Sources on Chinese Fiction]. 1936. Reprint. Taibei: Zhonghua shuju, 1957.

Lang Ying 郎瑛. *Qi xiu lei gao* 七修類稿 [Encyclopedia of Seven Divisions]. Beijing: Zhonghua, 1961.

Li Fang 李昉, ed. *Taiping guang ji* 太平廣記 [The Taiping Miscellany]. Shanghai: Zhonghua, 1960.

Li Jiarui 李家瑞. *Beiping fengsu lei zheng* 北平風俗類徵 [Inquiry into the Customs of Beijing] Shanghai: Commercial Press, 1937.

Li Shizhen 李時珍. *Bencao gangmu* 本草綱目 [Compendium of Materia Medica]. 4 vols. Beijing: Renmin weisheng chubanshe, 1981.

Ling Mengchu 凌濛初. *Chuke pai'an jingqi* 初刻拍案驚奇 [Clapping the Table in Amazement, First Collection]. 2 vols. Xining: Qinghai renmin chubanshe, 1984.

———. *Erke pai'an jingqi* 二刻拍案驚奇 [Clapping the Table in Amazement, Second Collection]. Shanghai: Shanghai guji chubanshe, 1983.

Liu Ruoyu 劉若愚. *Zhuo zhong zhi* 酌中志 [Monograph on Pouring to the Mark]. Congshu jicheng, vol. 85.616. Shanghai: Commercial Press, 1937.

Liu Tong 劉侗. *Dijing jingwu lue* 帝京景物略 [A Sketch of Scenes of the Imperial Capital]. Shanghai: Gudian wenxue, 1957.

Lü chuang xinhua 綠窗新話 [Tales of the Green Window]. Edited by Huangdu fengyue zhuren 皇都風月主人. Taibei: Shijie shuju, 1959.

Lu Rong 陸容. *Shu yuan za ji* 菽園雜記 [The Bean Garden Miscellany]. Congshu jicheng, vol. 12.629. Shanghai: Commercial Press, 1937.

Lü Xiong 呂熊. *Nüxian waishi* 女仙外史 [The Unofficial History of a Female Immortal]. 2 vols. Tianjin: Baihua wenyi chubanshe, 1985.

Lu Yunzhong 盧允中. *Zhongguo lidai xiaohua yibai pian* 中國歷代笑話一百篇 [Collection of Jokes of Historical Periods]. Hong Kong: Commercial Press, 1985.

Mao Jin 毛晉. *Liu shi zhong qu* 六十種曲 [Sixty Plays]. Shanghai: Kaiming shudian, 1935.

Mao Xiang 冒襄. *Ying mei yan yi yu* 影梅庵憶語 [Recollections from the Shaded Plum Hermitage]. Zhaodai congshu. Edited by Zhang Chao 張潮. (*juan* 3227-3230). Shanghai: Shanghai guji chubanshe, 1990.

Miao Yonghe 繆詠和. *Feng Menglong he sanyan* 馮夢龍和三言 [*Feng Menglong* and the "Three Words" Collections]. Shanghai: Shanghai guji chubanshe, 1979.

Ming shi 明史 [Official History of the Ming]. Edited by Zhang Tingyu 張廷玉. Beijing: Zhonghua shuju, 1974.

Otsuka Hidetaka 大塚秀高. "Kunai bungaku no nagare-shōsei den o ronjite Ri Gyo ni oyobu" 懼內文學の流れ小青伝玄論して李漁に及ふ [On Literature of Fearing the Wife, the Story of Xiaoqing and the Works of Li Yu]. *Saitama daigaku kiyō, kyōyō gakubu* no. 25 [1989]: 82,108.

Peng Pai 澎湃. *Zhongguo lidai nüjie* 中國歷代女傑 [Female Exemplars Throughout Chinese History]. Taizhong: Xueren wenhua, 1980.

Pu Songling 蒲松齡. *Liaozhai zhiyi* 聊齊志異 [Strange Tales from Liaozhai]. Edited by Zhang Youhe 張友鶴, 2 vols. 1962. Reprint. Shanghai: Shanghai guji chubanshe, 1983.

Qian Qianyi 錢謙益, ed. *Lie chao shiji* 列朝詩集 [Collected Poetry from the Dynasties]. 81 *juan*. 1652. Reprint. Shanghai: Guoguang yinshuashuo, 1910.

———. *Lie chao shiji xiao zhuan* 列朝詩集小傳 [Short Biographies of Poets through the Ages]. Shanghai: Zhonghua, 1959.

Qu You 瞿佑. *Jiandeng xinhua* 剪燈新話 [New Tales Told as the Lamp Burns]. In *Jiandeng xinhua, wai erzhong* 剪燈新話外二種 [New Tales Told as the Lamp Burns, and Two Other Collections]. Shanghai: Shanghai gudian wenxue chubanshe, 1957.

Shan hai jing jiao zhu 山海經校注 [The Classic of Mountains and Seas with Collected Commentaries]. Yuan Ke 袁珂, ed. Chengdu: Bashu shushe, 1993.

Shen Bang 沈榜. *Wanshu za ji* 宛薯雜記 [Administer to the Wanping District]. Beiping difang yanjiu congshu. Edited by Gao Xianzhi 高賢治. Taibei: Guting shushi, 1960.

Shen Defu 沈德符. *Wanli ye hu bian* 萬歷野獲編 [Unofficial Gleanings from the Wanli Period]. Beijing: Zhonghua, 1959.

Shi Diantou 石點頭 [The Stones Nod Their Heads]. Henan: Zhongzhou guji chubanshe, 1985.

Sun Shuyu 孫述宇. "*Shuihu zhuan* beihou de wangminghan" 水滸傳背後的亡命漢 [The Bandit Heroes Behind *The Water Margin*]. In *Zhongguo gudian xiaoshuo yanjiu zhuanji* 中國古典小說研究專集 [A Special Issue of Studies in Classical Chinese Fiction]. Vol. 1. Taibei: Lianjing chubanshe, 1979.

Tan Zhengbi 譚正壁. *San Yan Liang Pai zi liao* 三言兩拍資料 [Source Materials on the "Two Claps" and "Three Words" Collections]. Shanghai: Shanghai guji chubanshe, 1980.

———. *Zhongguo nüxing de wenxue shenghuo* 中國女性的文學生活 [The Literary Lives of Chinese Women]. Taibei: Zhuangyan chubanshe, 1982.

———. *Zhongguo nüxing wenxue shihua* 中國女性文學史話 [A History of Chinese Women's Literature]. Tianjin: Baihua wenyi chubanshe, 1984.

Wang Chunyu 王春瑜 and Du Wanyan 杜婉言. *Ming chao huanguan* 明朝宦官 [Eunuchs in the Ming Dynasty]. Beijing: Ci Jincheng chubanshe, 1989.

Wang Jianzhang 王建章. *Liedai xianshi* 列代僊史 [History of Immortals]. Changshu baofangke, 1881.

Wang Kentang 王肯堂. *Zheng zhi zhun sheng* 證治準繩 [Standards of Diagnostics and Treatment]. Taibei: Hai hong bao chai, 1974.

Wang Liqi 王利器. *Lidai xiaohua ji* 歷代笑話集 [An Anthology of Jokes from Various Periods]. 1957. Reprint. Hong Kong: Zhongliu chubanshe, 1975.

Wang Mao 王楙. *Ye ke congshu* 野客叢書 [Collected Comments of the Outsider]. Shanghai: Shanghai guji chubanshe, 1939.

Wang Qi 王圻. *San cai tu hui* 三才圖會 [Illustrated Encyclopedia]. Taibei: Chengwen, 1993.

Wang Qimo 王起謨. *Quan Ming zhong yi biezhuan* 全明忠義別傳 [Complete Ming Biographies of the Loyal and Righteous]. Suzhou: Guanglu guji chubanshe, 1991.

Wang Shunü 王書奴. *Zhongguo changji shi* 中國娼妓史 [A History of Chinese Performers and Geishas]. Preface 1933. Reprint. Shanghai: Shanghai Sanlian shudian, 1988.

Wang Xiuqin 王秀琴 and Hu Wenkai 胡文楷, compilers. *Lidai mingyuan shujian* 歷代名媛書簡 [Letters by Distinguished Women through the Dynasties]. Changsha: Shangwu, 1941.

Wu Youru 吳友如. *Wu Youru huabao* 吳友如畫寶. [Treasury of the Art of Wu Youru]. Shanghai guji chubanshe, 1981.

Xie Guozhen 謝國楨. *Ming Qing biji tancong* 明清筆記談叢 [A Discussion of the Ming and Qing Biji]. Shanghai: Zhonghua shuju, 1962.

Xie Zhaozhe 謝肇淛. *Wu za zu* 五雜俎 [The Five-fold Miscellany]. Taibei: Xinhua shuju, 1971.

Xu Daling 許大齡. "Mingdai Beijing de jingji shenghuo" 明代北京的經濟生活 [Economics of Ming Dynasty Beijing]. In *Beijing daxue xuebao* 北京大學學報. Nagoya: Renmin kexue lishi bian, 1967.

Yagisawa Hajime 八木澤元. "Fū Shōsei densetsu to sono gikyoku" 馮小青伝説と其戲曲 [The Feng Xiaoqing Legend and Dramas]. 2 pts. *Kangakkai zasshi* 漢學會雜志 4, #3 (1936): 81,91; 5, #2 (1937): 72,89.

———. "Mingdai joryū gekisakka Yō Shōgan ni tsuite" 明代女流劇作家葉小紈について [Ye Xiaowan, Ming Dynasty Woman Dramatist]. *Tōhōgaku* 東方學 5 [1982]: 85,98.

Yanyi bian 豔異編 [A Compendium of the Beautiful and the Uncanny]. Compiled by Wang Shizhen 王世貞, 2 vols. Shanghai: Shanghai Zhongyang shudian, 1936.

Yao Guangxiao 姚廣孝, ed. *Ming Shi lu* 明實錄 [Veritable Records of the Ming]. Beijing: Academia Sinica, 1940.

Yin Dengguo 殷登國. *Jia yan* 閨艷 [Female Beauty]. Taibei: Qidai shudian, 1984.

Youxiang liexian quanji 有像列仙全集 [Illustrated Collection of the Immortals]. Taibei: Xiesheng shuju, 1989.

Yu Huai 余懷. *Ban qiao zaji* 板橋雜記 [Wooden Bridge Miscellany]. Zhaodai congshu. Edited by Zhang Chao 張潮. (*juan* 3147-3153). Shanghai: Shanghai guji chubanshe, 1990.

Yu Jianhua 俞劍華. *Zhong guo meishujia renming cidian* 中國美術家人名詞典 [A Lexicon of Chinese Painters]. Shanghai: Renmin meishu chubanshe, 1981.

Yu Songqing 喻松青. "Ming Qing shiqi minjian zongjiao jiaopai zhong de nüxing" 明清時期民間宗教教派中的女性 [Women of Local Religious Sects during the Ming and Qing Periods], *Nankai xuebao* 南開學報, no. 5 [1982]: 29-33.

Yuan Hongdao 袁宏道. *Yuan Zhonglang quanji* 袁中郎全集 [Collected Works of Yuan Zhonglang]. Shanghai: Dafan shuju, 1935.

Zhang Dai 張岱. *Tao'an meng yi* 陶庵夢憶 [Dreamy Reminiscence from Tao'an]. Taibei: Jinfeng chuban, 1986.

Zhang Huijian 張慧劍. *Ming Qing Jiangsu wenren nianbiao* 明清江蘇文人年表 [Chronological Tables of Jiangsu Literary Figures during the Ming and Qing]. Shanghai: Shanghai guji chubanshe, 1986.

Zhang Jue 張爵. *Jingshi wu cheng fangxiang hutongji* 京師五城方巷衚衕集 [Beijing: Its Five Buroughs, District Streets and Alleys]. Beiping shiji congshu, vol. 2. Beijing: Beiping yanjiu yaun, 1936.

Zhang Zhongjiang 張忠江. *Jinu yu wenxue* 妓女與文學 [Geishas and Literature]. Taibei: Kangnai sheng, 1971.

Zhao Shijie 趙世杰 and Zhu Xi 朱錫, eds. *Lidai nüzi shiji* 歷代女子詩集 [Collections of Women's Poetry]. Taibei: Kuangwen, 1972.

Zhao Shijie 趙世杰 compiler. *Lidai nüzi wenji* 歷代女子文集 [Collected Literary Works of Women]. Beijing: Saoye shan fang, 1928.

Zheng Guangyi 鄭光儀, ed. *Zhongguo lidai cainü shige jianshang cidian* 中國歷代才女詩歌鑒賞辭典 [A Critical Explanatory Guide to Poetry by Talented Women through the Dynasties]. Beijing: Zhongguo gongren chubanshe, 1991.

Zou Shu 鄒樞. *Shi mei ci ji* 十美詞紀 [Records of the Ten Beauties]. Zhaodai cong shu, edited by Zhang Chao 張潮.(*juan* 3227-3230). Shanghai: Shanghai guji chubanshe,1990.

Index

About the Author

Victoria Cass has studied and worked in China. She has a Ph.D. in Chinese literature from the University of California at Berkeley, where she taught Chinese language and Chinese literature. She has also taught at the University of Washington and the University of Minnesota; she is associate professor of Chinese language and literature at University of Colorado, Boulder.